Stereotypes, Distortions and Omissions in U.S. History Textbooks

- A Content Analysis Instrument for Detecting Racism and Sexism

- Supplemental Information on Asian American, Black, Chicano, Native American, Puerto Rican, and Women's History

The Council on Interracial Books for Children

Racism and Sexism Resource Center for Educators

This book was made possible by a grant from the Carnegie Corporation of New York. The statements made and the views expressed are solely the responsibility of the Council on Interracial Books for Children.

Published by the
Racism and Sexism Resource Center for Educators
A Division of the
Council on Interracial Books for Children, Inc.
1841 Broadway, New York, N.Y. 10023

CONTENTS

Although this volume reflects the knowledge, insights and effort of the people listed below, the Council on Interracial Books for Children bears sole responsibility for the information and viewpoints contained herein.

Robert B. Moore, Ed. D., for the Council

CONTRIBUTORS

Dr. Beryle Banfield	Bank Street College of Education
Katherine B. Baxter	Writer, Teacher, Friends School, Philadelphia
Frances M. Beal	Afro American Institute, Richmond College C.U.N.Y.
Jean Carey Bond	Author, Coordinating Editor, CIBC *Bulletin*
Bradford Chambers	Director, Council on Interracial Books for Children
Dr. John Henrik Clarke	Afro American Studies, Hunter College C.U.N.Y.
Dr. Michael Dorris	Native American Studies, Dartmouth College
J.B. Durham	Director, International Indian Treaty Council
Dr. Rusty Eisenberg	History Department, Dartmouth College
Dr. Luis Nieves Falcón	Department of Sociology, University of Puerto Rico
Lyla Hoffman	Director, Foundation for Change
Dr. Gloria Joseph	Social Science Department, Hampshire College
William Loren Katz	Author, Teacher's College, Columbia U.
Merle Levine	Teacher, Wheatley Hills H.S., N.Y., Consultant for Feminist Press
Elizabeth Martinez	Author, Chicano Communications Center, Albuquerque
Dr. Robert B. Moore	Director, Racism & Sexism Resource Center for Educators

Dr. Alan Moriyama   Asian American Studies Center, U.C.L.A.

Dr. Franklin Odo   California State U., Long Beach

Benjamin Ortiz   Puerto Rican Studies, Hunter College, C.U.N.Y.

Dr. Morgan Otis   Department of Teacher Ed., California State U., Sacramento

Carmen Puigdollers   Puerto Rican Studies, Lehman College, C.U.N.Y.

Armando Rendón   Author, Latino Institute, American U.

Dr. Porfirio Sanchez   Mexican American Studies, California State College, Dominguez Hills

Dr. Albert V. Schwartz   Division of Educational Studies, Richmond College, C.U.N.Y.

John Silva   Chinatown Health Clinic, N.Y.

Amy Swerdlow   Women's Studies, Sarah Lawrence College

Ralph Tavares   Center for Urban Education

Janice Law Trecker   Feminist Author, Consultant

Kal Wagenheim   Author, Consultant, Puerto Rican Labor Dept.

Marli Weiner   Graduate Student, Women's Studies, Sarah Lawrence College

Legan Wong   Hunter College, C.U.N.Y.

Richard Wong   Asian American Resource Center, Basement Workshop, N.Y.

Special appreciation is due as well for the patience and efforts of Susan Bodenstein, Nessa Darren, Lynn Edwards, Nellie Hester, Nancy Nedwell, Virginia Sterling, Barbara Saturnine, Elsa Velasquez Sein and Anita Stark. Their work was essential to making this book a reality.

TEXTS USED IN THIS PROJECT

1. **America: Its People and Values,** Harcourt Brace Jovanovich, 1975.

2. **The American Experience,** Addison-Wesley, 1975.

3. **American History for Today,** Ginn and Company, 1970.

4. **The Challenge of America,** Holt, Rinehart and Winston, 1973.

5. **The Free and the Brave,*** Rand McNally and Company, 1967.

6. **A Free People: The United States in the Twentieth Century,** Macmillan Company, 1970.

7. **History of the American People,** McDougal, Littell and Company, 1975.

8. **The Impact of Our Past,** McGraw-Hill, 1972.

9. **In Search of America,** Ginn and Company, 1975.

10. **Man in America,** Silver Burdett, 1974.

11. **The Pageant of American History,** Allyn and Bacon, 1975.

12. **Rise of the American Nation,** Harcourt Brace Jovanovich, 1972.

13. **The Shaping of America,** Holt, Rinehart and Winston, 1972.

***The Free and the Brave** is the only pre-1970 text used in this study. It was considered an advanced text when it appeared and is still widely used. Quotations from this text have been kept to a minimum.

TERMINOLOGY

Our terminology is inconsistent, political and evolving. We state this not as an apology, but in the belief that the same holds true for everyone's terminology. The explanation published previously in our analysis of children's trade books, *Human and Anti-Human Values in Children's Books,* applies here:

> Language, reflecting society, is no more static nor sacred than is anything else in the political arena. In our racist and sexist society, our decisions about word usage are political decisions. When one uses the male pronoun to mean both sexes, one is making a political statement. The use of "Negro" or "Colored" today has clear political connotations. Both the words we use and the connotations those words imply are in a constant state of change, as our society's consciousness of racism and sexism develops.

Entire books, as well as numerous articles, about sexism in the English language have appeared recently. Extensive reports have been written on racism in language as well. (We have published a booklet called *Racism in the English Language.*) Since space limitations preclude a full discussion of these two topics, the following merely offers a brief explanation of a few terms used in this book. We urge interested readers to explore these fascinating topics more extensively.

To conclude, using words as political weapons is a mind stretching exercise. We recommend it.

FEMINIST—a person who has undertaken to play an advocacy role on behalf of women's social and economic rights. (By this definition a male can be a feminist.)

HERO—any heroic person, male or female. We deliberately avoid "feminine" word endings because, historically, such suffixes have been used to connote something "lesser than" the male meanings.

CHICANA is used to mean a female while CHICANO is used to mean a male, or males and females combined as a group. (Both these words refer to those people who once generally called themselves Mexican Americans but now, for reasons outlined on page 55, prefer to be known as Chicanos.) The "feminine" word ending in this instance is used because it is characteristic of the Spanish language; all nouns in Spanish are either masculine or feminine.

AMERICA and AMERICAN—as explained in the introduction of the Chicano section, refer respectively to a hemisphere and to all the people (e.g., Chileans, Mexicans, Canadians) who live in that hemisphere. Therefore, we have avoided use of those terms (except in quotes) when the reference is exclusively to the U.S. or to citizens of the U.S. The Puerto Rican section uses the term "North America," in reference to the U.S.

ASIAN AMERICAN, AFRICAN AMERICAN and NATIVE AMERICAN—are terms used, self-descriptively, by persons within those groups who are actively involved in liberation struggles. These are the labels they now choose to use for themselves. Since we respect a people's right to self-definition, we have used these terms in this book.

EURO AMERICAN—refers to European settlers in —and immigrants to—the United States, and to their descendants.

PILIPINO, or PILIPINO AMERICAN—are spellings used to refer to people who came from the Philippines, or to their descendants in the U.S. Again, we use this term because it is being used by Pilipinos as the way to designate themselves. (Technically, the spelling reflects the lack of phonetic "ph" or "f" sounds in the Philippine language.)

BLACK—is spelled with an upper-case "B" and white with a lower-case "w" because we are using Black in this book to mean a specific group of U.S. citizens: African Americans. When we refer to a specific group of white U.S. citizens, i.e., Polish Americans, Irish Americans, we capitalize those names. When we generalize about whites in the U.S. we use the lower-case. If we were to generalize about blacks, i.e., African Americans and Africans and Papua New Guineans, we would also use the lower case "b."

THIRD WORLD—refers to "minority" or "non-white" peoples in the U.S. While people of color *are* a minority within the U.S., they are the vast majority of the world's population, in which white people are a distinct minority. Use of "minority" to describe people of color in the U.S. tends to lose sight of the global majority/minority reality—a fact of increasing importance in the interconnected liberation struggles of people of color inside and outside the U.S. To describe people of color as "non-white" is to use whiteness as the standard or "norm" against which all others are defined.

NEO-COLONIAL—a "new form" of colonialism which exists after a colony achieves political and governmental independence from the colonizing country, but remains economically dependent. Neo-colonized nations do not control their own wealth, resources and industry, and are still basically controlled from outside.

INTRODUCTION

Why the Council Undertook This Project

Until recent years, most U.S. history textbooks presented a picture of our society that was virtually all-white and all-male. Gross omission of third world peoples and women was the rule and, where exceptions did occur, references to the presence and activities of these latter groups were cursory and often demeaning.

During the 1960's, the centuries-old movement for social change escalated to high levels of activism, and African Americans, Asian Americans, Chicanos, Native Americans, Puerto Ricans, and feminists mounted organized campaigns to "integrate" the content of textbooks to more truthfully represent this nation's history. This social pressure made it increasingly difficult for educators and publishers to disregard the role of women and third world people in the development of U.S. society. The educational establishment responded by accepting the concept of multicultural, pluralistic education.

Almost ten years have passed since that time. Over five years have passed since the educational establishment acknowledged the need for greater inclusion of women in textbooks. What changes have occurred?

Background of the Project

During the last decade and a half, excellent studies of pre-1970 U.S. history textbooks have examined the portrayal of third world people and women. Among these studies are those by the Indian Historian Press, the National Association for the Advancement of Colored People, the Mexican American Education Commission, a State-appointed task force of ethnic scholars in California, and numerous feminist analysts, including Janet Law Trecker and the Feminist Press.

Various instruments and criteria have been developed for analyzing textbooks. Frequently, these have focused on one particular third world group, or on women. Since the Council routinely reports and teaches about racism and sexism in educational materials, we have long been interested in developing a comprehensive instrument for analyzing the content of U.S. history texbooks in terms of their treatment of both women and third world peoples. In addition to providing criteria against which textbooks may be checked, we wanted this instrument to be informative, and to provide important facts frequently omitted or distorted in texts. Such an instrument, we felt, would also be a helpful consciousness-raising and teaching tool.

We were fortunate to have access to an unfinished work by the U.S. Civil Rights Commission which sought to identify stereotypes, distortions and omissions in history textbooks. We adapted this unfinished instrument for use in teacher training courses, sponsored by the Council, at Penn State and Columbia University. During these courses, we expanded the instrument to include women, Puerto Ricans and Asian Americans. Then a long process of refinement began. We sought the expertise of ethnic and feminist scholars from different regions of the country to analyze the textbooks, to add to the information, and to provide reference sources.

Before publishing the work, we wanted to make sure that our criteria were applicable to the newest textbooks—those published since 1970. Therefore we requested major publishers to send their latest history texts. The ones received are those excerpted from in this volume. Prompted by the changes we found in these texts, we again revised the criteria, in consultation with additional experts and historians. Finally, we condensed, compiled and edited all of the accumulated material, with the ultimate product being the instruments and other sections that comprise this book.

What You Will Find in This Book

The recently published textbooks sent to our offices by major publishers were examined for their treatment of six groups: Women, African Americans, Asian Americans, Chicanos, Native Americans and Puerto Ricans. In this volume, we seek to provide the following:

1. Observations and insights gained in reviewing the newer textbooks.

2. Guides to racist and sexist stereotypes and distortions common in recent textbooks.

3. Important information that is still missing from the newer textbooks.

4. Alternative ways of viewing past and present events.

5. Rating instruments for evaluating any history textbook.

6. A bibliography of resources for further study.

The six sections in this volume highlight significant aspects of each people's particular historical experiences in the U.S.—experiences which tend to be omitted from, or distorted in, textbooks. Each section begins with a short introductory essay and is followed by criteria designed to evaluate the information provided by textbooks. Under each of the criteria appear three columns: the first column quotes a passage from a sample textbook; the second column comments on what is right, wrong, or missing from that excerpt; and the third column offers one or more references for the new information provided in column two. These reference sources comprise a useful bibliography that fills in some missing pages of U.S. history. At the end of each section is a checklist for reader use in rating any textbook's performance with regard to racism and sexism. A glossary of terms appears on page 131 and an explanation of the terminology on page seven.

All but one of the sample textbooks were published in the first five years of the 1970's. The one exception, published in 1967, was widely heralded for its "advanced" presentation. Because of its widespread use and favorable reputation, we included it, but minimized its use since it pre-dates the other samples.

We have made every effort to insure that passages from the sample texts were excerpted without distorting the textbook's presentation. In some instances, the excerpt consists of a text's entire discussion of a particular point; in others, the excerpt constitutes a portion of the text's discussion, but the unquoted portion did not change the basic meaning. Further, since the textbooks varied greatly in quantity and quality of presentation, we deliberately selected quotes that best illustrated the omission, distortion or stereotype being discussed in a given category.

What You Will Not Find in This Book

We have separated the discussions of the six groups of people in order to most effectively design an instrument for measuring the textbook treatment of each. In doing so, we have partially obscured the fact that the histories of these groups in the U.S. share much in common—particularly regarding the exploitation they face and the struggles they share. Likewise, the information presented in the essays provides only a partial history of the peoples discussed. Those histories are too complex and varied to be comprehensively covered in one volume. Nor do we claim to have covered the most important aspects of each people's experience or to have delineated the essence of each people's cultural identity.

In this book, we have focused primarily on each people's relationship with white male society—the oppression which has characterized that relationship, and the resistance to that oppression. Despite this focus, readers should understand that we are fully aware that each people's identity is critically defined not only by their experiences with whites and with white and/or male oppression, but also by culturally distinctive factors. Our specific concern with third world people and women is not meant to imply that we feel textbooks accurately portray the experiences of the average, white workingman. Indeed, similar content analysis of labor history and its treatment in textbooks is critically needed.

The struggles of people for independence and/or self-determination are also too varied and widespread to be fully covered in a single volume. Instead, we have tried to cull significant highlights from those efforts which history texts have traditionally relegated to the background. The selected highlights are intended to illuminate the relationship between subordination and privilege, powerlessness and power, poverty and affluence.

In attempting to present information that is generally omitted from, or distorted in, most of the recently published textbooks, we have not covered all of the pervasive distortions and omissions of older texts (in fact, space limitations have prevented us from dealing fully with the omissions and distortions of even the newer texts). However, enough has been included to assist readers in evaluating their own textbooks and, hopefully, to supplement their knowledge and broaden their perspectives.

What You Can Do About Textbooks

We urge readers to consider that our purpose in challenging the traditional, unicultural perspective on U.S. history is not to foster negativism about the dynamic society in which we live. On the contrary, we seek—for ourselves and our readers—to stimulate thought about, and engender respect for, the experiences, viewpoints and aspirations of third world people and women throughout our history—and today. There is much in this history to inspire us all: the determination of people to be free, the survival of the human will against enormous odds, and the affirmation that human beings will ceaselessly struggle for their humanity and their dignity, for justice and liberation.

A PROJECT FOR PARENTS

First, read and rate portions of the textbooks your children are using. Choose the sections of greatest interest to you. This can be done individually, or collectively as a project with other concerned parents.

1. Discuss your findings with your child. This can be an important learning experience for both of you. Urge your child to initiate classroom discussion by raising questions about textbook assumptions.

2. Arrange a meeting with the classroom teacher, social studies chairperson and/or school principal. In the meeting, you might request:

A. Classroom discussion and assignments on racism and sexism as manifested in textbooks and in society.
B. Supplemental reading assignments offering alternative viewpoints to textbook presentations.
C. Invitations to third world people and feminists who can present their viewpoints to a class or student assembly.
D. Consultation by the teachers and/or school administrators with feminists, and with third world educators and parents before purchase of new history textbooks.

3. Send letters to local newspapers, parent-teacher groups and local feminist and third world organizations that can organize support for your work. You can ask their assistance in exerting pressure, if needed, on school authorities. (Many textbooks under consideration for purchase or adoption are rejected because of effective protest by feminist and/or third world groups. An alliance of third world and feminist organizations is most effective.)

4. Send a letter to the publisher of the textbook, summarizing both your objections regarding the book's content and your actions. Publishers are always considering revisions or new editions, and this is a very important method of persuasion.

5. Inform yourself about existing state laws or about adoption of new state laws which mandate the use of multicultural, bias-free textbooks.

A PROJECT FOR TEACHERS

Evaluate your textbook. Whether or not your school allows you the textbook of your choice, there is little doubt any text will provide endless examples of racism and sexism. Until truly bias-free, multicultural textbooks are written, available books can be utilized as tools to expose bias, as well as to teach history.

1. Select a number of particularly racist and sexist passages and consider how to use these to raise your students' consciousness. Suggestions:

A. You might assign an alternative reading source, written by third world or feminist historians, which contradicts a particular passage. Reading assignments can be followed by class discussion. Insights gained can, of course, be linked to relevant current events.

B. Devise role-playing exercises to reveal how women and/or third world people view a particular historical event described in a textbook passage. These exercises can be fun and instructive for students, once they are encouraged to probe for alternative perspectives.

C. Assign students to rewrite offensive passages, so that the racism or sexism is eliminated. They can proceed, on their own, to find other passages which they feel are biased.

2. Invite outside speakers to address your class, or a larger group of students, to present alternative viewpoints on historical and current events.

3. Make your voice heard when textbook purchases are being considered by your school.

4. Write letters to the textbook publisher. The publishers want to keep you happy because they want to sell more textbooks.

AFRICAN AMERICANS

A bronze Goddess of Liberty stands atop the Capitol dome in Washington, D.C. She was cast in 1859 by enslaved African Americans and, ever since, has symbolized the fundamental contradictions of the "world's greatest democracy."

The mockery continues. In 1976, during the U.S. Bicentennial celebration, a distinguished foreign visitor stood in the Capitol building, under the statue cast by his forbears. He was the President of Liberia, a nation founded by ex-slaves from the U.S., and he was the first African head of state to address a joint session of the U.S. Senate and House of Representatives. The one and only Black member of the U.S. Senate was about to introduce him to the assembled guests.

Sitting on the dais, as unaware of the symbolism of the Liberty Goddess overhead as they were of a live microphone accidentally transmitting their conversation, the Vice-President of the United States and the Speaker of the House of Representatives lightly traded racist banter about both the Black Senator and the people of Liberia. They had plenty of time to talk because the entire session was delayed while a southern Senator concluded his filibuster against a Civil Rights Bill.

The great historian and scholar, W.E.B. DuBois, once remarked that U.S. history, in large measure, can best be understood by studying the status and treatment of Black people and their response to that treatment. While his statement has validity for *all* oppressed third world people in this country, it is especially relevant to Afro Americans.

AN EMBARRASSING ENIGMA

The Afro American experience, to an even greater degree than other third world groups in the U.S., represents an enigma which establishment historians have found embarrassing to deal with. The very documents which proclaimed the birth of this nation explicitly accepted chattel slavery and very consciously condemned the Afro American population to generations of degradation and exploitation.

Historians have chosen to solve this moral dilemma by omissions, distortions and rationalizations about the nation's past. As recently as 1965, the "dean" of U.S. historians, Samuel Eliot Morison, wrote a best-selling history of the U.S. in which Black people were barely mentioned, except as happy slaves. But since U.S. national politics, morality, religion, culture and economy have all been inextricably linked to the Black experience, it follows—as DuBois claimed—that history books which do not honestly explore the "color-line" bear little resemblance to reality.

SLAVE LABOR

The European presence in the Americas gave a tremendous impetus to the commerical enterprises of Europe. To profitably use the land and resources which they conquered, an abundant work force had to be procured. The people whose land it was were unavailable for numerous reasons, among which were the genocidal practices of Europeans and the alien diseases they had introduced. European settlers and indentured servants were also insufficient in number, and so it was that the European merchants and bankers turned their eyes towards the African continent for the labor power they desired.

This uncompensated labor of millions of Africans laid the base for the agricultural development of the South in rice, indigo and tobacco. It created the cotton kingdom. It provided the skills and people-power necessary to maintain southern society. The slave trade itself, together with the commodities produced by slave labor, became the decisive factor in the swift development of U.S. commerce and capital. And it was thus, by the coerced "contribution" of Black people's labor, that the New England merchants built their initial fortunes—fortunes which were later used to expand and to industrialize the nation.

UNDERPAID LABOR

After the Civil War, Black people—reduced to serfdom by the sharecropping system—were recruited as a low-paid work force for northern industry. With the curtailment of large-scale European immigration and the impetus of WW I production, massive Black internal migration changed the existence of Afro American people from a predominantly rural to a predominantly urban population. Black workers became an underpaid, reserve labor pool—profitable to employers but always burdened by racism, discrimination and unemployment.

BLACK INFLUENCE

The lives and the labor of Afro Americans have strongly shaped the economic, moral, political, social and cultural reality of present day U.S. society. Today, Black people represent over 12 percent of the population. Unlike other third world people, they have long shared a common language with whites—albeit a language forced upon them as part of the slave experience. Their sizable presence, wide geographic dispersement and creative energies have combined to leave an indelible stamp upon this nation's literature, language, music, theatre, art and dance, as well as upon its scholarship and science. These achievements represent the perseverance and strength of individuals, sparked by the communities from which they came. They are, as well, evidence of the vast potential talent that was lost to this society by its destructive practice of racism.

The struggles of Black people for justice and liberation have had a profound influence on the country as a whole, and a domino effect on other groups oppressed by U.S. society. Alone, cooperating with other third world people or collaborating with progressive whites, Black people have been in the forefront of efforts for human dignity. Black insistence on free public education during Reconstruction gave poor white Southerners their first opportunity to attend school, just as recent Black struggles for open admission to colleges have given working-class white youth a chance for higher education. The fight for Civil Rights legislation was an impetus for other third world groups and for women to raise their own long struggles to a higher plateau, just as Black pressure for equal-pay-for-equal-work, which sparked a similar movement by women, has set an upwards wage pressure beneficial to all working people.

WHITE RATIONALIZATIONS

White people needed to assauge the guilt and counter the criticisms aroused by their treatment of Black people. This was accomplished by development of a particularly virulent ideology of white supremacy. The rationale was that the enslaved people were so inferior that they did not need or merit human treatment. To justify the treatment of the African slave, and later of the Afro American citizen, white society encouraged an army of propagandists to "scientifically" prove the inferiority of Black people. While this ideology of racism was applied to all people of color with whom Euro American society came into contact, its severest application was against Afro Americans. Because they were the most physically different from whites, because their numbers were the second largest to whites, and because of their geographical and social proximity to whites, Black people have been perceived as the greatest threat.

White supremacist ideology has infected every level of national life. Government officials, social scientists, ministers, teachers, journalists and doctors have all played a part, as new and more sophisticated revisions of the myths and rationalizations of white supremacy keep reappearing. Whether it is religious leaders in colonial days pointing to Biblical passages damning Ham; biologists of a hundred years ago "studying" cranial structures; Social Darwinists utilizing theories of evolution and survival of the fittest; geneticists of the 1920's "proving" inborn moral inferiority; Moynihan-like theories of Black "pathology;" recent genetic pronouncements of Shockley and Jensen about Black IQ—all serve as pseudo-scientific apologies for the ongoing oppression directed against Black people.

These theories, initiated originally to justify a system of chattel slavery, were later revised to rationalize the continued subjugation of freed Afro Americans in inferior schools, substandard housing and low-paying jobs. In turn, this mythology created a climate that condoned cruel and vicious treatment of Afro Americans. The climate of violence continues today—in Boston and other cities experiencing school desegregation, in Chicago and other areas experiencing neighborhood desegregation. The white working class is a protagonist in many anti-Black battles because it has been conditioned to the mythology of white supremacy which serves to divide people by race and prevents them from uniting around their common class interests and their common grievances.

The challenge to U.S. history textbooks is clear. They must report honestly on the status and treatment of Black people; they must include the Black response to, and perspective on, that treatment; and they must eliminate all rationalizations which serve to excuse the responsibility of white society.

TEXTBOOK FLAWS

Textbooks, too, have played their part in legitimizing theories of white superiority. While it is true that newer texts do include more information about Black people, this is usually offered from a white perspective, and barely touches upon Black oppression. One result is that Afro Americans are presented as "problems" for white society. There is another textbook fault—more pronounced in the coverage of the Black experience than with the coverage of other third world groups—and that is the focus on famous Black individuals. While this is an improvement over older texts which usually included only Booker T. Washington and George Washington Carver, it still omits the crucial element of the oppression of Black people in the U.S. James Oliver Horton effectively summed up these problems in the March, 1976 issue of *Black Scholar:*

> *Although the study of great black leaders could foster a certain racial pride, the study of the exceptional provided little understanding of the experience of blacks as a people in America. . . . The careers of black heroes became valuable illustrations of social mobility in American society. . . . Such integrated history, however, usually amounts to no more than spot appearances of black heroes in the dramatic production of the great American epic. Serious study of the experience of black people in America through a concentration on the black community, on the other hand, brings confrontation with the American myth. The black experience cannot be fully illuminated without bringing a new perspective to the study of American history. The black experience, much like that of women, Indians and some other minorities, is distinctly "un-American." . . . If the careers of many black leaders illustrate the American myth, the experience of black people in America illustrates the failure of the American system.*

Textbooks and African Americans

QUOTATION	COMMENT	REFERENCE

1. African, as well as European, culture forms an integral part of the U.S. heritage.

. . . in 1497, the Portuguese sailed around the tip of Africa and on to India. . . .

. . . Portuguese sailors began exploring the west coast of Africa as early as 1420. For half a century, Portuguese mariners worked their way down the coast until in 1484 Bartholomew Diaz had reached the southern tip of Africa. Then, in 1497, the Portuguese trading empire was launched when Vasco da Gama rounded Africa and sailed on to India.

Although Africans came from a complex and highly artistic culture, it was one that Englishmen could not easily understand.

The Shaping of America, p. 3, p. 4, p. 16

While this text provides 10 pages discussing socio-economic conditions in Europe prior to colonization of the Americas, its treatment of Africa prior to the slave trade consists of the quotes in column one.

Textbooks reinforce racism by presenting Africa as little more than a physical obstacle which European navigators had to "sail around." Africa is a large continent where many civilizations, political institutions, cultures and religions have flourished. The diversity of the "high" civilizations, such as Ghana, Mali and Songhay, as well as some of the less complex societies, should be discussed.

African Americans, Puerto Ricans and Chicanos can trace all or part of their own heritage to Africa. African values, history, folk tales, music, and speech styles are vital to their self-identification and are also important aspects of the total U.S. culture.

A Glorious Age in Africa: The Story of Three Great African Empires. Daniel Chu and Elliott Skinner.

A Guide to African History. Basil Davidson.

Great Rulers of the African Past. Lavinia Dobler and William A. Brown.

The World and Africa. W. E. B. DuBois, pp. 98-225.

From Slavery To Freedom. John Hope Franklin, pp. 3-41.

The Peoples of Africa. Colin Turnbull.

2. Africans were in the Americas prior to 1619.

The first Negroes were shipped to America—to Jamestown—in 1619, the year before the Mayflower arrived. . . . the first of millions of Africans who were transported toward these shores in the next two hundred years.

The Free and the Brave, p. 140

Free Africans, as well as slaves, were in the Americas before 1619. They accompanied Spanish, Portuguese and other explorers, serving in a variety of roles. They were seamen, explorers, farmers, guides and shipbuilders. Estevanico, who came to North America with Cabeza de Vaca, was the best known African explorer of that period. A slave rebellion is recorded in 1526 in what is now South Carolina. Because of that rebellion, the Spanish settlers returned to Haiti, leaving the Africans as the first permanent, non-indigenous settlement in what was later to become the U.S.

American Negro Slave Revolts. Herbert Aptheker, p. 163. Description of 1526 revolt.

The God-Kings and the Titans. James Bailey, pp. 146-153 and 183-195. Discussion of pre-Columbian African voyages to the Americas.

QUOTATION	COMMENT	REFERENCE

2. (Continued)

	Increasing evidence suggests that Africans traveled to the Americas centuries before Columbus. Skeletons, carvings and other archeological evidence found throughout Central and South America; the nautical skills and instruments of some ancient African civilizations; and the pattern of ocean currents between the continents combine to indicate that Africans traveled to the Americas during several historical periods.	*Introduction of African Civilizations.* John G. Jackson, pp. 232-264. *They Came Before Columbus.* Ivan Van Sertima.

3. The North American slave trade created enormous profits, became the most brutal system of slavery known, and disrupted African civilization.

QUOTATION	COMMENT	REFERENCE
The Triangle Trade was also known as the trade in rum, slaves, and molasses. It is hard to believe that men would treat their human brothers in such a way, just to make money. Yet the cruel African slave trade was nothing new. Slavery is as old as history. American History for Today, p. 62	This textbook naively questions "man's inhumanity to man" when the reason is "just to make money." At the same time the book rationalizes U.S. slavery, since "slavery is as old as history." Making money has historically been the root cause of most oppression and exploitation, yet textbooks neglect to analyze the profit motive underlying much of our history. Enormous wealth was created for the South by African labor and, for the North, by the slave trade itself. Much of that wealth was later invested in early industrialization and became a major source of this nation's economic power. That slavery existed in Africa, and elsewhere, does not justify the U.S. practice. Moreover, U.S. slavery was far more oppressive than any known to other civilizations. U.S. slavery sought to totally dehumanize Africans by classifying them as property; denied them basic human rights of marriage and family; cut them off from society by placing them totally at the mercy of slaveholders; and developed an ideology of racism that strictly enforced color distinctions to justify the practice of owning people. While Africans were involved in selling other Africans, it was Europeans who directed the trade, supplied the guns and reaped the profits. The slave trade increased existing hostilities and warfare in Africa. This, coupled with the loss of millions of its people, made the continent more vulnerable to division by European powers in the last part of the 19th century. Africa today still suffers from the destructive effects of European colonization.	*Slave Trade & Slavery.* John **Henrik Clarke and Vincent** Harding (eds.), pp.1-21. Particulars of U.S. slavery. *The African Slave Trade: Precolonial History, 1450-1850.* Basil Davidson. Effects of European slave trade on African life. *From Slavery to Freedom,* pp. 42-69. *The World the Slaveholders Made.* Eugene D. Genovese, pp. 3-21. *The Great White Lie: Slavery, Emancipation, and Changing Racial Attitudes.* Jack Gratus, pp. 23-87. Economics of U.S. involvement in the slave trade. *Black Cargoes: A History of the African Slave Trade, 1518-1865.* Daniel P. Mannix. Chapters 7, 11 and 12 include information on slave trade activities of Northerners. *Capitalism and Slavery.* Eric Williams, pp. 30-51. Thorough examination of the economics of slavery.

QUOTATION	COMMENT	REFERENCE

4. The significance of the Revolution, to Blacks, goes beyond participation in combat.

Five thousand Negroes, slave and free, fought for American independence. Negroes were in the first battles at Lexington, Concord, and Bunker Hill. They were also in the last battle at Yorktown. . . . There were no all-Negro units in the American Revolution. Negro soldiers and sailors fought side by side with whites. Many states passed laws freeing all honorably discharged Negroes.

American History for Today, p. 101

The inherent contradiction posed by white colonists fighting for freedom, while maintaining a slave society, was to cast an indelible imprint on the emerging nation. The actions and statements of the many people, Black and white, who raised the contradiction of maintaining slavery while promoting the principles of the Revolution, are important to any discussion of the period.

While some slaves who fought won their freedom, others were forced back into slavery. Many thousands of Black people fled to British lines to escape "patriot" slaveholders. In 1780, South Carolina enacted a law offering a Black person as a slave to any white man who volunteered to serve the cause of "independence," while both South Carolina and Georgia made it a practice to partly pay their officers' salaries by giving them Black people held in bondage.

Such actions and issues were of greater significance to Black people during and after the Revolution than was the fact that 5,000 Blacks fought to establish independence for white society.

The American Revolution. Herbert Aptheker, pp. 207-228.

Slaves Without Masters: The Free Negro in the Ante-Bellum South. Ira Berlin, pp. 15-29.
Discusses British and colonists' use of Black men and the effects of revolutionary philosophy on slavery.

The Negro in the American Revolution. Benjamin Quarles.
Black roles in the war, colonists' and British attitudes toward Blacks, and changes in Black lives at the close of the war.

5. The Constitution was a pro-slavery document and remained so for 78 years.

Actually the delegates [to the constitutional convention] were more than good politicians. They were really statesmen. A statesman does what is best for his nation. He works unselfishly for the good of all the people . . . they must figure out ways to do the most good for the most people without hurting the rights of anybody. . . . The men who wrote our Constitution were able to compromise and solve many big problems.

American History for Today, p. 117

The delegates also wrote into the Constitution another rule concerning slavery. It stated that, 20 years after the ratification of the Constitution, no more slaves could be brought into the United States from overseas.

America: Its People and Values, p. 192

Twenty-five of the fifty-five white men who wrote the Constitution held African people as slaves. Black people, who constituted 17 percent of the population, had no representation. To state that the delegates worked "unselfishly for the good of all the people" without "hurting the rights of anybody" ignores not only the approximately 680,000 people held in bondage at that time, but the millions of African people who were yet to be enslaved.

The Constitution included three pro-slavery provisions. Article 1, Section 2, Clause 3 contained the 3/5ths compromise which guaranteed extra representation in Congress for slaveholders. Article IV, Section 2, Clause 3 gave federal support to slaveholders in reclaiming their runaway "property." Article IV, Section 2, Clause 3, did *not* mandate that the slave trade would end in 20 years—as some texts assert it did. Rather, it guaranteed at least twenty more years of the trade in African people by prohibiting any Congressional action against the trade until 1807. The delegates could have no certainty in 1787 that 20 years later, Congress would vote to end the trade—an assertion made by other texts. While the trade was banned by Congress in 1808, the illicit importation of African people as slaves continued.

From Slavery to Freedom, pp. 141-144.

Class Conflict, Slavery, and the United States Constitution. Staughton Lynd, pp. 153-183.

Forever Free. Dorothy Sterling, pp. 83-89.

QUOTATION	COMMENT	REFERENCE

6. Slavery was inherently cruel and inhuman.

One important thing to remember about slavery is that it was a long and brutal episode in our history. It was a terrible system, basically, but many kinds of slaves, from the most oppressed field hand to the talented cabinet-maker, were able to earn money and buy their freedom. There were also many different masters. There were brutes who beat their slaves, but there were also kind men like George Washington who met their responsibilities well and freed their slaves.

The Impact of Our Past, p. 121

A kind master would often divide his slaves among his children. In his will he would give to his son or daughter one or more slaves to serve them for life.

The Pageant of American History, p. 205

New textbooks do not describe happy, content slaves, but they tend to minimize the barbarity of the system. Treatment of slaves varied from one plantation to another depending on the temperament of the owner and/or overseer, but extreme cruelty was not uncommon and humane treatment was rare. But even under the mildest conditions, the master was a person who kept other human beings as chattel—in itself an act of great cruelty.

The testimony of many observers bears witness to the degrees of abusiveness—from sheer neglect of basic living conditions to whippings, maimings, and incredible forms of torture. The notion that masters protected their property because of its value has little recorded foundation. It was more common to force a sick slave to work than to call a physician, more common for the slave to be the target of the master's anger or lust than to be protected. It was only by force that the system of slavery could be maintained at all.

American Negro Slave Revolts, pp. 53-78.
Details machinery of control over the slave population.

The Shaping of Black America. Lerone Bennett, Jr., pp. 145-169.

The Slave Community: Plantation Life in the Ante-Bellum South. John W. Blassingame, pp. 154-184.

The Peculiar Institution. Kenneth Stampp, pp. 141-191.

American Slavery As It Is. Theodore D. Weld.

7. Rebellion and slavery went hand in hand.

While no single slave revolt succeeded, records show that Negroes were most unhappy. Between 1663 and 1865, more than 100 slave revolts took place on land. At sea there were 55 revolts.

American History for Today, p. 227

Why did the slaves so seldom revolt. . . . First, the slaves knew that the masters held all the power. . . . Also, many slaves had learned the lessons of the plantation too well. They had learned the rules of slavery so well they hardly thought of rebelling.

The Challenge of America, p. 335

At least 250 insurrections and conspiracies within the continental U.S.—North as well as South—have been documented. Two known rebellions—the 1839 revolt on the "Amisted" led by Cinque and the 1841 revolt aboard the "Creole" led by Madison Washington—resulted in freedom. While such success was difficult if not impossible on land, the varied forms of resistance to oppression were continuous from the inception of slavery in the Americas.

Large conspiracies and revolts received the greatest publicity, but small-group and individual acts of resistance were everyday occurrences. These included slowing down on the job, sabotage, self-mutilation, infanticide, suicide, theft, arson, murder of overseers and masters, and escape. Female slaves were leaders of some revolts. While rebellions resulted in tighter controls, resistance to slavery ended only when slavery itself was abolished in 1865.

American Negro Slave Revolts.

Before the Mayflower: A History of the Negro in America. Lerone Bennett, Jr., pp. 97-126.

American Slavery: The Question of Resistance. John M. Bracey et al.

From Slavery to Freedom, pp. 205-213.

The Peculiar Institution, pp. 86-140.

QUOTATION	COMMENT	REFERENCE

8. While there were differences in the institution between North and South, slavery was never a regional issue.

The second, and by far the most important, difference between the North and the South was slavery. . . . By 1800, slavery was outlawed throughout most of the Western world. It was rapidly dying in the North. Yet it flourished in the South of the United States of America.

Man In America, p. 299

In most of the Northern states, the Negro slaves gained their freedom and some of their rights of citizenship. The United States government, under the Articles of Confederation, prohibited slavery in the Old Northwest. But no effort was made to end slavery in the Southern states or in the Old Southwest.

America: Its People and Values, p. 371

Slavery affected everyone in the U.S.—Northerner or Southerner, Black or white, slave or free—plunging them into war, and leaving a deep racial division which continues today. Slavery existed in all of the colonies. Abolition came to the northern states gradually, so that some northern Blacks were still enslaved until 1860. More significant was the role of the slave trade as a vital part of northern economy and the profitable links between northern economic institutions (factories, banks, etc.) and the plantation system.

Slaveowners and their supporters who occupied the Presidency, the Congress, the Supreme Court and other offices dominated national policy until the time of the Civil War. Opposition to slaveholding interests was frequently a dangerous undertaking. The racism created to justify slavery based on color found its way into every part of the country. Discrimination and segregation were common in the North, and most Northerners believed the African American to be inferior. Northern attitudes toward freedom for the slaves can be seen as liberal only when compared to southern attitudes.

Let My People Go: The Story of the Underground Railroad and the Growth of the Abolition Movement. Henrietta Buckmaster.
See especially pp. 9-10 and 221-255 for discussion of national pro-slavery dominance. See pp. 20 and 176-177 for discussion of repressive fugitive slave laws.

The Slave Catchers: Enforcement of the Fugitive Slave Law, 1850-1860. Stanley W. Campbell.
National effect of pro-slavery legislation.

The Negro in Colonial New England 1620-1776. Lorenzo Johnston Greene.

Black Cargoes, pp. 153-170, 245-247, 274, 283-285.
Northern slavery and involvement in the slave trade:

Black Bondage in the North. Edgar J. McManus.

9. Blacks initiated anti-slavery activity and were central to the abolition leadership.

There was a third force behind the new movement for immediate abolition after 1830. It was a stirring among black Americans—both the approximately 320,000 Negroes who were free and the 2 million slaves.

The Impact of Our Past, p. 354

Black people, as the oppressed group, *initiated* anti-slavery activity. Resistance and rebellion from the earliest times were actions aimed at abolishing slavery. Petitions for freedom are recorded as early as 1661. Petitions to the Massachusetts legislature in the 1770's from people held in bondage, based the argument for abolition of slavery on the principles of freedom and justice enunciated in the struggle with Britain. While white people of conscience generally had resources to publicize their efforts, it was Blacks who were at the heart of abolitionist activity and played leading roles throughout.

Abolitionists did not all share the same views. Some believed in the

Great Negroes Past and Present. Russell L. Adams.
Biographical sketches include Tubman, Truth and Douglass.

To Be Free: Studies in American Negro History. Herbert Aptheker, pp. 41-74.
Analyzes the roots and scope of militant abolitionism.

QUOTATION	COMMENT	REFERENCE

9. (Continued)

Abolitionists were very active and very forceful. But they never won wide support either in the North or South. Most Americans were in favor of the Constitution and disliked those who were not. The public did not approve of abolitionists who urged lawbreaking in the name of a "higher law."

American History for Today, p. 193

use of "moral suasion" to eradicate slavery, while others advocated political activity and/or armed resistance. But they were united on one point: their advocacy of the immediate, uncompensated overthrow of slavery. Many people, including Abraham Lincoln, were opposed to slavery but were not abolitionists.

The first abolition society was formed in Philadelphia in 1775. The movement became national in the 1830's, and by 1850 was a dominant force in U.S. political life. Its participants were not all Northerners. People such as David Walker and Angelina and Sarah Grimke were Southerners whose hatred of slavery had been nurtured in the slave states, but who wrote and spoke from the North.

Pioneers in Protest. Lerone Bennett, Jr. Includes Samuel E. Cornish, John B. Russworm, Garrison, and Wendell Phillips.

Let My People Go.

Documents of Upheaval: Selections From William Lloyd Garrison's The Liberator, 1831-1865. Truman Nelson.

The Black Abolitionists. Benjamin Quarles.

10. The life of the free African American was often only a slight improvement over the life of a slave.

. . . laws hampering free Negroes were made even stricter. The first United States census in 1790 counted more than 750,000 Negroes in the total population of nearly 4,000,000. Of the Negroes almost 700,000 were slaves.

The Impact of Our Past, p. 102

This text, like some others, provides very limited information on the situation of free Blacks. In 1790 there were 59,000 free Blacks in the U.S. (By Civil War time, the number had climbed to nearly 500,000, half of whom lived in the South.) Life for the free Blacks was increasingly precarious after the Revolutionary War. They were refused voting rights in many states, and lost prior voting rights in others. Employment was generally limited to menial jobs. They had difficulty in obtaining an education, often being required to pay taxes in support of the public schools they were not allowed to attend. Some states prohibited free Black immigration while others required entering Blacks to post bonds as guarantees of good conduct, or to be registered, or even to have a white guardian. All southern states required free Blacks to carry a pass. The possibilities of being kidnapped and sold into slavery, or of being falsely identified as a runaway, were always present. The notorious Fugitive Slave Law of 1850 increased the chances of enslavement so greatly that thousands of free Blacks went to Canada.

Slaves Without Masters, pp. 51-132.

From Slavery to Freedom, pp. 214-241.

A Pictorial History of the Negro in America. Langston Hughes and Milton Meltzer, pp. 52-83.

North of Slavery. Leon F. Litwack. The repression of free Blacks in the ante-bellum North, their accomplishments and struggles for justice.

Black Bondage in the North, pp. 180-188.

11. Blacks who participated in the take-over of the West were also oppressed by white society.

In spite of many hardships and dangers, hundreds of pioneers completed the trip to the Oregon country. There they started new farms, new homes, and a new life.

Man In America, p. 270

Textbooks frequently fail to mention that Black people took part in the take-over of the West, as trappers, missionaries, explorers, Pony Express riders, railroad laborers, cowboys and members of the U.S. Army. Some participated in the suppression of Native Americans. Other Black people who had escaped slavery and found refuge with Native American nations, fought alongside them against the whites.

Negroes in the Early West. Olive W. Burt.

QUOTATION	COMMENT	REFERENCE

11. (Continued)

| | But while Black people were involved in the exploration of the West that preceded U.S. settlement (and the area was prohibited to slavery), discrimination against Black people persisted. In 1844, a provision was added to Oregon's constitution expelling Black people within three years and decreeing that any Blacks who entered should be flogged. After the establishment of the Republic of Texas, the Texas Congress ordered all free Black people out of the Republic. The 1850 Indiana Constitution barred Black people from entering or settling in the state. Western states barred Black men from voting and adopted a variety of other discriminatory practices. | *The Negro Cowboys*. Philip Durham and Everett L. Jones.

From Slavery to Freedom, pp. 265-270.

The Black Frontiersmen. J. Norman Heard.

The Black West. William Katz.

North Into Freedom. John Malvin, pp. 1-22. |

12. The lack of land redistribution was the fundamental failure of Reconstruction.

| *[The freedpeople] would need food, homes, and jobs. They would need education and training. But they did not get these things along with freedom. What they got was the opportunity to work as free men.*

The most serious problem facing Southerners— white and black alike—was how to get the farms producing again. . . . An important part of the problem was to develop a new relationship between the races. Before the war, the slave system provided most of the labor needed to farm the land and harvest the crops of the South. Now, a new solution to the labor problem had to be found.

America: Its People and Values, p. 476, p. 487 | Texts do state that freedpeople needed voting rights, food, homes and education. However, they neglect to explain that they also needed an economic base upon which to build their political "rights" and social "freedom." Since it was the uncompensated labor of four million freedpeople and their forebears that had developed the economy of the South, they had a right to compensation. Without an economic base, independence from white control was impossible, since Black "labor" was totally at the mercy of white capital.

Many proposals for land distribution were made, involving either the confiscation of the rebels' plantations or the division of publicly held southern lands to freedpeople. At the time these proposals were made and in the years that followed, the federal government gave millions of acres to homesteaders and to railroad tycoons, although neither group could justify their acquisition as compensation for past labor. | *A documentary History of the Negro People in the United States, Vol. II*. Herbert Aptheker (ed.), pp. 633-636, 652-654.

"Black Struggle For Land During Reconstruction," Milfred C. Fierce, in *Black Scholar*, February, 1974.

Black Reconstruction in America, 1860-1880. W.E.B. DuBois.

The Betrayal of the Negro. Rayford W. Logan, pp. 125-146.

The Era of Reconstruction. Kenneth M. Stampp, pp. 122-131, 186-215. |

13. When freedpeople had land, they displayed incentive and skill, establishing productive lives.

| *. . . three and a half million blacks became free men. Many southerners did not know how to live without slaves. Many former slaves did not know how to live without their former masters.* | The portrayal of freedpeople as "helpless," child-like, rootless wanderers needing leadership and benevolence is a distortion. As after any major war, there was much destruction and confusion—plus the additional factor of liberation for four million people. | |

QUOTATION	COMMENT	REFERENCE

13. (Continued)

The law had made them free but had left them helpless.
Most slaves could neither read nor write. . . .
Some slaves thought that freedom meant they would no longer have to work. Others abruptly left the plantation to crowd southern cities. . . . After a period of homeless and jobless wandering, most had to settle for work as farm laborers.

The Pageant of American History, pp. 281-282

Only about a million acres of confiscated land was distributed to freedpeople, but most of this was later taken from them. There are numerous examples of their successful farming and of their organization of civil governments that provided necessary services. These examples illustrate the potential of land distribution that could have revolutionized the South.

In 1863, the plantations of Jefferson Davis and his brother were divided and seventy freedpeople were given 30 acres each, while a Black regiment protected them from Confederates. This "Davis Bend" program was so successful that by 1865 another 5,000 acres were given to 1,800 Blacks organized into 181 companies. The government supplied equipment and supplies which were repaid when crops were sold. The people opened stores, established a school, set up a government, and provided free medical services to all who could not afford a doctor. In 1865, they cleared $160,000 after paying expenses.

Eyewitness: The Negro in American History. William Loren Katz.
See pp. 245-246 for reference to James Island and General Saxton, and pp. 258-259 for Hampton, Virginia.

Mississippi: Conflict & Change. James Loewen and Charles Sallis (eds.).
See pp. 136-137 for discussion of Davis Bend.

To improve their status they would need education, prosperity, and able leadership. Yet almost no ex-slave in 1865 had even the skills, tools, or land needed just to support himself.

The Impact of Our Past, p. 397

A visitor to Hampton, Virginia, another such development, wrote: "I found it a thrifty village, occupied chiefly by freedmen [with] sash-factory and blacksmith's shop, shoemakers' shops and stores. . . . I found no idleness anywhere. . . . On one estate of six hundred acres there was a thriving community of 800 freedmen."

These and other successful ventures were destroyed when rebel Confederates received pardons from President Johnson and were allowed to regain "their" land. General Saxton, commanding the Department of the South, pleaded in vain for Congress to buy such land and let the freedpeople remain. He wrote that on the islands off the coasts of Georgia and South Carolina, "the freedmen have established civil governments with constitutions and laws, with all the different departments for schools, churches, building roads, and other improvements." On one of these islands, freedpeople used arms to resist the return of pardoned rebels.

14. Sharecropping resulted in the economic re-enslavement of Black people.

The problem of operating the farms in the South was solved by the sharecropping system. . . . The man who did the handwork was called the sharecropper. Since the owner provided the

Sharecropping only solved the "problem of operating the farms" for the benefit of white landowners and bankers. The freedpeople and poor whites who became sharecroppers became totally dependent. Sharecropping was an effective re-imposition of white control over

Freedom Bound.

Black Reconstruction.

QUOTATION	COMMENT	REFERENCE

14. (Continued)

land, the work animals, the seeds, and the tools, he received the larger share of the crop.

America: Its People and Values, p. 487

the labor of Black people and of white profit from their labor. It marked the failure of Reconstruction—well before the withdrawal of federal troops in 1877 and the establishment of Jim Crow policies.

The Betrayal of the Negro.

The Era of Reconstruction.

---

15. The Reconstruction governments were more progressive and democratic than later southern governments.

In some cases, blacks and white northerners did not run the state governments well. Some men took bribes. Others stole public money. In some elections, blacks were allowed to vote more than one time. Each time they used a different name. On the whole, however, blacks who had never before had a part in government did well. Schools were built and attempts were made to have blacks own land. The important thing was that blacks now had a voice in their government.

History of the American People, pp. 255-256

Black officeholders included both ex-slaves and educated men who had never been enslaved.

The Impact of Our Past, p. 400

While newer texts do present more information on the positive activities of the Reconstruction period, the negative myths of corruption and incompetence are emphasized too frequently. The Reconstruction governments were generally less corrupt than were later all-white Democratic governments or northern governments of that time.

Tax reform, penal reform, voting rights without regard to race or property, free public education, reapportionment of legislatures and greater rights for women were some of the advances made. These reforms benefitted poor whites as well as Black people.

While it is true that most of the freedpeople could not read or write, neither could many white Southerners, or many immigrants who voted in the North. Most of the Black office holders—ex-slaves or not—were educated. They included artisans, ministers and businessmen. Half of the Black men elected to the U.S. Congress during that period were college educated.

Black Power USA: The Human Side of Reconstruction. Lerone Bennett, Jr. See especially chapters 6 & 7.

Freedom Bound.

Black Reconstruction.

Reconstruction After the Civil War. John Hope Franklin. See especially pp. 152-173, 194-217.

---

16. Post-reconstruction brought a rigidly segregated society, with full federal support.

In the 1880's and 1890's . . . the [Supreme] Court ruled in a number of decisions that state segregation laws did not violate the Fourteenth Amendment. The Supreme Court, however, did set one requirement. If a state law required segregation in schools or on railroads, the facilities provided for whites and blacks must be equal.

America: Its People and Values, pp. 490-491

This textbook does not challenge the alleged equality of facilities set aside for Blacks. While some texts do give scattered statistics on the blatant hypocrisy involved in the "separate-but-equal" doctrine, none reveals the human and social toll caused by inferior education, health care, housing, etc. The continuous struggle against racism and segregation by Black people and some whites for decades prior to the "Civil Rights" movement should be discussed.

After Reconstruction, the South passed a rash of Jim Crow laws in the space of a few years. In 1883 the Supreme Court declared the anti-segregation Civil Rights Act of 1875 unconstitutional. The 1896 Supreme Court decision, *Plessy* v. *Ferguson*, gave more specific

Civil Rights: The Challenge of the Fourteenth Amendment. Peter Goldman.

Black Protest: History, Documents and Analysis, 1619 to the Present. Joanne Grant.

The Thin Disguise: Turning Point in Negro History, Plessy v Ferguson—A Documentary Presentation (1864-1896). Otto H. Olsen (ed).

QUOTATION	COMMENT	REFERENCE

16. (Continued)

federal sanction to segregation. The "separate-but-equal" doctrine, established as national policy, continued until the 1954 Supreme Court decision proclaimed separate education to be unequal.

The complicity of various government agencies and officials, always a factor in the maintenance of segregation, continues to postpone the death of Jim Crow. Segregation as a legal force has ended, but it persists "de facto"—in fact.

The Black American. Benjamin Quarles, pp. 364-489.

Crusade For Justice: The Autobiography of Ida B. Wells. Ida B. Wells.

The Strange Career of Jim Crow. C. Van Woodward.

---

17. The racism of organized labor has harmed Black people and disrupted the potential for working-class unity.

The A.F. of L. got its start in 1886 . . . The American Federation of Labor is a combined organization, or federation, of craft unions. A craft union is made up of workers in a single craft or trade. Carpenters, for example, have a craft union. So do plumbers, electricians, and so on. Carpenters in a community belong to a local union. *The local carpenters' union, in turn, belongs to a* national union *of carpenters. The same is true of plumbers, electricians, and other craft workers. . . . From the earliest days of the organization, the A.F. of L. membership was made up almost entirely of skilled workers.*

America: Its People and Values, pp. 649-650

Most textbooks present the development of trade unionism without analyzing the impact of the unions' racial policies. In 1866 the National Labor Union decided to organize Black workers, but in 1869 developed a policy of separate Black unions. Isaac Myers, a Black labor leader, then organized the National Colored Labor Union which adopted a statement saying: ". . . we make no discrimination as to nationality, sex or color. Any labor movement based on such discrimination . . . . will be suicidal, for it arrays against the classes represented by it all other laboring classes which ought to be rather allied in the closest union and avoid these dissensions and divisions which in the past have given wealth the advantage over labor." The statement then called on the white worker, ". . . so long ill-taught and advised that his true interest is gained by hatred and abuse of the laborers of African descent, as well as the Chinaman . . . having one and the same interest . . . to join us in our movement and thus aid in the protection and conservation of their and our interests."

Because of exclusionary union practices, strikebreaking was often the only means of employment open to Black people, although Black workers sometimes refused to be used in such a role. There were instances of Black-white unity, notably the successful strike of 10,000 longshoremen in New Orleans at the turn of the century. But the practice of white unions, particularly the craft unions, was one of exclusion and racism. The racist policies and practices of those developmental years are reflected today in the leadership and practices of many unions, such as those mentioned by the textbook: plumbers, carpenters and electricians.

A Documentary History of the Negro People in the United States.
Includes many documents relating to labor. See especially pp. 632-633 for full statement of the National Colored Labor Union.

"The Racial Practices of Organized Labor—The Age of Gompers and After," Herbert Hill, in *Employment, Race & Poverty.*

The Betrayal of the Negro, pp. 147-162.

QUOTATION	COMMENT	REFERENCE

18. Wilson's "progressive" policies were meant "for whites only."

The frequent failure of textbooks to present the racist views and actions of Woodrow Wilson is symptomatic of their general disinclination to present the racist views and actions of this nation's leaders and presidents.

Reluctant Reformers: Racism and Social Reform Movements in the United States. Robert L. Allen.

Woodrow Wilson had gained national prominence as a foe of privilege and as a person with extraordinary powers of leadership. . . . A southerner who had lived most of his life in the North . . . a scholar who knew the past as well as the present, Wilson was able to see public questions in perspective. As befitted the son and grandson of clergymen, he approached public questions with high idealism. Wilson's inauguration, like that of Jefferson or of Jackson, represented a peaceful revolution on behalf of the common people.

A Free People, p. 125

Wilson was a Southerner, as were half of his Cabinet and a high proportion of Washington functionaries. He told an African American delegation which was protesting his policies, "Segregation is not humiliating, but a benefit, and ought to be so regarded by you gentlemen." Both as President and historian, Wilson manifested white supremacist views. His writings on southern history and his firm support for the blatantly racist film "Birth of a Nation," of which he said, "It's like writing history with lightning . . . and is all so terribly true," raise serious questions about this textbook's claim that he "knew the past," and about what perspective he used to view questions about race.

Under the Wilson administration, the Post Office, the Treasury, the Bureau of Printing and Engraving, the Interior Department, the Senate and the Library of Congress segregated their facilities, restaurants or offices. Many Black employees of the federal government in the South were downgraded or fired.

The White Savage: Racial Fantasies in the Postbellum South. Lawrence J. Friedman, pp. 150-172.

Early American Views on Negro Slavery. Matthew Mellon. Discusses views of Franklin, Washington, Jefferson and Madison.

Lincoln and the Negro. Benjamin Quarles.

Fathers and Children. Michael Paul Rogin. Discusses Jackson's views.

19. Discrimination faced by European immigrants was different from the racism faced by Blacks.

When textbooks compare the immigrant experience to the Black experience, the implication is that Blacks can "make it" too, if they only would work hard enough. The effect of color is ignored.

Like other poor immigrants from Europe . . . many poor blacks had a hard time finding jobs and decent housing, staying healthy and out of trouble with the law. In 1910 concerned blacks founded the National Urban League to help such Negro newcomers with the problems of city living that they faced in common with other Americans.

The Impact of Our Past, p. 413

Many European ethnics faced intense prejudice for varying periods in the U.S., but were eventually accepted at most levels of society. Ethnic prejudice never reached the social, cultural and institutional scale practiced against Black people. Racist attitudes were quickly assimilated by white ethnics upon their arrival in this country. No matter how poorly they were paid, it was still possible for them to look down upon Black and other third world peoples. This racism was useful to employers as a tool to keep labor divided and wages low. Linking the immigrant experience to the Black experience encourages students to blame the latter for not achieving as much as the former. It encourages "blaming the victim."

Report of the National Advisory Commission on Civil Disorders, pp. 278-282. A flawed but concise discussion of the differences between the Black and the immigrant experiences.

Blaming the Victim. William Ryan. A provocative study of the mythology that results from the syndrome of blaming the victim.

QUOTATION	COMMENT	REFERENCE

20. Institutional racism, not merely individual prejudice, causes and perpetuates racial inequality.

Separate schools were generally the rule in both the North and the South. In the North blacks and whites were separated mainly because of segregated neighborhoods. Children from black neighborhoods went to schools which were nearly all black in student population. Children from white neighborhoods went to schools in which nearly all were white. In the South, regardless of neighborhood, blacks, by law, had to go to all-black schools.

The Pageant of American History, p. 459

Low-income families have little choice in where they can live. Racial prejudice has kept minority groups out of the better neighborhoods and forced them into run-down sections of the cities.

Man In America, p. 624

Textbooks do report segregation in housing and schooling, but they rarely delve into the interconnected racist practices of all institutions. The entire gamut of institutions—business, unions, education, health, church, government, media—are controlled by whites, and function in ways which subordinate third world people. The prejudice of individual whites—while destructive—plays a secondary role.

It is circuitous to state that segregated schools resulted from segregated neighborhoods, without discussing the practices and policies of real estate agencies, banks and zoning boards in the maintenance of segregated housing. Even when the causes of segregated housing are analyzed, northern school segregation must also be related to educational practices such as site selection and the setting of district boundaries, mechanisms through which northern communities establish and perpetuate segregated schools.

Textbooks mislead students to believe that racism can be destroyed merely by changing individual attitudes, rather than explaining the need to change institutional policies and practices.

Black Power: The Politics of Liberation in America. Stokely Carmichael and Charles V. Hamilton.

Fact Sheets on Institutional Racism.

Institutional Racism in America. Louis L. Knowles and Kenneth Prewitt.

21. The myth of "progress" obscures the existing reality of the majority of Black people.

Black Americans thus entered the 1900's handicapped by problems they had not anticipated during the first hopeful years of freedom. Yet despite those handicaps they made impressive advances. . . . *Negroes won* increasing success *in every field of activity—science, medicine, the professions, business, music and art, entertainment and sports. By the end of World War II they had made* marked—*although still drastically limited—progress toward fuller political, legal, and social rights. During the postwar years the movement to end discrimination in government, business, education and sports began to accelerate. President Truman took steps to* insure equal opportunities *for black Americans, and a number of barriers*

Progress has been achieved in ending Jim Crow practices and enacting civil rights laws. But the textbook images of "marked progress," "impressive advances," or "insured equal opportunity" do not reflect reality for the majority of Black people.

While average income for Blacks has increased as a result of general economic growth and inflation, the gap between the median white and median Black income widened from $1,576 in 1950 to $2,846 in 1959, and to $5,548 in 1974. Black unemployment has consistently been twice as high as white. Black business receipts are 0.3 percent of all business receipts. Blacks are still less than 3 percent of all professionals. Black officeholders represent less than 1 percent of the total of elected officials. In spite of new laws, the national scope of segregation in schools and housing has not changed significantly.

"Black Prosperity Image Found to Be Superficial," in *New York Times,* May 31, 1976.

"Blacks Have Made Political Gains But Signs of Frustration are Widespread," in *New York Times,* June 1, 1976.

"Are Most Blacks In the Middle Class?" Herrington J. Bryce, in *Black Scholar,* February, 1975.

Fact Sheets on Institutional Racism.

QUOTATION	COMMENT	REFERENCE

21. (Continued)

began to break down. . . . Under President Eisenhower progress in civil rights continued. (emphasis added)

Rise of the American Nation, pp. 823-824

Perhaps the greatest success of the civil rights movement was the achievement of greater political rights for black citizens. . . . In 1974, more than 2,700 black Americans were elected to government offices in the United States, including seventeen elected to Congress. The number of black office holders doubled between 1968 and 1973.

America: Its People and Values, pp. 790-791

And economic, political and social power remain firmly entrenched within white institutions. The oppressed condition of the masses of Black people, and the precarious economic and social status of others, defines a reality for Black people as a whole that is not reflected in textbooks.

AFRICAN AMERICAN TEXTBOOK CHECKLIST

Title _____

Publisher _____ Year _____ Grade Level _____

There are 21 criteria to be scored. The highest possible rating is +42. The lowest is –42. This text scores _____ .

	Incorrect Information	No Information	Omits This Period	Limited Information	Full Information
	−2	−1	0	+1	+2
1. African, as well as European, culture forms an integral part of the U.S. heritage.					
2. Africans were in the Americas prior to 1619.					
3. The North American slave trade created enormous profits, became the most brutal system of slavery known, and disrupted African civilization.					
4. The significance of the Revolution, to Blacks, goes beyond participation in combat.					
5. The Constitution was a pro-slavery document and remained so for 78 years.					
6. Slavery was inherently cruel and inhuman.					
7. Rebellion and slavery went hand in hand.					
8. While there were differences in the institution between North and South, slavery was never a regional issue.					
9. Blacks initiated anti-slavery activity and were central to the abolition leadership.					
10. The life of the free African American was often only a slight improvement over the life of a slave.					
11. Blacks who participated in the take-over of the West were also oppressed by white society.					
12. The lack of land redistribution was the fundamental failure of Reconstruction.					
13. When freedpeople had land, they displayed incentive and skill, establishing productive lives.					
14. Sharecropping resulted in the economic re-enslavement of Black people.					
15. The Reconstruction governments were more progressive and democratic than later southern governments.					
16. Post-reconstruction brought a rigidly segregated society, with full Federal support.					
17. The racism of organized labor has harmed Black people and disrupted the potential for working-class unity.					
18. Wilson's "progressive" policies were meant "for whites only."					

	−2	−1	0	+1	+2
19. Discrimination faced by European immigrants was different from the racism faced by Blacks.					
20. Institutional racism, not merely individual prejudice, causes and perpetuates racial inequality.					
21. The myth of "progress" obscures the existing reality of the majority of Black people.					
Total					
Textbook Final Score					

ASIAN AMERICANS

Who are Asian Americans? There is an ongoing discussion among Asian Americans about exactly *who* is described by that classification. The broadest definition includes the peoples of all "Asian" countries, including China, Japan, the Philippines, Korea, Indonesia, Malaysia, the Pacific Islands, Cambodia, Laos, Vietnam, Thailand, Burma, Pakistan, India, etc., who live in the U.S. While recognizing the cultural diversity of each of these peoples, the term "Asian American" has come to symbolize a sense of common Asian heritage, pride in Asian cultures and a recognition of similar historical experiences and present-day problems in the U.S. The Asian Americans whose historical experiences will be discussed in this book are people of Chinese, Japanese and Pilipino* descent—as they are the three largest Asian American population groups in the U.S. and have the longest history in this country.

The 1970 census recorded 591,000 people of Japanese descent; 435,000 of Chinese descent; 343,000 of Pilipino descent; 100,000 of Hawaiian descent; 76,000 of Indian descent; 70,000 of Korean descent; 9,000 of Pakistani descent and 506,000 "other" Asians. Over 100,000 Vietnamese were added to the Asian American population after the U.S. defeat in Vietnam.

TERMINOLOGY

Textbooks often refer to Asian Americans as "Orientals" or "Asiatics." Many Asian Americans consider the term "Oriental" a pejorative word that evokes images of the "exotic Orient"—a "land of spices, silk and jade." "Oriental" as well as "Asiatic" also evokes the image of "un-American" foreigners. Neither term takes into account that Asian Americans are both U.S. citizens and people of Asian descent—and are aware of these two aspects of their heritage.

Examination of Asian American history sheds interesting light upon the present functioning of racism in the U.S. In 1848, when the first Chinese arrived, white society had subjugated large numbers of third world peoples through force. Native Americans were decimated by disease, genocide and warfare and were already well on the way to total segregation on reservations. African Americans were enslaved and kept in bondage by law and by force. Chicanos were subjugated by armed force after the military defeat of their country. But such methods were neither practical nor desirable in the new situation posed by Chinese immigrants. Therefore, white society's previous models of total racial oppression began to change.

NEW MODEL FOR RACISM

The Chinese were recruited by U.S. business interests that wanted a large, mobile and low-paid labor force to develop the newly conquered western regions. The Chinese therefore became a model for the later treatment of other "free" third world peoples—a mobile yet controlled group as part of a racial-labor caste system. Instead of the total repression heretofore practiced, the new mode was: to encourage the arrival of work forces when business needed them, but to pay them less than whites; to discourage their arrival when business did not need extra labor; and to prevent interracial working-class unity, by encouraging friction among groups of third world workers and divisions between them and white workers, in order to keep down wages paid to all labor.

Thus, Asian Americans served as the test group to develop and refine the system of institutional racial oppression operating through business, labor unions, education, employment practices, etc.—the system that continues to exploit third world people in the U.S. today.

Asian immigration evolved into a cyclical pattern of recruitment, exploitation and exclusion—at least in terms of Chinese, Japanese and

* While most texts use "Filipino" we will use "Pilipino" because there is no phonetic "ph" or "f" sound indigenous to the Philipine language, and also because many Pilipino groups prefer this term.

Pilipino immigration. First, Chinese laborers were recruited as a source of low-paid, exploitable labor. When there was a temporary business recession, the Chinese were scapegoated, subjected to racism and violence, and ultimately excluded. However, when the desire of employers for a source of cheap labor arose again, large-scale recruitment of Japanese laborers resulted and the entire pattern was repeated. Exclusion of Japanese as a source of low-paid labor led to recruitment of Pilipino laborers. The cycle continued until they, too, were restricted from immigrating. All three groups were victimized by exclusionary racist legislation—Asians being the first to be excluded from this country. And all three groups were characterized by predominantly male immigration and a high sex imbalance caused by that exclusion.

Textbooks, for the most part, omit this history of Asian Americans—their role as workers in a wide variety of occupations; the institutionalized oppression, economic exploitation and anti-Asian violence they faced; their long history of resistance and struggle; and the present-day problems that confront them.

FOREIGN AND DOMESTIC POLICIES TIED

Textbooks often lead one to believe that the U.S. established the Open Door Policy in order to protect the sovereignty of China. Omitted is discussion of the profits and privileges received by the U.S. as the West divided China into spheres of influence. The U.S. is said to have "opened the doors of Japan in 1853," but students often do not understand that it was done under the intimidation of Commodore Perry's gunboats. Textbooks tell us that the U.S. helped "liberate" the Philippines from Spanish rule, but often fail to mention or fully describe the Pilipinos' strong fight against U.S. control. These ethnocentric portrayals not only evade the imperialistic nature of U.S. Asian policy, but also omit the effects of those policies on Asians in the U.S.

The treatment of Asians in the U.S. has often reflected the state of relations between the U.S. and the Asian countries of origin. The internment of tens of thousands of Japanese in the U.S. during WW II is the most obvious example of this connection. The earlier action of Theodore Roosevelt in response to Japan's protests against the segregation of Japanese students in San Francisco, and the fact that anti-Japanese legislation never actually referred to the Japanese by name, reflected the U.S. respect for the power of Japan. On the other hand, the failure to respond to China's protests about anti-Chinese activity and the adoption of anti-Chinese legislation that specifically named the Chinese, reflected the U.S. disdain of China as a weak nation. The 1943 Magnuson Act providing a minimum immigration quota for Chinese resulted from China's position as a war-time ally. The systematic repression of Chinese American political activists in the late 1940's and the 1950's resulted from the anti-communist fervor of the cold-war period, the 1949 victory of communism in China and China's position during the Korean War. Since the Philippines was a U.S. colony, Pilipinos were classified neither as aliens nor as citizens of the U.S., but as "nationals." Thus, for a period of time after other Asians were excluded, Pilipinos were accorded unlimited rights of immigration to the U.S.

IMAGES OF ASIAN AMERICANS

Asians have been portrayed in the dominant U.S. culture as treacherous, evil and lacking in respect for their own lives. Images of "banzai attacks," "hara-kiri" and "yellow hordes" created the perception that Asians consider life cheap. This had the effect of legitimizing the decision to drop atomic bombs on Japanese cities and to napalm and defoliate Vietnam.

Textbooks perpetuate two interrelated stereotypes of Asian Americans. Asian workers are repeatedly described as "willing" to work for low wages, evoking an image of "coolie" laborers who are faceless beasts of burden. This stereotype ignores the oppression which forced Asian laborers to take any available work in order to survive. Related to this distortion is the stereotype of Asians as "docile," "complacent" or "subservient." This stereotype "explains" their supposed willingness to be exploited. Both stereotypes are reinforced because textbooks do not present the persistent labor struggles and legal battles carried on by Asian Americans.

Textbooks and Asian Americans

Chinese Americans

QUOTATION	COMMENT	REFERENCE
1. Multiple reasons caused the Chinese to come to the U.S.		
While adventurous nineteenth-century Americans sought their fortunes in China, thousands of Chinese crossed the Pacific in the opposite direction for the same reason. At first they came to look for gold in California in 1849. The Impact of Our Past, p. 547	Natural disasters, famines and corruption plagued China. Social, economic and political life was disrupted because of colonization by Western powers. Peasants were taxed exorbitantly for the importation of opium forced upon them by the British. Industrial and agricultural interests in the U.S. wanted cheap labor to exploit western resources. Representatives actively recruited Chinese by telling them of supposed opportunities in the U.S., describing a "Mountain of Gold." Because of poverty and starvation in China, the effort was successful. Most who came were men, intending to return to China. Families remained behind. As early as 1852, Chinese women started arriving in the U.S. They were kidnapped, or bought, and sold here as prostitutes. They were kept as prisoners and, if they attempted escape, their "owners" bribed San Francisco police and courts to return them.	*Contacts and Conflicts—The Asian Immigration Experience.* *Ethnic Americans—A History of Immigration and Assimilation.* Leonard Dinnerstein and David Reimers. "Causes of Chinese Emigration," Pyau Ling, in *Roots: An Asian American Reader* "Forgotten Women," Gayle Louie, in *Asian Women.* *Asians in the West.* Stanford Lyman, pp. 9-26.
2. Anti-Chinese bias existed in the U.S. prior to the time Chinese arrived.		
For some years, Chinese laborers had been welcome additions to the labor supply. . . . in 1873 when the depression hit the country . . . workmen feared that the Chinese would take their jobs at low wages. Fear and insecurity were intensified because the Chinese, for reasons not always of their own choosing, lived entirely to themselves, and did not learn American ways of living. Rise of the American Nation, p. 500	Negative images of Chinese people had been shaped by U.S. traders, missionaries and diplomats, who often described them as immoral, dishonest, superstitious and intellectually inferior. Such accounts were widely circulated through the press and literature. After 1840, this older Sinophobia was supplemented by sensational newspaper coverage of events in China, such as the Tai Ping Rebellion and Arrow Wars, including accounts of "massacres" of Christians and traders.	*Images of Asia: American Views of China and India.* Harold Isaacs. *Chinese Americans.* Stanford Lyman, pp. 55-58. Analyzes Chinese experience in U.S. *The Unwelcome Immigrant—The American Image of the Chinese, 1785-1882.* Stuart Miller.

QUOTATION	COMMENT	REFERENCE

3. The Chinese experienced both suffering and exploitation in building the railroad.

They were the backbone of the construction gangs that built the western section of the first transcontinental railroad.

Rise of the American Nation, p. 500

The Central Pacific, plagued by a labor shortage, initially hired 50 Chinese as an experiment (it was thought the Chinese were too "small" for such labor). Ultimately, over 12,000 Chinese laborers were hired. They worked from sunrise to sundown, six days a week for $26 a month. They built the railroad over incredibly difficult terrain and were forced to work through the West's worst recorded blizzard. It has been estimated that at least 1,200 Chinese died during the construction of the railroad. The railroad owners received free land, plus $16,000 to $48,000 from the government for every mile constructed.

Outlines: History of the Chinese in America. H.M. Lai and Philip Choy, pp. 55-60.

Chinese Working People in America. Wei Min She Labor Committee.

4. Chinese worked at many occupations and were instrumental in developing some industries.

For a time, Chinese workers were in great demand. They helped build the transcontinental railroads. They also worked as household servants or as waiters and launderers.

America: Its People and Values, p. 551

Most texts, if they mention Chinese laborers at all, discuss their work in the railroads and service industries. With the completion of the railroad, Chinese began to enter other areas of employment: garment and footwear manufacturing, fishing, canneries, cigarmaking, land reclamation, agricultural work, and construction, as well as domestic and service industries.

Chinese were instrumental in the development of many of these industries. They were the mainstay of the early woolen and cigar industries of the West. Thousands of acres of wasteland were turned into rich, productive agricultural fields by Chinese, and they constituted over half of the farm labor in California in the 1880's.

A History of the Chinese in California. H.M. Lai and Philip Choy, pp. 30-64.
Outlines: History of the Chinese in America, pp. 47-88.

Both books offer an excellent description of the many occupational areas Chinese were involved in.

Asians in the West, pp. 57-80.

5. Racism systematically excluded Chinese from entering into, or remaining in, some fields of work.

Few had the money to buy a farm, and so many Chinese became cooks and laundrymen. American pioneers often thought such jobs unmanly, but Chinese men did not think it was only women's work to feed people or do laundry.

The Impact of Our Past, p. 547

This quote is misleading. Since most Chinese were saving money to return to China, few wanted to buy farms. Moreover, this text—like many—omits the systematic exclusion of Chinese laborers from urban industries and agriculture.

Exclusion was brought about through boycotts, "anti-coolie clubs," and physical violence. The success of this policy became evident with the near disappearance of Chinese—by 1910—from any occupation that was competitive with whites. Chinese were forced into service jobs looked down upon by white workers.

The cigar industry provides an example. Chinese first appeared in that industry in the 1850's and by 1866 owned half the cigar

"Anti-Oriental Agitation and the Rise of Working Class Racism," Herbert Hill, in *Society.* January 1973.

To Serve the Devil: Vol. II Jacobs, Landau and Pell, pp. 66-166.

Chinese Americans, pp. 58-85.

The Indispensable Enemy—Labor and the Anti-Chinese Movement in California. Alexander Saxton, pp. 3-19. Description of the labor force in California.

QUOTATION	COMMENT	REFERENCE

5. (Continued)

production in San Francisco. By 1870, they comprised 90 percent of the labor force. In 1874, white cigar makers adopted a made-by-white-labor cigar label. Under the "leadership" of Adolph Strasser and Samuel Gompers, the Cigar Makers International Union, in 1884, organized a boycott of brands produced by Chinese labor, and by the late 1880's Chinese had been driven out of the industry.

---

6. Chinese workers organized to resist exploitation.

Because they were willing to work for lower wages, there was fear that they would take jobs away from Americans.

The Pageant of American History, p, 415

Many books state that Chinese were "willing" to work for low wages. Thousands of miles from home, impoverished, facing racism and violence, Chinese *had* to work to survive. Employers exploited their predicament and paid them less. To state that Chinese were "willing" is to blame the victims. This same textbook then contradicts itself, and states that Chinese were "forced" to take low-paying jobs because they were unskilled. This is also a distortion, as both skilled and unskilled Chinese were paid less than comparably qualified whites.

Chinese Working People in America.

They were unskilled and were forced to take jobs that paid very little.

The Pageant of American History, p. 423

The actions of Chinese workers themselves counteract this myth of "willingness." In 1867, for example, 7,000 Chinese railroad workers struck for a 10 hour day, higher wages and an end to the whipping of workers. The strike failed because the isolated workers were starved out by the Central Pacific. Nevertheless, Chinese formed labor guilds in many industries and effectively utilized strikes to win better working conditions.

---

7. Racism was utilized to divide Chinese from other workers.

The Chinese were willing to work for what other laborers considered very low wages. Naturally, employers wanted to hire the lower paid Chinese. As a result, other workers called on the federal government to forbid further Chinese immigration.

America: Its People and Values, p. 551

This text not only blames Chinese for a "willingness" to work for low wages, but additionally blames white workers for the exclusion of Chinese. Employers appear as blameless. They just "naturally" wanted to hire those "willing" to work for less pay.

By the beginning of the 1870's, a depressed economy and increased immigration from Europe created a pool of surplus labor. Utilizing anti-Chinese sentiments, employers and labor "leaders" scapegoated the Chinese, telling white workers that Chinese were the cause of widespread unemployment and inflation. In many instances employers used Chinese laborers to threaten other workers. Boston's Chinatown began in 1875 when Chinese workers were brought from California to break a strike by shoe factory workers. Mississippi's

The Mississippi Chinese. James W. Loewen.

Chinese Working People in America.

QUOTATION	COMMENT	REFERENCE

7. (Continued)

Chinese population—the largest of any southern state—originated in 1870, when Chinese were brought in as sharecroppers to hold Black labor "in line."

Samuel Gompers, the "Father of the American Federation of Labor," and other labor "leaders," were instrumental in driving Chinese out of many industries. In 1902, Gompers co-authored a pamphlet for the Chinese Exclusion Convention entitled "Some Reasons for Chinese Exclusion: Meat vs. Rice, American Manhood Against Asiatic Coolieism—Which Shall Survive?" Rather than working for interracial working-class unity, such "leaders" collaborated with those who divided workers to keep wages down.

---

8. The widespread violence against Chinese was backed by institutional support.

. . . in 1873 . . . a depression hit the country. As unemployment mounted, California workmen feared that the Chinese would take their jobs at low wages. . . . Ill feeling, already running high, was fanned into violence.

Rise of the American Nation, p. 500

Often, there was trouble between the Chinese and other workers.

America: Its People and Values, p. 551

Textbooks generally fail to describe the extensiveness of or the institutional support for the anti-Chinese violence, implying that a few racist individuals were responsible for the troubles that did occur. The anti-Chinese violence predated the 1873 depression (which is when the first quote implies it began) and occurred in the East as well as on the West Coast. Examples include the 1885 massacre of 28 Chinese at Rock Springs, Wyoming, and similar violence in Eureka, California, and Denver, Colorado. In 1886 the entire Chinese populations of Tacoma and Seattle, Washington, were forcibly driven out.

Both state and federal courts supported anti-Chinese activities. For example, Chinese were denied the right to testify against whites in 1854 (*People v. Hall*). With this ruling, individuals were given free reign to rob, assault, and even murder Chinese without fear of legal punishment. In 1882, California declared a legal state holiday for anti-Chinese demonstrations. After the Civil War, anti-Chinese sentiment made it politically advantageous for both the Democratic and Republican parties to take anti-Chinese positions.

"Anti-Oriental Agitation and the Rise of Working Class Racism."

To Serve the Devil: Vol II.

Outlines: History of the Chinese in America.

A History of the Chinese in California.

Asians in the West, pp. 9-26.

Chinese Americans.

The Indispensable Enemy. Chapter II offers an excellent account and analysis of the role of political parties in the anti-Chinese movement.

"*Chink!*." C.T. Wu (ed).

---

9. There were numerous national, state and local anti-Chinese laws.

In 1882 Congress ended all further Chinese immigration.

In Search of America, p. 54-C

Many texts note the 1882 Chinese Exclusion Act and ignore the other local, state and national laws created to victimize Chinese. Examples of such laws fall into three types:

Immigration Legislation—"An Act to Prevent the Further Immigra-

QUOTATION	COMMENT	REFERENCE

9. (Continued)

tion of Chinese or Mongolians to this State" (California), 1858; Scott Act, 1888—Chinese who left were forbidden to return to the U.S.; Geary Act, 1892—extended 1882 immigration restrictions for another decade and required all Chinese laborers to carry certificates of residence; Act of April 29, 1904—extended exclusion indefinitely. *Occupational Restriction Legislation*—Foreign Miners Tax, 1853— designed to drive Chinese from mining; San Francisco Anti-Ironing Ordinance, 1880—prohibited Chinese from ironing at night; California Fish and Games Act, 1893—prohibited use of Chinese fishing nets. *Punitive and Harassing Legislation*—San Francisco Queue Ordinance, 1875—shaving of queues of Chinese in jail; San Francisco Cubic Air Law, 1873—Chinese could be arrested for living in crowded rooms; Anti-Miscegenation Laws—14 states included Chinese in such laws.

A History of the Chinese in California.

Outlines: History of the Chinese in America.

Chinese Americans.

"The Chinese In American Courts," Connie Yu, in *Bulletin Of Concerned Asian Scholars.* Fall, 1972.

---

10. The 1882 Chinese Exclusion Act had extensive ramifications.

In the 1880's, the government acted. Chinese immigration was stopped by a new law passed by Congress.

America: Its People and Values, p. 551

This book, like many others, fails to report that the Act of 1882 stipulated the exclusion of Chinese laborers for a period of 10 years— and denied Chinese in the U.S. the right to become naturalized citizens. Subsequent acts extended the exclusion until 1943. In that year the Magnuson Bill provided a token immigration quota of 100 and permitted the naturalization of Chinese immigrants. (Some assert that this action was a propaganda tool, since the U.S. could not exclude Chinese while China was an ally in WW II.) Most texts also fail to report that the 1882 Act contravened the Burlingame Treaty of 1868. (In that treaty, China and the U.S. had pledged to allow free entry of one another's citizens to each country.)

A History of the Chinese in America.

Outlines: History of the Chinese in America.

Chinese Americans, pp. 54-85.

"Chink!"
Reprints several of the anti-Chinese laws.

---

11. Sixty years of exclusion had devastating social consequences to Chinese in the U.S.

. . . in 1882 Congress enacted a new Chinese Exclusion Act which, with several extensions, continued in effect until World War II.

Rise of the American Nation, p. 500

Because most Chinese men had originally planned to return to China, they left their families behind. Therefore, exclusion resulted in predominantly male communities, husbands separated for years from wives and children, illegal practices to unite families, and the delay of a major U.S.-born generation of Chinese until the 1930's and 1940's. By 1890 there were 2,678 males for every 100 females in the Chinese American population of 107,288. Many Chinese (mostly men) returned to China to be with their families and by 1920 there were only 61,639 Chinese left in the U.S. With this decline (plus some

"Chinese Immigrant Women," Betty Jung, in *Asian Women.*

The Chinese in the United States of America. Rose Hum Lee, pp. 203-218.

Chinese Americans, pp. 86-118.

Longtime Californ': A Documentary Study of An American Chinatown. Victor and Brett DeBary Nee.

QUOTATION	**COMMENT**	**REFERENCE**

---

11. (Continued)

other factors) the ratio in 1920 was 695 males to 100 females. However, it was not until 1943, with amendments to the 1924 Quota Act and the repeal of the Exclusion Act, that a number of Chinese women entered the U.S. and the sex imbalance improved. A high sex imbalance in certain age categories of the Chinese American population remains today, as a legacy of those years of exclusion.

---

12. Chinatowns in the U.S. suffer the problems common to other urban ghettos.

A dragon dance in San Francisco's Chinatown was something new for visiting rural Americans to see. . . . The largest number of immigrants from Asia—primarily from Japan and China—settled in California. Many chose to live in San Francisco's Chinatown and to continue cultural traditions like the dragon dance. . . .

The Impact of Our Past, pp. 469-470

In many cities there remains the evidence of the waves of immigration to this country. . . . Chinatown draws crowds of visitors when it exuberantly celebrates the Chinese New Year.

The Pageant of American History, pp. 412-413

It should not be implied that familiar institutions and customs were the only reasons that Chinese "chose" to live in Chinatowns. Another reason was protection from the hostility and violence encountered in other areas.

Chinatowns are incorrectly portrayed as exotic communities free of social or economic problems. In the 1960's, "urban renewal" destroyed much existing old housing, while, at the same time, the removal of immigration quotas (1965) resulted in an increase of newcomers. As a result, housing—much of which is substandard—is in great demand and is overpriced. Inadequate health care leads to high rates of T.B., anemia, and mental health problems. In 1966, Boston's Chinatown had an infant mortality rate two and a half times that of the rest of the city. The incidence of new T.B. cases was 192 percent greater and the general death rate was 129 percent greater than elsewhere in Boston.

Employment in these communities is limited mainly to restaurant and garment work, both of which suffered serious setbacks in recent years and cannot support the growing population. A 1970 report on Boston's Chinatown showed a median family income of $5,170 per year—the lowest of the city's neighborhoods—with 63 percent of families earning less than $6,000 and 21 percent less than $3,000. In most families, women work to supplement income. More than 75 percent of the women in New York City's Chinatown work in garment factories, which are located in unsafe and poorly ventilated lofts. In 1972 the Department of Labor filed injunctions against 52 Chinatown shops for improper time-and-pay records. Workers were often earning 65 cents an hour for a 50 hour week and—in addition—were not being paid for all of the hours worked. Language difficulties and discrimination keep many Chinatown residents from working outside of the community.

Three books about Chinatown's social institutions:
The Chinese in the United States of America, pp. 132-184.
Ethnic Enterprise in America. Ivan Light, pp. 81-100.
Chinese Americans, pp. 8-51.

"Need For Awareness: An Essay on Chinatown San Francisco," Buck Wong, in *Roots: An Asian American Reader.*

"Chinatown, Their Chinatown: The Truth Behind the Facade," Ron Chernow, in *New York Magazine*, 6/11/73.

"The Chinatown Sweatshops: Oppression and an Alternative," Dean Lan, in *Amerasia Journal*, November, 1971.

"Boston's Chinese: They Have Their Problems Too!" Betty Murphy, in *Chinese-Americans: School and Community Problems.*

Longtime Californ', pp. 253-357.

Chinese Americans, pp. 151-157.

"New York Chinatown Today: Community In Crisis," Rocky Chin, in *Roots: An Asian American Reader.*

QUOTATION	COMMENT	REFERENCE

13. Chinese have a long history of struggle against oppression.

Chinese Americans have been stereotyped as passive and complacent due to their "traditional Asian values." This distorts the history of Chinese, both in China and in the U.S. The ancestors of most Chinese Americans came from the southeastern provinces of China—an area with a tradition of fighting oppression. The revolution which brought an end to the Ching dynasty began there, as did the Tai Ping and Boxer rebellions.

Dramatic—if less evident—changes have been taking place in traditionally "quiet" Asian communities. . . . Asian youths in the early 1970's were no longer willing to play "good, well behaved citizens" if it meant accepting a subservient, stereotyped role. Neither, apparently, was the older generation. . . . In San Francisco the historically compliant Chinese aggressively resisted attempts to bus their children to schools outside of Chinatown.

The American Experience, p. 643

"The 1938 National Dollar Strike," Patricia Fong, in *Asian American Review.* Vol. 2, No. 1, 1975.

The gains achieved by Chinese in the U.S. resulted from persistent struggle. Chinese frequently fought anti-Chinese legislation in the courts. The formation of Chinese labor guilds and unions was common in the second half of the 19th century. Two examples from the first half of the 20th century are the 1933 organization of the Chinese Hand Laundry Alliance in New York to oppose discriminatory license fees and the 14-week strike by Chinese women garment workers in 1938 against the National Dollar Store chain to win the right to unionize. More contemporary examples are the struggles against discriminatory hiring practices of the construction industry and demonstrations against police brutality.

A Historical Survey of Organizations of the Left Among the Chinese in America," H.M. Lai, in *Bulletin of Concerned Asian Scholars.* Fall, 1972.

Asians in the West, pp. 99-118.

Longtime Californ'.

Whereas elderly Asian Americans have been content to maintain life styles based on the traditional values of their cultures, the youth have been growing increasingly rebellious. This rebellion has been against the docile acceptance of discrimination by their elders, against whites for their discriminatory practices, and against traditional Asian values.

The American Experience, p. 645

The hysteria of the anti-communist, cold war era had a paralyzing effect on the Chinese American community, particularly during the tense relationship between the U.S. and the People's Republic of China during the Korean War. The McCarran Act of 1950 (stipulating that people could be apprehended and detained by the government in time of "internal security emergency") and memories of the incarceration of Japanese Americans during WW II, created fear. This period became known as the "silent years," as progressive forces were systematically suppressed by the FBI and Immigration officials, and a conservative leadership became entrenched.

"The Ghetto Of the Mind: Notes On the Historical Psychology Of Chinese America," Ben Tong, in *Amerasia Journal,* November, 1971.

Chinese Working People in America.

The present militancy among Chinese Americans is not a rejection of Asian values or of previous generations, but represents the re-emergence of a long tradition of struggle.

Japanese Americans

QUOTATION	COMMENT	REFERENCE

---

1. U.S. sugar interests in Hawaii recruited and exploited Japanese laborers.

Immigrants also came [to Hawaii] *from China and Japan. Over the years, Americans developed sugar plantations on the islands. Sugar growing soon became the main industry, and Hawaiian sugar was sold at good prices in the United States. . . . New groups were added to the islands' population as Americans, Chinese, and Japanese came to live there.*

America: Its People and Values, p. 678

U.S. business interests in Hawaii desired a large labor force for the expanding sugar industry. Because Western diseases were decimating the native population, labor was sought overseas. In 1852, Chinese laborers were imported but refused to extend their contracts after five years. Then the first group of Japanese contract laborers was brought to Hawaii in 1868. However, complaints of mistreatment led Japan to ban further emigration.

In the 1880's, economic and political turmoil in Japan led the government to resume migration. By 1896, 20,000 Japanese were in Hawaii, constituting the largest single ethnic group on the islands. Organized protests against the harsh conditions they faced occurred between 1890-1920. In 1919, the Federation of Japanese Labor called a strike to end the ten-hour work day for 77¢ pay. The workers and their families were forced out of their company-owned housing during the long strike and more than 1,200 died. The Hawaii Sugar Planters Association spent $12 million to crush the strike.

The rights of Japanese decreased as U.S. influence increased. Japanese had been eligible for citizenship and suffrage under the original Hawaiian constitution. Pro-U.S. annexation groups feared the rising numbers of Japanese as a potential threat to their own power. Their solution was to limit Japanese civil rights by forcing a new constitution on the Hawaiian monarchs, in 1887, which denied citizenship and suffrage to Japanese.

"Asian Immigration to Hawaii," in *Contacts and Conflicts— The Asian Immigration Experience.*

Hawaii Pono: A Social History. Lawrence Fuchs. Excellent description of the Japanese experience in Hawaii.

"R.W. Irwin and Systematic Immigration to Hawaii," Yukiko Irwin and Hilary Conroy, in *East Across the Pacific.* Hilary Conroy and Scott Miyakawa (eds.).

To Serve The Devil: Vol II— Colonials & Sojourners. Paul Jacobs, Saul Landau and Eve Pell, pp. 3-65.

"First Year Immigrants to Hawaii and Eugene Van Reed," Masaji Marumoto, in *East Across The Pacific.*

---

2. Japanese undertook a variety of occupations in the U.S.

Around 1900 Japanese immigrants began to arrive in the West. They became farm workers and gardeners; many soon owned their own farms and businesses.

The Impact of Our Past, p. 548

It is a common misconception that people from "crowded" Japan were "land hungry" and became involved only in farming. At first they became cooks, waiters, gardeners or domestics. Following the Chinese exclusion, however, they were recruited for many of the occupations in which Chinese had formerly been employed. Japanese worked in fish, fruit and vegetable canneries, lumbering, mining, and farm labor. Many became tenant farmers and accomplished impressive achievements in transforming swamplands into productive farmlands.

"Early Issei Socialists and the Japanese Community," Yuji Ichioka, in *Amerasia Journal,* U.C.L.A., July, 1971.

Asians In The West. Stanford Lyman, pp. 57-80.

"One Hundred Years of Japanese Labor in the U.S.A." Karl Yoneda, in *Roots: An Asian American Reader.*

QUOTATION	COMMENT	REFERENCE

3. There was extensive legal, social, and economic persecution of Japanese in this country.

Japanese immigrants ran into many of the same difficulties that the Chinese had faced earlier. Often, other Americans did not treat them fairly.

America: Its People and Values, p. 560

Arriving in the U.S. in large numbers during the 1880's, Japanese inherited the anti-Asian legacy developed against Chinese. Perceived as part of the "Yellow Peril," they were subjected to beatings, lynchings, expulsion from areas in which they lived, and looting and burning of their communities.

But unlike anti-Chinese legislation, anti-Japanese laws did not usually specify the target population. An 1867 Federal District Court had declared Chinese "ineligible for citizenship" and this policy was applied to foreign-born Japanese and upheld by the Supreme Court in 1922. That same year Congress passed the Cable Act, stipulating that " . . . any woman who marries an alien ineligible for citizenship shall cease to be an American citizen." This meant that if a Nisei (second generation, U.S. born citizen) or Caucasian woman married an Issei (first generation, born in Japan), she lost her citizenship.

In 1913, California passed an Alien Land Law, and other western states subsequently did the same. These laws denied the right to own or lease agricultural land to persons ineligible for citizenship. Japanese were the unnamed, but specific targets. Although the constitutionality of these laws was frequently tested, it was not until 1952 that California abolished its Alien Land Law, and 1967 when Washington did likewise. A 1943 California statute barred "aliens ineligible for citizenship" from obtaining commercial fishing licenses. The Supreme Court struck this law down in 1948. Miscegenation laws, school segregation policies and other anti-Asian legislation also were applied to Japanese.

"The Anti-Japanese Land Laws of California and Ten Other States," Dudley McGovney, in *California Law Review*. Exellent reviews of laws against Japanese. For discussion of other anti-Japanese laws, see: *Hirabayashi v. U.S. 320 U.S. 81 (1943); Korematsu v. U.S. 89 Lied. 194 (1944); Oyama v. Calif. 322 U.S. 6A2 (1947); Takahasi v. Fish & Game Commission 334 U.S. 410 (1947).*

The Politics of Prejudice: The Anti-Japanese Movement in California & The Struggle For Japanese Exclusion. Roger Daniels.

4. Theodore Roosevelt manifested anti-Japanese sentiments and actions.

In 1906 San Francisco political leaders . . . segregated San Francisco's schools by placing the city's ninety-three Japanese students in a separate school. At the time, President Theodore Roosevelt was trying to improve trade and establish good relations with Japan. He was embarrassed by the action in San Francisco and called it "wicked" foolishness. He persuaded San Francisco to integrate its schools again.

The Challenge of America, p. 508

Roosevelt intervened in the school controversy because of Japan's diplomatic protests. In trying to satisfy both Japan and anti-Japanese forces in the U.S., he made promises to both sides.

He convinced San Francisco schools to accept Japanese students. In return, he attached an amendment to a proposed immigration bill giving the President power to prohibit aliens from migrating to the U.S. via an intermediate stopover. After enactment, he issued an executive order which barred immigration of Japanese from Hawaii, Mexico or Canada. This action *preceded* the frequently discussed "Gentlemen's Agreement" and was the initial step leading to

"The Issei Generation," Roger Daniels, in *Roots: An Asian American Reader*.

The Politics of Prejudice: The Anti-Japanese Movement in California and The Struggle For Japanese Exclusion, pp. 34-35. Quotes Roosevelt's letter.

QUOTATION	COMMENT	REFERENCE

4. (Continued)

exclusion of Japanese.

In a personal letter, Roosevelt wrote that anti-Japanese groups were right " . . . to protest as vigorously as possible against the admission of Japanese laborers, for their very frugality, abstentiousness, and clannishness makes them formidable to our laboring class . . . . I would not have objected at all to . . . a resolution, courteous and proper in its terms, which would really have achieved the object they were after."

Japanese Americans. William Peterson. A good general text but has several weaknesses in its perspectives, particularly relating to "success" and to the reasons for the concentration camps.

5. The U.S. broke the Gentlemen's Agreement, in 1924, by excluding Japanese.

Californians now demanded that the Japanese, like the Chinese, be excluded as "undesirable." The government of Japan prevented this embarrassment by signing a "Gentlemen's Agreement" with the U.S. in 1907. Under it Japan itself would not allow its laborers to emigrate to America, so no insulting anti-Japanese law was needed.

The Impact of Our Past, p. 548

The "Gentlemen's Agreement" stipulated that Japan would voluntarily prevent all but a few categories of its people from emigrating to the U.S. However, in 1924, the U.S. broke the Agreement by passing an Immigration Act which contained a clause excluding *all* Asians (except Hawaiian and Pilipino farm laborers). In 1952, the McCarran-Walter Act partially rectified this racist exclusion by assigning a quota of about 100 immigrants a year to Japan and allowing Japanese aliens to become citizens.

It is a gross distortion for the text to state that "no insulting laws" were needed, when, in fact, numerous U.S. laws were insulting, both to Japan and to Japanese in the U.S.

"The Issei Generation."

"Japanese Immigrants on a Western Frontier: The Issei in California," Roger Daniels, in *East Across The Pacific.*

To Serve The Devil: Vol. II, pp. 166-270.

6. Curtailment of immigration had harmful social consequences upon Japanese in the U.S.

. . . in 1907, Japanese immigrants also were largely shut out.

The Impact of Our Past, p. 467

Early immigrants were mainly male laborers. By 1900, of 24,326 Japanese in this country, only 985 were females—a ratio of 24 to 1. By 1920, the ratio had improved to 5 to 1. Some Japanese men were married before they immigrated and others returned to Japan to find a wife. For the majority of single males who could not afford to travel to Japan and back, "picture brides" were the method of marriage. This practice was in line with Japanese social customs and was common within Japan. Because most of the "picture-brides" became laborers in order to provide support for their families, the U.S. complained that they violated the Gentlemen's Agreement— which excluded laborers. Japan stopped issuing passports to the brides in 1920. This action, along with the 1924 Quota Act, left 42.5 percent of the adult male Japanese American population single.

"Early Asian Women in America," in *Contacts and Conflicts: The Asian Immigration Experience,* pp. 23-25.

"Issei: The First Women," Emma Gee, in *Asian Women.* Asian American Studies Center.

QUOTATION	COMMENT	REFERENCE

7. Placing Japanese in concentration camps during WW II was an action consistent with the long history of U.S. racism.

Japanese-Americans living on the Pacific Coast were especially hard hit. They were victims of hysteria brought on by the war.

In Search of America, p. 79-D

In one way there was more home-front unity in World War II than in 1918. There were almost no anti-war radicals. It was also taken for granted that all but a tiny minority of German-Americans were loyal. Thus American pluralism (a pattern of many faiths and different nationalities living peacefully together) seemed stronger in the 1940's than ever. But there was a glaring exception. On the West Coast lived 110,000 Americans of Japanese birth or descent. . . . Forced to sell their homes and property at once, for whatever price was offered, the Japanese-Americans obeyed orders. . . .

The Impact of Our Past, p. 704

It was the long practiced racism against Japanese on the West Coast and not war-time "hysteria" or "national security" that led to the internment of over 110,000 Japanese living on the mainland. In Hawaii, a more militarily vulnerable area with a far larger proportion of Japanese, no internment took place. The economic interests of whites on the West Coast, who pressured for the removal of their Japanese competitors, and the racist implications in the fact that German and Italian Americans received dissimilar treatment, are important related factors. It should also be noted that the Internal Security Act of 1951, which attempted to legitimatize the WW II concentration camps and which authorized the future establishment of such camps, was not repealed until 1971.

The following is a selective listing of a few of the many excellent books and articles on the "camp" years.

Executive Order 9066. Maisie & Richard Conrat. Collection of photos taken during those years—excellent and moving visual collection.

Concentration Camps USA: Japanese Americans and WW II. Roger Daniels. Good bibliography of readings on various aspects of the camps.

8. Alien and native born Japanese, as well as some Japanese from outside the U.S., were interned.

Japanese born in the United States are called Nisei. When West Coast residents got panicky after Pearl Harbor, the Nisei were rounded up. Even though they were citizens, the Nisei were sent to camps as a "safety measure." There Japanese-Americans were put behind barbed wire and guarded by soldiers. . . . Within a year, however, most Nisei were allowed to leave the camps. They went to college or to harvest crops. Many volunteered for armed duty. . . .

American History for Today, p. 452

This book implies that only Nisei were in camps and that most left after a year. Approximately 47,000 Issei were also placed in the concentration camps. The only group allowed to leave the camps were 4,000 Nisei students sent to mid-western or eastern colleges. Temporary work releases were allowed for agricultural laborers. They left the camps under armed guard and most were returned each evening. Over 33,000 Nisei fought during WW II while their families and friends were behind barbed wire. Their unit suffered the highest casualties, and won the most medals, of any similar unit during the war.

Also in the camps were 2,100 South Americans of Japanese ancestry. The U.S. engineered their deportation to this country in an abortive plan to exchange them for U.S. prisoners of war. After the war, the U.S. tried to deport them to Japan. Peruvian Japanese sued in court, to prevent deportation, and won. While some returned to Peru, thirteen families won a court case allowing them to remain.

Prejudice, War and the Constitution. Jacobus ten Broek. Excellent, scholarly book on the reasons for the camps.

The Spoilage: Japanese American Evacuation and Resettlement During WW II. Dorothy Thomas and Richard Nishimoto.

QUOTATION	COMMENT	REFERENCE

9. Japanese Americans received less than 10 cents on the dollar as compensation for their property losses.

To make up partially for the injustice committed, the United States repaid the Nisei $35,000,000 for losses suffered in relocation.

The Pageant of American History, p. 538

The evacuees lost their homes, land, businesses and possessions. In 1948, President Truman signed the "Japanese American Evacuation Claims Act" designed to provide reparations for losses. Some 23,000 Japanese filed claims for about $131 million. The claims processing was slow and inefficient, and claims had to be based on 1942 dollar value, with no interest. Although the Federal Reserve Bank placed the property losses at $400 million, only about $38 million was paid to claimants.

The following is a selective listing of a few of the many excellent books and articles on the "camp" years.

Executive Order 9066. Maisie & Richard Conrat. Collection of photos taken during those years—excellent and moving visual collection.

10. Japanese Americans have not forgiven or forgotten the concentration camps.

. . . the Japanese-Americans seem not to have lost faith in the United States. Most appear to have forgiven the government for violating their rights during World War II. Some of them even say that the whole affair was a "helpful catastrophe." It permitted young men to prove their loyalty by going to war. Those remaining at home showed their willingness to go along with American concepts of law and order, even if this meant removal from their community and detainment in a relocation center.

Man In America, p. 572

Many Japanese Americans designate time by referring to "before camp years" or "after camp years." Each December, many Japanese American newspapers contain sections devoted to accounts of camp experiences, as well as articles debating whether Japanese should have allowed themselves to be interned. Japanese communities in California organize annual pilgrimages back to the camps. It is estimated that 4,700 to 8,000 people of Japanese descent emigrated to Japan after the war—an action attributed to their wartime treatment.

Concentration Camps USA: Japanese Americans and WW II. Roger Daniels. Good bibliography of readings on various aspects of the camps.

Prejudice, War and the Constitution. Jacobus ten Broek. Excellent, scholarly book on the reasons for the camps.

The Spoilage: Japanese American Evacuation and Resettlement During WW II. Dorothy Thomas and Richard Nishimoto.

11. Describing Japanese Americans as a "successful minority" is a stereotype.

In Hawaii today, about a third of the population are Japanese-Americans. They work as farmers and in all kinds of businesses, and they are important in the political life of the state. In California, descendants of Japanese immigrants have become very successful farmers. A number of Japanese-Americans are now outstanding photographers, architects, and professors in American universities.

America: Its People and Values, p. 561

Though the comparative situation of Japanese Americans has improved, the "success" myth obscures problems they still face. Middle-class Japanese Americans are often denied advancement opportunities. While the median income for Japanese American families is higher than the national average, in over 50 percent of most families both wife and husband work, as compared to 39 percent of other U.S. families.

In Nihonmachi (the Japanese equivalent to Chinatown) elderly Issei and Nisei are often unable to obtain necessary social services or medical care. "Urban renewal" has destroyed large sections of many such communities, which are the cultural and social centers of the Japanese population. The "fat Jap" remark of Spiro Agnew and the "little Jap" remark made during the Senate Watergate hearings are indicative of the prejudice Japanese Americans still confront.

Japanese American Identity Dilemma. Minako Maykovich.

"The 'Quiet Minority'—Tokyo-U.S. Differences Stir Fear and Militancy in Japanese Americans," Norman Pearlstone, in *Wall Street Journal,* Aug. 8, 1972.

"Asian Americans: A Success Story?" Stanley Sue and Harry Kitano in *Journal of Social Issues.* Vol. 29, No. 2, 1973.

Pilipino Americans

QUOTATION	COMMENT	REFERENCE

1. Pilipinos had struggled against Spanish rule, and were almost victorious before the U.S. arrived.

The 7,100 islands [of the Philippines] *supported a population of 7,500,000, divided into 43 ethnic groups, speaking 87 different languages and dialects. Culturally the Filipinos ranged from primitive peoples in the jungles to highly literate inhabitants in the cities. When Dewey reached Manila Bay, an uprising against Spain had just begun, and Filipino patriots, besieging Manila, assisted the American forces.*

A Free People, p. 70

Spain's rule of the Philippines began in 1565. Since that time there were at least 200 sporadic revolts by Pilipinos. By 1872, under the leadership of Andrea Bonifasio, a secret independence organization called Katipuran was formed. Armed struggle began in 1896. Because upper-class Pilipinos controlled many leadership positions and disliked Bonifasio, who came from a poor background, he was replaced by Emilio Aguinaldo, who was more willing to compromise. In 1897 an agreement was reached. Spain promised reforms, and Aguinaldo accepted a sum of money and agreed to go into exile. Because the Spanish did not institute any reforms, the rebellion resumed with new vigor in February, 1898.

By May, when Dewey sailed into Manila Bay and destroyed the Spanish fleet, Pilipinos had virtually defeated the Spanish land forces and had the last hold-outs surrounded in Manila. On June 12, 1898, Aguinaldo declared the Republic of the Philippines. However, a stalemate continued until August when the Spanish, preferring to surrender to the U.S. rather than to Pilipinos, yet wanting to preserve their "honor," staged a mock battle with—and surrendered to—the U.S. In December, the U.S. and Spain—without Pilipino representation—signed the Treaty of Paris, ceding the Philippines to the U.S.

"The First Vietnam: The Philippine-American War, 1899-1902," Luzviminda Francisco, in *Letters In Exile.*

The Philippine Revolution. T.M. Kalaw.

"The Philippines and Martial Law," Domingo Vicente, in *Bridge: The Asian American Magazine.* April, 1974.

2. The U.S. may have instigated a battle with Pilipino forces to influence the U.S. Senate vote on the Treaty of Paris.

Once it became apparent . . . that the United States intended to annex the Philippines, a new uprising broke out, led by the able guerrilla chieftain Emilio Aguinaldo. It required over 60,000 troops—four times the number sent to Cuba—and three years of fighting to suppress the Filipino patriots.
A Free People, p. 70

Fighting between Pilipino and U.S. forces broke out in February 1899. Some believe that the U.S. instigated the fighting to influence the Senate, where ratification of the Treaty of Paris was stalemated by those who opposed U.S. imperialism. When news of the fighting—reported as having been instigated by Pilipinos—reached Washington, the Senate ratified the treaty by two votes.

"The First Vietnam: The Philippine-American War, 1899-1902."

3. The U.S. spent hundreds of millions of dollars and three years to brutally suppress the Pilipino independence effort.

[The Pilipinos] *were weak and defenseless. They had no experience in governing themselves. If left alone, they might be taken over by one of*

Economic and military considerations were the real reasons for the U.S. take-over. The "cover" for this was the Manifest Destiny ideology of helping "inferior," "backward" people to learn "Ameri-

QUOTATION	COMMENT	REFERENCE

3. (Continued)

the empire-building European nations. . . . After months of waiting, President McKinley and Congress finally accepted responsibility for governing the islands of the Philippines. . . . American officials established public schools and taught the people how to read and write. Americans helped to set up hospitals and taught modern health practices. . . . The United States tried to help the Filipinos to develop their land into a democratic nation. Step by step, the Filipinos learned to govern themselves.

America: Its People and Values, p. 683

can" ways. Incredibly, this textbook totally perpetuates the myth of U.S. "benevolence." Most other textbooks at least mention Pilipino resistance to U.S. imperialism.

The U.S.-Philippine war—fought over three years—was a classic guerrilla war. There was popular support for those fighting foreign domination. The U.S. responded with a scorched earth policy, destruction of villages, killing of non-combatants, torture, and relocation into concentration camps. General Shafter reflected the U.S. policy when he stated: "It may be necessary to kill half the Filipinos in order that the remaining half of the population may be advanced to a higher plane of life than their present semi-barbarous state affords." An estimated one million Pilipinos—out of a population of seven million—died during the war.

Press censorship was widely practiced to keep such information from the U.S. public, but letters sent home by U.S. troops were sometimes printed, adding fuel to the anti-imperialist sentiment in the U.S. Over 75,000 troops and hundreds of millions of dollars were used to suppress Pilipino independence. This suppression was described by President McKinley as "benevolent assimilation."

"The First Vietnam: The Philippine-American War, 1899-1902."

---

4. The U.S. exploited the Philippines in a classic colonial fashion.

Genuinely devoted to the interests of the "little brown brothers," as he called them, Taft started a program to prepare the Filipinos for self-government and to protect them from foreign exploitation.

A Free People, p. 71

Textbooks frequently credit the U.S. with a desire to "protect" the Philippines from foreign exploitation. More accurately, it was a desire to protect U.S. business from competition with foreign business in the Philippines. The Payne-Aldrich Act of 1901 allowed U.S. goods to be imported to the Philippines free of tariff, in exchange for export of raw materials. This retarded the development of Pilipino manufacturing, stimulated the production of export crops such as sugar, bananas, pineapple, coffee, coconut and tobacco, and diverted land from food production for local consumption, resulting in the necessity to import food. U.S. industries were established to use cheap Pilipino labor, with profits returning to the U.S. All this created economic conditions which forced Pilipinos to immigrate to the U.S. in order to survive.

Compadre Colonialism: Studies on the Philippines Under American Rule, Norman G. Owens.

"Pilipino Immigration," in *Contacts and Conflicts: The Asian Immigration Experience.*

The Philippines to the End of the Military Regime. Charles B Elliot.

QUOTATION	COMMENT	REFERENCE

---

5. Pilipinos were recruited to the U.S. as low-paid labor when other Asians were excluded.

American workers were opposed to unrestricted immigration of Filipinos, fearing job competition.

The American Experience, p. 389

The 1907 Gentlemen's Agreement with Japan resulted in the decline of Japanese immigration to Hawaii. The Hawaiian sugar planters recruited 160 Pilipino laborers in 1907, and by 1919, had recruited 25,000 Pilipinos to Hawaii. In the early 1920's, California faced a labor shortage. Recruitment, in Hawaii and the Philippines, led to a significant migration of Pilipinos to the U.S.A. By 1930, there were 45,200 Pilipinos in the U.S. and 63,000 in Hawaii.

Chinese and Japanese immigration to the U.S. was reduced drastically by restrictive legislation based on their "ineligibility for citizenship." Although a 1925 Supreme Court ruling defined Pilipinos as "ineligible for citizenship" (unless they served three years in the U.S. Navy) they were not considered "aliens." Because the Philippines was a U.S. colony, Pilipinos were considered "subjects" or "nationals" and were allowed to immigrate.

Pilipinos were often employed as low-paid "stoop" laborers in lettuce and asparagus fields, as well as pickers of grapes, tomatoes and berries. They traveled to farming regions during the growing season and, in the winter, worked in urban areas as houseboys, cooks, dishwashers or domestics. Some went north, particularly to Alaska, and were employed in fishing and canning industries.

"California's Discrimination Against Filipinos 1927-1935," M. Brett Melendy, in *Letters In Exile.*

"Filipinos In The U.S.," M. Brett Melendy, in *Pacific Historical Review.* November, 1974.

"Filipino Immigration: The Creation of a New Social Problem," Violet Rabaya, in *Roots: An Asian American Reader.*

"An Exercise on How To Join The Navy and Still Not See The World," in *Letters In Exile.*

---

6. Pilipinos in the U.S. were subjected to violence, institutional racism and immigration restrictions.

In the Tydings-McDuffey [sic] Act of 1934, provision was made for the independence of the Philippines in ten years.

The Pageant of American History, p. 359

This book ignores the treatment of Pilipinos in the U.S. and the effect of the Tydings-McDuffie Act on Pilipino Americans. Pilipino immigration was highest in the 1920's and the immigrants inherited the existing anti-Asian hostility. Additionally, when the great depression hit the country, it created a huge pool of surplus white labor, forced to work in low-paid agricultural jobs they had rejected in the past. Violence against Pilipino workers was common, exacerbated because the largely male Pilipino population dated white women. In 1933, the California legislature amended the State's miscegenation law to include "members of the Malay race," and by 1939, 10 states specifically included Pilipinos in miscegenation laws.

Pressure for exclusion of Pilipinos built, and the 1934 Tydings-McDuffie Act limited Pilipino immigration to 50 each year. The Repatriation Act of 1935 enabled the U.S. government to pay for the transportation of Pilipinos back to the Philippines, but stipulated that they would not be allowed to return except as part of the 50-a-year quota.

"Anti-Miscegenation Laws and the Pilipino," in *Letters In Exile.*

"Anti Filipino Race Riots," Emory S. Bogardus, in *Letters In Exile.*

"California's Discrimination Against Filipinos 1927-1935."

"Filipinos In The U.S."

"Filipino Immigration: The Creation of a New Social Problem."

QUOTATION	COMMENT	REFERENCE

7. Pilipino workers have a long history of struggling for their rights.

In California a new union of almost entirely Mexican-American grape-pickers struck against working conditions in 1965.

The Impact of Our Past, p. 736

The 1965 strike was initiated by the Agricultural Workers Organizing Committee (predominantly Pilipino), which later merged with the National Farm Workers Association (predominantly Chicano) to form the United Farm Workers. This multi-national union overcame the racial divisions promoted by growers, and its successes have been the result of this unity.

Prior to that time Pilipino workers struggled for their rights through organizations like the Pilipino American Labor Association, the Pilipino Labor Union and the Agricultural Workers Organizing Committee. In 1924, they waged an unsuccessful eight-month strike against Hawaiian sugar plantations. In 1934, 3,000 Pilipinos struck the lettuce fields of Salinas, California, for higher wages and better working conditions. Pilipinos were active in the successful 1937 effort of Alaskan cannery workers to form a union.

"An Interview With Philip Vera Cruz," in *Roots: An Asian American Reader.*

"Agbayani Village," Chris Braga & Barbara Morita, in *Letters In Exile.*

Pinoy Know Yourself: An Introduction to the Filipino American Experience. Canillo, et al. (ed).

8. Pilipinos in the U.S. today still suffer from racism and exploitation.

Maintaining a close identity with others of their ethnic backgrounds, groups such as the Puerto Ricans in New York City and the Filipinos in several West Coast cities form additional urban sub-populations which keep the nation's cities seething with discontent and conflict.

The American Experience, p. 646

Projections show that if current immigration is maintained through the 1970's, Pilipinos will be the largest Asian group in this country. Yet textbooks provide scanty information about Pilipino Americans. Thus this quote, implying that Pilipinos are responsible for urban conflict, is particularly disparaging.

Pilipinos suffer most of the conditions shared by other third world groups—high unemployment, poor housing, etc. Some 40 percent of all employed Pilipino men in the U.S. work in low-skill, low-pay jobs (compared to 19 percent of men as a whole). Twelve percent of employed Pilipino men are farm workers (compared to 5 percent of all employed men). The average income level of Pilipino families is about equal to the U.S. average, yet 38 percent contain five or more members and 61 percent have more than one wage earner (compared to 51 percent of all U.S. families). Forty-six percent of all Pilipino wives in husband/wife families work (compared to only 39 percent of all U.S. wives). It should be noted that a large number of Pilipinos are college-educated professionals who have immigrated since 1965.

"Filipinos: A Fast Growing U.S. Minority—Philippines Revolution," in *Roots: An Asian American Reader.*

"Pilipino Highlights," in *Letters In Exile.*
Provides data from a 1974 HEW study of 1970 census figures.

America Is In The Heart. Carlos Bulasan.

"Health Care Problems of the Elderly," James L. Weaver and James Alan Constantine, in *Letters In Exile.*

QUOTATION	COMMENT	REFERENCE

9. On July 4, 1946 the Philippines became a neo-colony of the U.S.

For the first time in the world's history, a great power gave up a colony of its own free will. On July 4, 1946, the United States granted independence to the Philippine Islands. . . . Since freedom was granted in 1946, strong ties of friendship have bound the two nations.

American History for Today, p. 380

The Philippines was the first country to change from outright colonization to neo-colonization. The U.S. maintained economic and military control of the country, using much more than "ties of friendship" to bind the Philippines. A number of U.S. laws and treaties defined the new relationship.

Property Act—all real estate and other property acquired by the U.S. government, on or after July 4, 1946, would be respected.

Bell Trade Act—required a Parity Amendment in the Philippine constitution giving U.S. citizens "equal rights and opportunities with Pilipinos for the disposition, exploitation, development and utilization of any and all Philippine natural resources." Also established trade, tariff and currency regulations and gave the U.S. continued rights to define these areas.

U.S.-Philippines Military Bases Treaty of 1947—a 1934 pact had dictated that the U.S. would retain its 23 military bases in the Philippines after independence. This 1947 Treaty gave the U.S. extraterritorial rights to these bases for 99 years.

U.S.-Philippines Military Assistance Pact—maintained U.S. domination of the Philippine armed forces through the Joint U.S. Military Advising Group (JUSMAG), which trains and advises the Philippine armed forces and sells or lends them weapons.

U.S. corporations have controlling interests in the 900 largest Philippine businesses. They control key sectors of the economy, such as oil refining, mining, rubber, agriculture, timber and finance. U.S. corporate investments in the Philippines represent 80 percent of foreign investment in the country and 60 percent of all U.S. investment in Southeast Asia.

"The Lichauco Papers: Imperialism In The Philippines," Alejandro Lichauco, in *Monthly Review*, July-August, 1973.

"The Philippines: American Corporations, Martial Law and Underdevelopment," *IDOC*. Corporate Information Center, National Council of Churches, November, 1973.

"The Philippines and Martial Law."

ASIAN AMERICAN TEXTBOOK CHECKLIST

Title _____

Publisher _____ Year _____ Grade Level _____

Chinese Americans

There are 13 criteria to be scored. The highest possible rating is +26. The lowest is –26. This text scores _____ .

	Incorrect Information −2	No Information −1	Omits This Period 0	Limited Information +1	Full Information +2
1. Multiple reasons caused the Chinese to come to the U.S.					
2. Anti-Chinese bias existed in the U.S. prior to the time Chinese arrived.					
3. The Chinese experienced both suffering and exploitation in building the railroad.					
4. Chinese worked at many occupations and were instrumental in developing some industries.					
5. Racism systematically excluded Chinese from entering into, or remaining in, some fields of work.					
6. Chinese workers organized to resist exploitation.					
7. Racism was utilized to divide Chinese from other workers.					
8. The widespread violence against Chinese was backed by institutional support.					
9. There were numerous national, state and local anti-Chinese laws.					
10. The 1882 Chinese Exclusion Act had extensive ramifications.					
11. Sixty years of exclusion had devastating social consequences to Chinese in the U.S.					
12. Chinatowns in the U.S. suffer the problems common to other urban ghettos.					
13. Chinese have a long history of struggle against oppression.					
Total					
Textbook Final Score					

Japanese Americans

There are 11 criteria to be scored. The highest possible rating is +22. The lowest is –22. This text scores _____ .

	-2	-1	0	+1	+2
1. U.S. sugar interests in Hawaii recruited and exploited Japanese laborers.					
2. Japanese undertook a variety of occupations in the U.S.					
3. There was extensive legal, social, and economic persecution of Japanese in this country.					
4. Theodore Roosevelt manifested anti-Japanese sentiments and actions.					
5. The U.S. broke the Gentlemen's Agreement, in 1924, by excluding Japanese.					
6. Curtailment of immigration had harmful social consequences upon Japanese in the U.S.					
7. Placing Japanese in concentration camps during WW II was an action consistent with the long history of U.S. racism.					
8. Alien and native born Japanese, as well as some Japanese from outside the U.S., were interned.					
9. Japanese Americans received less than 10 cents on the dollar as compensation for their property losses.					
10. Japanese Americans have not forgiven or forgotten the concentration camps.					
11. Describing Japanese Americans as a "successful minority" is a stereotype.					
Total					
Textbook Final Score					

Pilipino Americans

There are 9 criteria to be scored. The highest possible rating is +18. The lowest is –18. This text scores _____ .

	-2	-1	0	+1	+2
1. Pilipinos had struggled against Spanish rule, and were almost victorious before the U.S. arrived.					
2. The U.S. may have instigated a battle with Pilipino forces to influence the U.S. Senate vote on the Treaty of Paris.					
3. The U.S. spent hundreds of millions of dollars and three years to brutally suppress the Pilipino independence effort.					
4. The U.S. exploited the Philippines in a classic colonial fashion.					
5. Pilipinos were recruited to the U.S. as low-paid labor when other Asians were excluded.					
6. Pilipinos in the U.S. were subjected to violence, institutional racism and immigration restrictions.					
7. Pilipino workers have a long history of struggling for their rights.					
8. Pilipinos in the U.S. today still suffer from racism and exploitation.					
9. On July 4, 1946 the Philippines became a neo-colony of the U.S.					
Total					
Textbook Final Score					

CHICANOS

Racially, Chicanos are a 450-year-old mixture of Native Americans and Europeans, with an addition of Africans brought to the American continent as slaves. In other words, Chicanos are an Indo-Euro-Afro people. Historically, their very birth as a people lies in conquest, colonization and exploitation. Chicanos did not exist until the conquest of the native peoples of Mexico by Spain, which created a mixing of peoples—the result being the mestizo, or La Raza, or Chicanos. It is not an exaggeration to say that, as a people, they were born from the act of physical, political and cultural rape. In this they are, of course, the same as all mestizos of Mexico. But for the Chicano, an added rape took place. Their homeland, northern Mexico, was invaded and occupied by the United States during the 1846-1848 war against Mexico. That area became the present-day Southwest of the U.S. Thus Mexicanos became Chicanos.

TERMINOLOGY

Any discussion of the treatment of Chicanos in textbooks must begin with the name itself. "Mexican-Americans" is the name most widely used in textbooks, in school systems, and by governmental agencies. However, many Chicanos reject the hyphenated term because it diminishes the sense of peoplehood which they feel. The term implies that Chicanos are an immigrant group, such as the Irish Americans or Polish Americans, and denies the historical fact that people of Mexican origin were actually settled in what is now the U.S. years before the Pilgrims landed.

Chicano is an increasingly popular term in the Southwest and other areas, although not nationwide. Other terms, such as Indo-Hispano, Hispanic, Latino, Mexicano, Mexican and Spanish are still used. The most broadly accepted term is probably Raza or La Raza—which literally means "the race," but without any implication of master-race. It might better be translated as "our people" or even "the folks," in relation to the speaker. However, Raza includes not only Spanish-speaking people in the U.S. but also the majority of people in Latin America—all who are a mixture of predominantly Native American and Spanish. Mexicans, Guatemalans, Colombians, Bolivians, and others are all Raza.

We will use the term "Chicano" to mean people of Mexican descent living in the U.S. While the origin of the term is obscure, it is thought to be a shortened version of Mexicano with a "sh" sound given to the "*x*" in accordance with 16th-century Aztec (Nahuatl) pronunciation. "Mexican" will be used to refer either to the inhabitants of northern Mexico before the U.S. take-over, or to citizens of Mexico at any time. The term "Anglo" refers to all non-Chicanos, but primarily to "white" people. It derives from "Anglo-Saxon" and is a neutral term that Chicanos use in referring to whites.

The discussion of terminology leads to one of the first areas of textbook problems: the meaning of "America." Most textbooks are written on the assumption that the history of America and the history of the U.S. are one and the same. However, America is a hemisphere, not a single nation. Texts do not recognize that Mexicans, Chileans, and Canadians are also "Americans" and consider the hemisphere to be theirs as well. The exclusive application of the term "American" to the U.S. is indicative of the general ethnocentrism of U.S. history textbooks. Convenience of usage does not excuse this error in the eyes of many other Americans—including many Chicanos.

INVISIBLE PEOPLE

Chicanos are the second largest group of third world people in the U.S., but in many pre-1970 U.S. history textbooks, Chicanos are not mentioned *at all* and Mexicans are presented only in connection with the Texas "War of Independence" and the "Mexican American War" of 1846-1848. When Mexicans are mentioned, it is frequently with distortion, ethnocentrism and stereotypes. Even such a noted historian as Samuel Eliot Morison attributed the 1846-1848 war to "Latin disinclination to acknowledge a disagreeable fait accompli"—the previous U.S. take-over of Texas. Mexico is too often portrayed as a half-civilized land of constant revolution. This negative image of Mexicans can too easily be transferred onto Chicanos. In some of the newer texts, there is little disparaging of Chicanos. The problem is that a whole people simply are not mentioned or that whole segments of the Chicano historical experience are ignored.

HISTORY OF RESISTANCE

Most textbooks describe the U.S. take-over of northern Mexico as occurring unopposed by the Mexican inhabitants. They fail to relate what happened to those Mexicans, to their property and to their way of life. If they mention people who did resist the take-over, it is as "bandits." By omitting the record of Anglo brutality, rapacity (including the Cart and El Paso Salt Wars), and a host of other events, the distortion of Chicano history is compounded.

Many of the newest texts mention recent Chicano "protest," asserting that it began in the 1960's. Such assertions ignore the long history of labor and civil rights struggles by Chicanos against exploitation and discrimination. The idea of the Chicano as the "sleeping Mexican who has at last. awakened" is pure myth.

CHICANO ROOTS IGNORED

Chicanos have very old roots in the territory of the U.S. Mexicans lived in what is now the Southwest as far back as the 1500's—before the settlements at Plymouth or Jamestown—and their Native American ancestors were the original inhabitants. The presence of at least 75,000 Mexicans when the U.S. conquered those lands in the 1846-1848 war is rarely recognized. They were not the "Spaniards" that some textbooks mention as living in the area. The vast majority were mestizos—the mixture of peoples called Raza—the original Chicanos.

The Chicano also has a second set of roots, dating from more recent migrations of Mexicans to the U.S., especially—but not only—since the early 1900's. Those arrivals supplemented the existing population. By ignoring the first set of roots and mentioning only the latter, textbooks inaccurately portray Chicanos as "foreign immigrants," facing the same problems faced by all previous "immigrants" and starting to "climb the ladder of opportunity." Thus, not only is the origin and much of the history of a whole people truncated, but the racist and colonialist nature of their oppression is ignored.

TIES TO MEXICO

Unlike other third world people in the U.S.—Native American nations excepted—Chicanos were citizens of an independent nation whose territory was forcibly incorporated as an integral part of the U.S. Half of Mexico was taken in the 1846-1848 war, an area that now forms one third of the U.S. That war was, from the Mexican viewpoint, a violation of national sovereignty and has been strongly criticized by some U.S. historians. (As late as the 1930's, some Mexican maps continued to identify the lost territories as part of Mexico, temporarily occupied by the U.S.) The border between Mexico and the U.S. which was imposed by that war had little reality to Mexicans or Chicanos until 1924, when it was patrolled for the first time.

A somewhat unique aspect of the Chicano situation is the close proximity of the "mother country," which facilitates the constant replenishment of Chicano culture. There are also heavy pressures to "Americanize," and a constant struggle takes place between the two forces. However, textbooks have a tendency to utilize the strong Chicano culture as a means of shifting the blame for oppression onto Chicanos themselves. According to this premise, if only Chicanos would learn English and acculturate, their problems would be solved. The shifting of blame serves to justify white supremacy and the exploitation of Chicano labor.

ANGLO ETHNOCENTRISM

Some textbooks seem incapable of understanding that Chicanos actually prefer their own culture to what they see of Anglo society. For example, many Chicanos do not accept the values of competitiveness and individualism as superior to their traditional values of mutual help and collectivity. They prefer the closeness of the Chicano family to the "generation gap" and other conflicts in many Anglo families. What the Anglo sees as weakness, softness, lack of "drive," the Chicano may see as warmth and humanism. There is, indeed, a lack of understanding of cultural pluralism in textbooks.

Furthermore, there is an ethnocentric expectation that Chicanos must learn English—"as the European immigrants did"—and little recognition of the fact that Chicanos speak a world language of major importance, the second most widely spoken language in the American hemisphere. It is a language that Anglos would do well to learn. Spanish is the foremost cultural bond of Chicanos. (While more and more young Chicanos use English to communicate, most are bi-lingual.) With the language goes a set of values and relationship styles. There is a tendency in textbooks to ignore all this.

The term "Raza" is a good example of the Anglo language problem. For Chicanos, it carries many subjective qualities and feelings, and its particular meaning or use (sometimes as singular, sometimes as plural) depends on the situation. Most textbooks cannot grasp these subtleties and so avoid using the term most widely used by the people themselves, in speaking of themselves.

In sum, textbooks still view Chicanos—in the past and in the present—through Anglo eyes.

Textbooks and Chicanos

QUOTATION	COMMENT	REFERENCE

---

1. The Native peoples of central and southern Mexico had attained high levels of civilization before the arrival of Spaniards.

QUOTATION	COMMENT	REFERENCE
. . . the Spanish contribution in return was very considerable. There is no question that the Spanish aimed to "civilize" the Indians as well as profit from them. Yet "civilizing" the Indians too often meant merely getting them to work. . . . They taught them the Spanish language and literature, Roman Catholic prayers, and the Roman Catholic catechism, and they showed them how to farm in European fashion. The Free and the Brave, pp. 40-41	Though critical of the Spanish, textbooks seem to agree on the superiority of Spanish civilization. Maya achievements in astronomy, mathematics and calendar computation were unmatched. Aztec achievements in city planning and administration stunned Cortez. Medical care and sanitation were further developed than in Europe. Most of the ancient cultures of Mexico had social systems without private property. Each individual was considered the responsibility of all the people. Much of Native customs and beliefs survive, co-existing with Spanish customs and beliefs. Since the Spaniards who came to Mexico were predominantly males, there was much mixing with the Native population. Out of this mixing came the mestizo, the people now known as La Raza. Both mestizos and Native Americans were worked like slaves by the Spanish, particularly in the mission farms of California. (Spanish attempts to establish missions and settlements in other areas were frequently thwarted by the resistance of Native people.) The Spaniards attempted to divide poor mestizos and Native Americans by encouraging hostility between them. However, during the 1680 Pueblo Revolt in Nuevo México, Mexican workers joined with Native peoples and drove the Spanish out.	*450 Years of Chicano History in Pictures.* Chicano Communications Center. Excellent resource for classroom use and a reference applicable to each criteria in this section. *Art Before Columbus.* Andre Emmerich. *Aztlan.* Luis Valdez and Stan Steiner (eds). *Aztecs of Mexico.* George C. Valliant. *Sons of the Shaking Earth.* Eric Wolf. *Viva La Raza!* Elizabeth Martínez and Enriqueta Vásquez.

---

2. Many cities in the Southwest U.S. were originally settled by La Raza.

QUOTATION	COMMENT	REFERENCE
Lying between the Oregon country and Texas was some rich, almost unpopulated land. Much of it was mountains and desert. This area had once been claimed by Spain, but now belonged to Mexico. American History for Today, p. 212	The impression is often given that Northern Mexico was an empty land. This totally ignores the large Native American populations. It also ignores the wide-ranging settlements in California, New Mexico and along the present Texas-Mexican border, under the rule of Spain and, later, of Mexico. Some settlements preceded the Pilgrims' landing. Some of the early colonizers were Spaniards by birth, but most were a mixture of Spanish, Native American and African people. (Spain brought tens of thousands of Africans to Mexico as	*North From Mexico: The Spanish-Speaking People of the United States.* Carey McWilliams. *The Chicanos.* Gilberto López y Rivas. *Los Primeros Pobladores.* Frances Swadesh.

QUOTATION	COMMENT	REFERENCE

2. (Continued)

. . . in 1609, Spaniards settled at Santa Fe, New Mexico. During this period Spaniards built ranches and missions in what is now northern Mexico and the southwestern United States.

Rise of the American Nation, p. 14

The Spaniards had established a capital city at Monterey, in 1769. . . . These Spaniards began building a series of missions. Eventually, there were 21 of these missions, stretching from San Diego to north of what is now San Francisco. . . . Except for these Spanish mission settlements, and a few outposts, most of California was unsettled land.

America: Its People and Values, p. 408

slaves.) The 21 persons who founded Los Angeles in 1781 were subjects of the Spanish crown, but only two were Spaniards; the rest were Native Americans, mulattos, mestizos, Africans and one Chinese. It would be more appropriate to call them Raza.

These early settlements are generally dismissed in a few words, while textbooks describe the European settlements in the East in great detail. Although life was simple and rugged, there was literature and art. The first newspaper west of the Mississippi and the first epic poem written in North America developed out of these settlements. By 1846, there were 75,000 Mexicans in the West.

3. U.S. citizens living in Texas were foreign guests of Mexico.

Mexico asked some Americans to move into its unpopulated territory of Texas. More and more Americans poured into Texas. . . . The Mexican government decided to close its gates to Americans and tighten up the laws. One law prohibited slavery in Texas. Things came to a head when the Mexican dictator Santa Anna swept away the freedoms guaranteed Texans by the Mexican Constitution.

American History for Today, p. 205

It was the "Americans" who asked Mexico for land grants in Texas. They were given with certain conditions, including respect for Mexican law and religion. These conditions were constantly violated—especially the 1829 Mexican law against slavery. The so-called "freedoms" that were "swept away" primarily involved the freedom to own slaves and to carry out unlimited settlement on Mexican land.

Occupied America: The, Chicano's Struggle Toward Liberation. Rodolfo Acuña.

The Mexican Side of the Texan Revolution. Carlos E. Castañeda.

4. The U.S. takeover of Texas was a conspiracy planned by pro-slavery forces.

Unhappy with Mexican rule, Americans in Texas declared independence in 1836 and set up the Lone Star Republic.

American History for Today, p. 205

Mexico's loss of Texas did not result from the "unhappiness" of Anglo settlers. It was planned secretly by President Jackson and other Southerners to expand slave-holding territory. President Grant later wrote: "The occupation, separation and annexation of Texas were, from the inception of the movement to its final consummation, a conspiracy to acquire territory out of which slave states might be formed."

Personal Memoirs. Ulysses S. Grant.

Origins of the War With Mexico. Glen Price.

QUOTATION	COMMENT	REFERENCE

5. Mexican forces were defenders, not invaders, of Texas.

QUOTATION	COMMENT	REFERENCE
In 1836 the Mexican leader Santa Anna invaded Texas. His army of more than 3,000 men defeated 200 Texans defending the Alamo. In Search of America, p. 66-B *Santa Ana returned to San Antonio with a huge army. His men slaughtered all 145 Texans trapped in the Alamo, a church and mission just outside the town.* History of the American People, p. 204	To call Mexicans the invaders is a total reversal of fact. Texas had been officially acknowledged as outside the U.S. by an 1821 treaty between the U.S. and Spain; in that same year, Texas (Tejas) became part of Coahuila, a state of Mexico. Though the Anglos were outnumbered, the Battle of the Alamo was far from a massacre. The Anglos had 21 cannons to the Mexicans' 8 or 10, as well as superior rifles and training. Many Mexican soldiers were killed in the fighting. The Anglo leaders included William Travis, a murderer who had allowed a slave to be tried and convicted for Travis' own crime and then fled to Texas, and James Bowie, a slave-trading adventurer. Davey Crockett and six others surrendered. They were later executed as traitors to Mexico.	*Occupied America.* *Olvidate De El Alamo.* Rafael Trujillo Herrera. "Myths and Realities of the Alamo," Walter Lord, in *The American West.*

6. Texas and California had large non-Anglo populations.

QUOTATION	COMMENT	REFERENCE
Before Polk could take office in 1845, Congress invited Texas to join the Union. Texans, who wanted to be with "their own people" in the United States, gladly voted to accept the invitation. American History for Today, pp. 207-208	This book ignores all Texans except Anglo settlers. Native Americans had no "vote" nor did the vast majority of Spanish-speaking people who had lived there for some 150 years. Texts similarly ignore the Native American and Mexican population of California when they discuss the revolt of John Fremont and other Anglo settlers. In both Texas and California Anglos were a minority of the areas' population.	*Occupied America.*

7. The war against Mexico was not caused by cultural conflicts, but by U.S. expansionism.

QUOTATION	COMMENT	REFERENCE
The annexation of Texas in 1845 moved the United States one step closer to war with Mexico. But other factors also led to the Mexican War which finally broke out in 1846. At the root of the conflict was the fact that two different ways of life met and clashed in the vast region west of Texas. . . . Rise of the American Nation, p. 324	This textbook errs about "the root of the conflict." The expansionist policy of the U.S. was the "root" cause of the war, a fact which historians have acknowledged. As President Ulysses S. Grant later wrote, "We were sent to provoke a fight, but it was essential that Mexico should commence it." President Polk wrote that his purpose in declaring war was "to acquire, for the United States, California, New Mexico and perhaps some other of the northern provinces of Mexico."	*The Chicanos.* *The Mexican War: Was It Manifest Destiny?* Ramon Ruiz. *Manifest Destiny: A Study In Nationalist Expansion.* Alfred Katz Weinberg.

8. The war against Mexico was considered unjust by many U.S. citizens of that time.

QUOTATION	COMMENT	REFERENCE
With about 10,000 men Scott sailed south to Veracruz on the Gulf of Mexico. By the end of March 1847, his troops had taken the city. Now, step by step, they began to march inland on a	Information is not usually presented on the unnecessary shellings, murder, rape, desecration of churches and other atrocities committed by U.S. troops in Mexico. Some U.S. Catholic troops who could not tolerate the atrocities deserted and formed a battalion to fight on the	

QUOTATION	COMMENT	REFERENCE

8. (Continued)

long, upward climb. The little army included many young officers trained at West Point. . . . They were proving the value of their training and getting experience that they would use on both sides of the Civil War a few years later.

The Impact of Our Past, p. 294

Mexican side. Textbooks often fail to mention the opposition of many U.S. citizens to the annexation of Texas and later widespread opposition to the war against Mexico. For instance, the Massachusetts Legislature passed a resolution in 1847 calling the war "unconstitutional, unjust," and Abraham Lincoln, then a Congressman, introduced repeated resolutions in Congress against the war.

North From Mexico.

Memoirs. General Winfield Scott.

---

9. The U.S. won almost a third of its present territory through the Mexican-American war.

. . . in the treaty of Guadalupe Hidalgo . . . Mexico was forced to give up Texas, New Mexico and Upper California. . . . In return . . . the United States gave Mexico $15 million and agreed to assume debts totaling over $3 million that Mexico owed to Americans.

Rise of the American Nation, p. 327

Such textbook descriptions are deceptive. Tejas, Nuevo Mexico and California, the ceded areas, included the current states of California, New Mexico, Texas, Nevada, Utah, most of Arizona and Colorado, and part of Wyoming—about a third of the U.S. The $15 million paid to Mexico by the U.S. should be compared to the vast wealth gained from the former Mexican lands. The mines of Arizona alone, in an 80-year period, produced three billion dollars worth of metal.

Occupied America.

---

10. The Treaty of Guadalupe Hidalgo was not honored by the U.S.

Under the terms of the treaty . . . we did not make Mexico pay a bill of over three million dollars that she owed us for damage to American property.

American History for Today, pp. 215-216

Most textbooks mention the three million dollar debt cancellation (which seems to put the U.S. in a favorable light), but fail to note other points in the treaty. Articles VIII and IX promised civil rights and respect for the property of Mexicans living in the ceded areas. These promises were swiftly broken. Anglos took 200 million acres of Mexican owned land by force or by legal trickery; stole Mexican cattle, homes, businesses; and drove Mexican miners from mining camps in California. Thousands of Mexicans were lynched throughout the Southwest.

Occupied America.

---

11. For many years after the end of the war, Chicanos resisted the U.S. takeover of their country.

After the Mexican war ended, many southwesterners [of Spanish, Mexican and Indian ancestry] stayed on as American citizens.

Rise of the American Nation, p. 359

The impression is that Chicanos docilely acquiesced or perhaps even welcomed the change. Although the Mexican Governor of New Mexico did surrender without resistance, his act was viewed as a betrayal by Chicanos and Native Americans, who began armed rebellion in 1847. In California, thousands of Chicanos supported the resistance struggle led by José Maria Flores. Until about 1910, so-called "bandit" leaders such as Joaquin Murieta, Juan Cortina and Gregorio Cortez waged guerrilla warfare against the land seizure.

Furia y Muerte: Los Banditos Chicanos. (English Text) P. Castillo and A. Camarillo (eds).

QUOTATION	COMMENT	REFERENCE

12. The development of the Southwest was not achieved solely by Anglos.

The cattle industry—and culture—developed naturally from the conditions of the last frontier: limitless supplies of pasturage. . . ; the availability of about 5,000,000 longhorn mavericks (wild cattle from earlier Spanish herds) free to the man who could brand them; and most important, railroads to get the beef to eastern markets.

The American Experience, p. 200

Textbooks often imply that Anglo "pioneers" built the Southwest in the face of a total lack of prior civilization. The wealth of the Southwest was unlocked by Mexican and Chicano know-how, which developed from both Native American and Spanish technology. The cowboy is of Mexican origin—an offspring of the *vaquero*. The skills and knowledge of the vaqueros were vital to the development of the U.S. cattle industry—from breeding, pasturing, branding and round-up techniques to the clothes worn and food eaten on the trail. Additionally, much of the cattle that Anglos began with was not "wild," but was stolen from Mexicans. Sheep-raising, another important livestock industry in the arid area, was developed by Chicanos. Irrigation, vital to the development of agriculture in the desert areas; mining techniques; and adobe construction were developed long before the arrival of the Anglo.

North From Mexico.

13. The recruitment and deportation of Mexican workers have reflected the needs of U.S. business.

. . . in the 1900's, many families moved across the border from Mexico. Most of them became workers in the orchards and on the farms, vineyards, and ranches of the southwestern United States.

America: Its People and Values, p. 561

During and after World War I hundreds of thousands of Mexicans poured across the border to seek jobs in the United States. . . . Some, called "braceros," came under contract. Others, called "wetbacks," entered the country illegally by swimming or wading across the Rio Grande.

Rise of the American Nation, p. 830

For many years, going to the U.S. was not a matter of immigrating, but simply "going north," for the border had little historical or cultural meaning and was not patrolled until the mid-1920's. Mexicans came in large numbers before the early 1900's, usually because of economic need. However, they did not simply "pour" across the border, but were actively recruited by labor contractors whenever cheap labor was desired. The post-WW I rapid expansion of the Southwest's economy created a labor shortage and, after the exclusion of Chinese and Japanese laborers, Mexican workers were a source of labor profitable for Anglo business. While Chicanos did provide a large percentage of farm labor, they were heavily involved in other occupations. It is estimated that between 1910 and 1930, 60 percent of the mine workers and 80 percent of the railroad workers in the western states were Chicanos. They suffered terrible living conditions in migrant camps, lack of educational facilities for children, employment discrimination and widespread Anglo hostility and violence.

During the Great Depression, nearly 500,000 Chicano-Mexicanos were deported, perhaps half of them U.S. citizens. They were considered surplus labor, and deportation of activist workers was often an attempt to crush labor agitation. When WW II created new demands for labor, the "Bracero" program was created to bring

Merchants of Labor—The Mexican Bracero Story. Ernesto Galarza.

The Chicanos. Matt S. Meier and Feliciano López.

Factories In The Field. Carey McWilliams.

North From Mexico.

QUOTATION	COMMENT	REFERENCE

13. (Continued)

hundreds of thousands of Mexicans to the U.S. Immigration officials have always responded to business interests by admitting, or by deporting, Mexicans.

"Wetback" is a derogatory term, as well as inaccurate; the Rio Grande is bone-dry in most places.

14. Racism and violence against Chicanos was widespread through World War II.

Other home-front nonwhite minorities had both good and bad experiences. . . . In Los Angeles Mexican-American civilian youths were beaten by mobs (including off-duty servicemen) in a 1943 outbreak.

The Impact of Our Past, p. 704

Few books mention the "Zoot Suit Riots" of 1943, and this text fails to describe the extent of the violence. Hundreds of young Chicanos were beaten and brutalized by white mobs in Los Angeles, with the complicity of the police and press. The "Zoot Suit Riots" were a part of the racism that led to the formation of many Chicano civil rights organizations. The anti-Chicano violence during WW II occurred while Chicanos were serving in the armed forces in numbers far greater than their proportion of the population.

Occupied America.

North From Mexico.

Among The Valiant. Paul Morin.

15. Chicanos have an ongoing history of resistance to oppression.

If textbooks discuss Chicano organization and protest, they generally mention only that which occurred in the 1960's. In 1903 Chicanos led a strike of 1,500 copper miners in Arizona. Chicano-Mexicano labor struggles and strikes in the 1920's and 1930's involved thousands of women and men, and many strong unions and labor organizations were formed. Attempts to crush the strikes led to violent repression of workers and deportation of strike leaders.

Occupied America.

450 Years of Chicano History In Pictures.

Viva La Raza.

In recent years under the leadership of Cesar Chavez [Mexican Americans] have begun to organize in order to win more rights and opportunities.

In Search of America, p. 150-D

Protest and resistance continued after WW II, led primarily by the G.I. Forum (Chicano) and the Community Service Organization. One result was the outlawing of segregated schools for Chicanos, although the practice frequently continued. The atmosphere of the McCarthy era led to further repression of Chicano protest—including the deportation of "subversives."

North From Mexico.

Chicano Manifesto. Armando Rendon.

La Raza—Forgotten Americans. Julian Samora.

The farmworkers' struggle is usually the only current struggle discussed. Other issues have involved thousands of Chicanos—for example, the successful two-year strike against Farah Manufacturing Company by 4,000 workers, 85 percent of them Chicanas (Chicano women). Chicanos have also organized against racism in schools, police brutality, judicial injustice, substandard housing, and forced sterilization of Chicanas.

QUOTATION	COMMENT	REFERENCE

16. The struggle of the United Farm Workers' Union has met violent resistance by a combination of powerful forces.

QUOTATION	COMMENT	REFERENCE
In California a new union of almost entirely Mexican-American grape-pickers struck against working conditions in 1965. . . . By 1970 the grape-growers gave in and recognized the union. For Chavez, a devoted believer in nonviolence, this was important proof that the way of peaceful protest did not lead to a dead end. The Impact of Our Past, p. 736	The United Farm Workers' Union includes Pilipino, Arab, and other third world workers. Historically, growers have utilized racial differences to divide the workers. One of the significant accomplishments of the Union has been to expose these divisive tactics and unite the multi-national workers. Textbooks often leave the impression that the UFW has been victorious. They ignore the violent tactics utilized in attempts to crush the Union. They do not mention the continuing complicity of agribusiness, government and the Teamsters' Union to prevent the farmworkers from winning decent work conditions.	*Forty Acres: Cesar Chavez and the Farm Workers.* Mark Day. *So Shall Ye Reap: The Story of Cesar Chavez and The Farm Workers' Movement.* Joan Landon and Henry Anderson.

17. Most Chicanos are urban dwellers and non-farm workers.

QUOTATION	COMMENT	REFERENCE
Unlike black Americans, who have spread to all regions of the United States, Mexican-Americans have stayed mainly in the Southwest. Man In America, p. 567 *Fed up with the limited opportunities afforded by the traditional agricultural occupations of their ethnic group, many younger Chicanos have moved to urban areas.* The American Experience, p. 645	Most Chicanos do live in the Southwest, but large numbers are in Michigan, Minnesota, Ohio, Washington and other areas. As long ago as 1950, 66 percent of Chicanos lived in cities. Less than 10 percent of the Chicano population are farm workers.	*Occupied America.* *The Mexican-American People, The Nation's Second Largest Minority.* Leo Grebler, Joan W. Moore, Ralph Guzman. *The Chicanos.*

18. Chicano poverty is the result of past and present racism.

QUOTATION	COMMENT	REFERENCE
There are at least four million people with Spanish last names living in the American Southwest. Nearly all of these are of Mexican descent. The great majority are unskilled, poorly paid workers. . . . they cluster in distinct communities called barrios. *The average Mexican-American male has completed only eight years of schooling. One in six has gone no further than the fifth grade. In most cases, unfamiliarity with the English language is responsible for this low level of education.* Man In America, pp. 547-54	Chicanos are typically described as suffering from poverty—usually attributed to their "unfamiliarity with the English language" or their tendency to "cling strongly to their own culture." Such statements are blatant examples of victim blaming. The root of Chicano poverty can be found in history—in the take-over of the lands which once supported Chicano society. With the loss of their land, Chicanos became an exploitable labor force, victimized by the racism of Anglo society.	*Occupied America.* *Factories In The Fields.*

CHICANO TEXTBOOK CHECKLIST

Title _____

Publisher _____ Year _____ Grade Level _____

There are 18 criteria to be scored. The highest possible rating is +36.
The lowest is –36. This text scores _____ .

	Incorrect Information −2	No Information −1	Omits This Period 0	Limited Information +1	Full Information +2
1. The Native peoples of central and southern Mexico had attained high levels of civilization before the arrival of Spaniards.					
2. Many cities in the Southwest U.S. were originally settled by La Raza.					
3. U.S. citizens living in Texas were foreign guests of Mexico.					
4. The U.S. takeover of Texas was a conspiracy planned by pro-slavery forces.					
5. Mexican forces were defenders, not invaders, of Texas.					
6. Texas and California had large non-Anglo populations.					
7. The war against Mexico was not caused by cultural conflicts, but by U.S. expansionism.					
8. The war against Mexico was considered unjust by many U.S. citizens of that time.					
9. The U.S. won almost a third of its present territory through the Mexican-American war.					
10. The Treaty of Guadalupe Hidalgo was not honored by the U.S.					
11. For many years after the end of the war, Chicanos resisted the U.S. takeover of their country.					
12. The development of the Southwest was not achieved solely by Anglos.					
13. The recruitment and deportation of Mexican workers have reflected the needs of U.S. business.					
14. Racism and violence against Chicanos was widespread through World War II.					
15. Chicanos have an ongoing history of resistance to oppression.					
16. The struggle of the United Farm Workers' Union has met violent resistance by a combination of powerful forces.					
17. Most Chicanos are urban dwellers and non-farm workers.					
18. Chicano poverty is the result of past and present racism.					
Total					
Textbook Final Score					

NATIVE AMERICANS

The term "Native American," as used in this book, refers to people living in the U.S. who trace their lineage to the original inhabitants of these lands and who consider themselves to be Native American. The term "Indian," a misnomer applied by Columbus to the enormously diverse people he met in this hemisphere, will not be used. Over the years, white society has applied such a wide range of negative stereotypes and characterizations to "Indian" that for many non-Native Americans, the term evokes images having little relation to the real human beings to whom it is applied.

Before the arrival of Europeans, the diverse societies of North America referred to themselves, in their own languages, as "the people," without negative connotations of inferiority or superiority. One group of people distinguished themselves from the next people—who had other land, other languages, other customs and other dress—by using the word in their own language that referred to themselves. For example, the Ani'uwiyah called themselves Ani'uwiyah ("the people") and still call themselves Ani'uwiyah, or use the European word, Cherokee, as their national name.

Native Americans have always preferred to identify themselves by their particular national name—e.g., Arikara, Cayuga, Chickasaw, Kiowa, Makah, Mattapony, Micmac, Pome, Potawatomi, Zuni. For that reason, the name of a specific group of people will always be used when possible and the term "Native American" will be used when generalizing about more than one Native society.

TRIBE OR NATION

Similarly, the terms "nation" and "tribe" are European in origin and concept. "Tribe" has assumed pejorative qualities evoking backward peoples living in a "primitive or barbarous condition" (Oxford English Dictionary definition). We will thus avoid use of the term "tribe" and use instead "people," "society" or "nation." The term "nation" was utilized by the U.S. government in many treaties with, and laws affecting, Native Americans. It has wide use among Native Americans today (as in "The Independent Oglala Nation" reaffirmed at Wounded Knee in 1973), particularly within the political context of demands for treaty rights, sovereignty and self-determination. Recognition of the legally binding treaties between Native American nations and the U.S. is a fundamental demand of Native American people today.

AUTHENTICITY

Finally, when we refer to individual Native Americans, we will try to use their actual names, rather than the names applied to them by Euro Americans. Metacom and Tatanka Iotanka may have less of an exotic ring than "King Philip" and "Sitting Bull," but that is precisely why these actual names should be used. The name Tatanka Iotanka has as much legitimacy as Mao Tse-tung or Kwame Nkrumah, and the authenticity and dignity of a name should not be challenged by attempting English translations.

THE "INDIAN" IMAGE

Native Americans, unlike other third world people in the U.S., have always been visible in history textbooks—or at least an objectified image of "Indians" has been visible. They were there, first to be "discovered" by Columbus, then to "lurk" in the "wilderness," "attack" wagon trains, "scalp" pioneers, and finally—with the buffalo—to "vanish from the scene." Granted, textbooks provided a few "friendly Indians" to offer food or guide services at critical moments, but these were the contrast to the "savages" who hindered, but never halted, the inexorable tide of Euro American "progress".

Such blatant stereotyping was once pervasive. While less frequent in the newer texts, stereotypes still appear: "braves," "massacre," "warpath," "swooped down on," "wild animals and unfriendly Indians" are examples of the terminology still applied to Native Americans in the newest of textbooks. Generally, the stereotyping is more subtle, but omission, distortion, Eurocentrism and ethnocentrism still are the rule.

Newer textbooks usually have an opening section giving information on the "First Americans"—before the arrival of Europeans. Focusing on "Indian cultures," these sections present over-simplified or distorted descriptions of the enormously diverse and dynamic Native American societies. They focus on a few "customs," material objects or foods which supposedly distinguished one generalized category ("Northeast Indians") from another generalized category ("Northwest Indians"). Complex societies and cultures may be written off as "warlike," as "gatherers" or as "nomads."

"INDIANS" VS "HUMANS"

Newer texts no longer describe Native people as "primitive" but, instead, as having a "simple" culture that was not "highly advanced." Their existence and development are said to have been at the mercy of the natural environment. Their societies are portrayed as static and unchanging. Their "lack of technology" insured their subjugation by "more advanced" European peoples. Their quality as human beings is lost, and they appear as fossilized relics in a museum display.

That analogy is heightened by the subsequent contrasting portrayal of the dynamic, ever-evolving European settlement. Those initial, inadequate descriptions of pre-Columbian cultures are replaced simply by "Indians," who seem to have no cultures or social organization. From then on, most "Indians" are portrayed as "unfriendly" obstacles to Euro-American settlement. Occasionally, they are described as unfortunate victims of Euro American encroachment, hopelessly attempting to defend their lands. While this presentation as victims is more sympathetic than that in older books, the encroachment is still perceived as an acceptable result of "progress."

In a few instances, the treatment "Indians" received is even called "cruel," although such a description is reserved for a few specific Native nations like the Cherokee. Invariably these were nations (so we are told), which had assimilated more of the "civilized" practices of Euro-Americans than had other Native nations. The implication is that the more "civilized" (less "Indian") a people were, the more deplorable it was to treat them cruelly.

The greed and profits, the trickery and deceit, the racism and genocide that have consistently shaped U.S. actions toward Native Americans are, for the most part, ignored. One is left with a sense of the inevitable triumph of *human* progress over "Indians."

RECENT HISTORY

Many of the newer texts provide a page or two about 20th-century national policies (usually described as benevolent in intent) toward Native Americans. These texts also mention protest activities of the 1960's and 1970's. But rarely do they analyze how today's events reflect a continuation of past policies. It was the profit motive that caused European commercial interests to promote colonization of Native lands. Later, this same motive resulted in driving the survivors of Native nations onto remnants of land then considered worthless. Similarly, it is the profit motive today which encourages corporations and the government to ignore treaty rights and to exploit these "worthless lands" for newly discovered minerals and resources. The present struggles of Native Americans are focused on preventing further loss of land and treaty rights, and on regaining previously lost land and rights.

UNIQUE EXPERIENCE

There are three distinct aspects of the experience of Native Americans that distinguish their history from that of other third world people in the U.S.

1. Native Americans were the original inhabitants of this continent. In 1492 there were an estimated 10 to 12 million in what is now the U.S. They were a diverse people, with a wide range of social, cultural and linguistic identities. During the next four hundred years, they were decimated by epidemic diseases introduced by Europeans, and by almost continuous warfare with the white invaders—until there were only a quarter of a million remaining in the U.S. Their decimation, along with that of the 50 to 100 million Native people estimated to have inhabited the entire Western hemisphere in the 15th century, has been termed "a demographic disaster with no known parallel in world history." Their land was stolen and their cultures and societies disrupted—some obliterated. That some survived, adapting where necessary, innovating when required and, most importantly, maintaining traditional values and cultures whenever possible, represents a sorely neglected but integral part of "American" history.

2. The relationship of Native Americans to the U.S. is the second unique aspect. That relationship is defined, in many instances, by treaties between sovereign nations. The first treaty signed by the new United States was with a Native nation, and by 1871 as many as 372 treaties with Native nations had been ratified by the U.S. Senate. Although frequently ignored or abrogated by the U.S., such treaties remain, to this day, the "supreme law of the land." As the U.S. Supreme Court ruled in the case of *Worcester v. Georgia* in 1832:

> The very term "nation," so generally applied to them, means "a people distinct from others." The constitution, by declaring treaties already made, as well as those to be made, to be the supreme law of the land, has adopted and sanctioned the previous treaties with the Indian nations, and, consequently, admits their rank among those powers who are capable of making treaties. The words "treaty" and "nation" are words of our own language, selected in our diplomatic and legislative proceedings, by ourselves, having each a definite and well understood meaning. We have applied them to Indians as we have applied them to the other nations of the earth. They are applied to all in the same sense.

The central concerns of Native Americans today are recognition of treaty rights, sovereignty and self-determination.

3. Self-determination is an issue of concern for all third world people in the U.S. Yet no other people in this country have their lives so closely controlled, and their powerlessness so carefully manipulated, as do Native Americans. For no other people have a massive government bureaucracy specifically established to control their lives. That Native American lands continue to be lost, year after year, is the responsibility of the Bureau of Indian Affairs, which holds these lands "in trust." That the destructive miseducation of Native American children continues, and that Native Americans suffer from the highest incidences of many diseases, are also the responsibility of the same federal bureaucracy. That Native Americans suffer disproportionately high rates of poverty and unemployment is, too, the responsibility of the BIA—for the BIA leases and manages the lands and resources it holds "in trust." Even the many corrupt or undemocratic "tribal governments" are the responsibility of the BIA, which establishes and oversees them.

A NOTE TO THE READER:

The following section has been designed to apply to textbooks' treatment of all Native Americans in a general manner. The histories of particular Native American nations are too diverse, and their relationship with the U.S. too complex and extensive, to provide criteria applicable for each people. In many instances, criteria do refer to a specific people or event but are also applicable to textbooks' treatment of other people and other events. They are designed not only to provide factual information, but to provide a perspective lacking in the textbooks: the perspective of the people whose homes and lands were the foundation upon which the U.S. was built.

Textbooks and Native Americans

QUOTATION	COMMENT	REFERENCE

1. Native Americans are the original inhabitants of North America.

It has often been said that the only native American is the Indian. Certainly it is true that the Indian has been native to America for a longer period of time than any other people. But even the Indian was an immigrant.

The Pageant of American History, p. 2

Many textbooks refer to Native Americans as the first immigrants, or the "First Americans," based on unproven theories linking them to people who migrated to Alaska over a "land bridge" from Asia. Assertions that Native Americans were merely the first among many groups of immigrants serve as subtle justification for European conquest, implying that they had no greater claim to the land than did later immigrants. Native Americans should be portrayed as the *original* inhabitants of the continent. In fact, evidence of "modern man" existing in the Americas over 70,000 years ago predates knowledge of such life in Europe.

Indians of the Americas. John Collier.

They Came Here First: The Epic of the American Indian. D'Arcy McNickle.

This Country Was Ours. Virgil Vogel.

"Coast Dig Focuses on Man's Move to New World," *New York Times,* August 16, 1976, p. 33.

2. Pre-Columbian Native American societies reflected great diversity and complexity.

The Eastern Woodland tribes lived in the region east of the Mississippi River, from Canada to Florida. . . . The Indians hunted for their food and clothing. . . . The Eastern Woodland Indians were farmers, too, and they grew corn, beans and squash. They lived in buildings called longhouses, which were rows of apartments, shared by several families. The men hunted and fished; the women tended the fields and gathered the fruit. They had money called wampum, which consisted of bits of seashells strung together like beads.

The Challenge of America, p. 11

Textbook attempts to describe the social, political and cultural fabric of pre-Columbian Native American societies are grossly oversimplified and ethnocentric. In North America there were over 300 distinct languages and about 500 separate cultures. Societies ranged from the urban complexes of the "Mound Builders" and the multi-national political alliances of the Iroquois and of the Huron, to the small hunting bands of the Inuit. Art, science and oral literature flourished in every society. Well developed systems of trade existed between many of the nations.

Emphasis should not be placed on material objects—such as wampum, moccasins and baskets—but on the alternative social relationships and value systems that were (and are) predominant among Native American peoples. Native religions and spiritual practices should be described as equally valid as other religions. Native American cultures should be presented as dynamic and changing, rather than static and primitive. To discuss Native cultures only in terms of the pre-European past suggests that the cultures disappeared and denies their continuity with Native cultures today.

Indians of the Americas.

The Indian in America's Past. Jack D. Forbes.

They Came Here First.

QUOTATION	COMMENT	REFERENCE

3. The myth of "discovery" is blatantly Eurocentric.

In reality, Columbus "rediscovered" the New World. Other Europeans had explored there many years before. The Norsemen were probably the first Europeans to reach the New World. . . . Other Europeans may also have "discovered" the New World before Columbus. . . .However, after Columbus' voyage the Americas stayed discovered.

Rise of the American Nation, p. 10

Evidence indicates that when Columbus arrived in the Americas, the Western hemisphere (North and South America) was occupied by 50 to 100 million people. While scholars may disagree over the exact numbers, it is Eurocentric to suggest that Europeans "discovered" a continent that had, perhaps, a larger population than did western Europe at that time. While the existence of the Americas may have been new information to Europeans, anthropological evidence suggests that Native Americans had previous contact with African and Chinese travelers, none of whom apparently claimed either "discovery" of—or rights to—the land.

Indians of the Americas.

Essays in Population History: Mexico and the Caribbean. Sherburne F. Cook and Woodrow Borah.

"The Tip of an Iceberg: Pre-Columbian Indian Demography and Some Implications for Revisionism," Wilbur R. Jacobs, in *William and Mary Quarterly,* January, 1974.

They Came Here First.

4. At least ten to twelve million Native peoples may have lived in what later became the U.S.

When Europeans first came to North America, there were probably about 750,000 Indians living in the land that is now the United States.

America: Its People and Values, pp. 563-564

In 1492 the number of Indians in all of North America north of Mexico was about equal to the number of people in the city of Detroit today. . . . When Columbus landed in America, there was one Indian for every 150 persons who now live in the United States. At that time the Indians within the present boundaries of the United States were only slightly greater in number than the people who live in Baltimore, Maryland, today [less than two million].

Man in America, pp. 31-32

Most texts provide very low figures—ranging from less than one million up to two million—for the Native American population of North America before the arrival of Europeans. Such figures, when compared to the number of people in the U.S. today, suggest that the vast continent was underutilized and imply that European settlement was justified. Regardless of the number of Native Americans at the time, such implications are unfounded. The low figures in textbooks are based on research by scholars who utilized, in part, the writings of European explorers and settlers. Other scholars, using different methodology, believe that the Native population of North America was actually between 10 and 12 million. Three-quarters of the Native population is thought to have been wiped out by epidemic diseases such as smallpox, measles, cholera and syphilis, brought to this continent by Europeans. Because Native Americans had developed no natural immunity to these foreign diseases, epidemics spread rapidly among them, carried into the interior by Native people who had contracted the diseases directly from Europeans. Thus, the population of many Native nations was drastically reduced before Europeans actually reached them and wrote of their encounters. While the transmission of these diseases was generally unintentional, occasionally a deliberate attempt at germ warfare was made by Europeans. One such device was to infect Native people by giving them blankets infested with smallpox.

"Estimating Aboriginal American Population: An Appraisal of Techniques with a New Hemispheric Estimate," Henry F. Dobyns, in *Current Anthropology,* VII, 1966. .

"The Tip of an Iceberg: Pre-Columbian Indian Demography and Some Implications for Revisionism."

Chronicles of American Indian Protest. Council on Interracial Books for Children.

QUOTATION	COMMENT	REFERENCE

5. "Advanced culture" is an ethnocentric concept and does not explain or justify European conquest.

A conflict of cultures. The Eastern Woodland Indians did not develop a highly advanced culture. But their culture did make it possible for them to live successfully in ways suited to their needs. . . . Beginning in the mid-1600's, the world of the Eastern Woodland Indians suddenly changed. The Indians faced Europeans, who were people with more advanced cultures. These Europeans had better weapons, better tools, and more advanced forms of political organization.

America: Its People and Values, p. 68

. . . Indians were limited by their natural environment. Wasn't this a weakness—a minus—for the Indians? . . . Beginning in 1492, groups with a higher technology invaded the New World. These groups soon used their knowledge to overcome the Indians.

Man In America, p. 40

"Advanced culture" is a highly relative term. Politically, most Native American societies were more democratic than those in Europe or the colonies. Decisions were generally made by consensus, women were usually actively involved and there was seldom a property requirement for participation. In fact, the colonies borrowed from the political organization of the six nations of the Iroquois Confederacy in designing their central authority. With few exceptions, Native American societies were more accepting of diversity, offered greater individual freedom, and were more "community" oriented and less competitive than European societies.

Prior to European contact, Native Americans utilized virtually all available medicinal plants and herbs. The enormous variety of foodstuffs cultivated by Native Americans—which Europeans came to depend on—demonstrates the agricultural knowledge of many of the societies. It was not until the development of the cartridge rifle that Euro American technology "overcame the Indians." The previous muzzle-loading, one-shot arms had been too slow and cumbersome against bows and arrows.

European survival in North America was heavily dependent on the technology and skills of Native Americans in agriculture, medicine, transportation and hunting. That Europeans prevailed over Native societies is attributable not to "advanced culture," but to epidemics, which had a tremendously disruptive and weakening effect on Native societies, and to the land greed of the Europeans. Neither of these factors reflects "advanced" culture.

Indians of the Americas.

God Is Red. Vine Deloria, Jr.

The Patriot Chiefs. Alvin Josephy.

They Came Here First.

The Great Law of Peace of the People of the Longhouse. White Roots of Peace. Authentic factual source of the social and political structure of the Mohawk Nation.

6. War and violence were not characteristic of Native nations.

War was part of the way of life of these southeastern Indians.

Man In America, p. 36

The Iroquois were a fierce and warlike people.

America: Its People and Values, p. 68

Descriptions of Native American nations as "warlike" must be treated with caution. Much of the available information on Native Americans was written by Europeans who naturally viewed those defending their lands and communities against European invasion as warlike. Native American nations had many non-violent, well-ordered processes for solving their international problems. While there were conflicts prior to the European invasion, they were generally for limited objectives rather than for total victory or conquest, and loss of life was minimal.

Indians of the Americas.

Who's The Savage? A Documentary History of the Mistreatment of the Native North Americans. D.R. Wrone and R.S. Nelson.

QUOTATION	COMMENT	REFERENCE

6. (Continued)

European encroachments forced some societies to move from their traditional lands into those of others. In some instances this caused conflicts (as when the Sioux moved into the territory of the Crow), while in other instances the new arrivals were assisted by the original inhabitants (as when the Sioux moved into the territory of the Mandan).

---

7. Native American technology and knowledge were achievements in their own right.

The Indian gave us the snowshoe, the canoe, and the moccasin. He gave us buckwheat cakes and maple syrup, root beer and sarsaparilla, pumpkins and pineapples, chicle (chewing gum) and tobacco. His skills as a naturalist and his knowledge of the environment are contributions the Indian made to America.

The Pageant of American History, p. 7

Textbooks commonly discuss "contributions of the Indians." The implication is that the sole value of Native Americans lies in what they "gave" to the U.S.

A much less ethnocentric implication would result if texts were to state that Europeans—of necessity—adopted much of Native American technology and knowledge for their own survival. Native American achievements in agriculture, transportation, medicine and social and political practices were admirable in their own right and should be an integral part of the discussion of Native American societies and cultures, apart from their value to white people. Also, this textbook's use of the male pronoun denies the primary role of Native women in agricultural achievements.

---

8. Missionary activities were an integral part of European conquest.

From the beginning, there were a few settlers who made friends with the Indians and tried to understand them. . . . Churches sent missionaries to teach their religion to the Indians, cure their sicknesses, and try to teach them new ways. The missionaries accomplished much, but there were never enough of them or of other settlers who wanted to help the Indians.

America: Its People and Values, p. 564

Missionary efforts principally benefited the Europeans by providing them with free labor in developing missions and farms, and with a source of converts. For the most part, missionaries operated from the perspective that Native Americans were "savages" in need of uplifting from "heathen" beliefs. European powers and the U.S. government encouraged missionaries to break down traditional Native American customs, beliefs and societies.

Under the administration of U.S. President Grant, reservations were parceled out among various religious denominations whose members were appointed as agents to supervise the Native people under their control. The missionary lobby succeeded in having Congress declare Native American religious practices illegal, a situation which existed until 1934. The fact that the traditional religious practices and beliefs survive attests to their vitality and importance to Native American people.

Akwesasne Notes. Vol. 7, No. 5. Early Winter, 1975.

Custer Died For Your Sins. Vine Deloria, Jr.

God Is Red.

The Indian In America's Past.

A Pictorial History of the American Indian. Oliver La Farge.

QUOTATION	COMMENT	REFERENCE

9. Native nations made alliances with European nations for their own strategic purposes.

[George Rogers Clark] *set out in 1778 to end once and for all the attacks by Indians who had been stirred up, apparently, by the British at Detroit.*

The Free and the Brave, p. 208

Indians! Along the frontier, from Maine to New York, the Indians are attacking. And English colonists fight back to defend their houses and their lives. . . . The Indian attacks along the frontier are part of a larger conflict. A bitter struggle is going on between England and France. Most of the Indians are fighting on the side of France. . . . The French encouraged the Indians to make many of these attacks. . . .

America: Its People and Values, p. 127

Textbooks often describe Native Americans as being "stirred up" by one European group to attack another. The impression is that they were pawns, manipulated by Europeans. Native nations were struggling to maintain their communities and lands and, like other people in similar circumstances, made whatever alliances seemed to offer them assistance. Alliances with various European nations need to be placed in the perspective of Native American survival objectives.

Bury My Heart At Wounded Knee. Dee Brown.

Chronicles of American Indian Protest

To Serve the Devil, Vol. I: Jacobs, Landau and Pell.

The Patriot Chiefs.

The American Indian Wars. John Tebbel and Keith Jennison.

This Country Was Ours.

Red Man's Land, White Man's Law. Wilcomb E. Washburn.

Who's The Savage?

10. Conflicting European and colonial economic interests in Native lands helped trigger the U.S. Revolution.

. . . [The French] had to drive off a little force of Virginia militiamen commanded by a colonel named George Washington . . . Washington and other Virginians believed the future lay in the rich, unsettled lands of the West.

The government in London quickly moved to clean up the wreckage of the war and pay its huge costs. Among the first steps was a 1763 ruling to forbid settlement west of a "Proclamation Line" running down the Alleghenies. The proclamation would hold back pioneers until an Indian policy could be worked out. This seemed especially necessary after a gifted Indian named Pontiac united many tribes in a rebellion in 1763 that took a year to subdue. But the measure angered the colonists.

The Impact of Our Past, pp. 146 and 150

Pontiac and the 18 nation confederacy he led almost defeated the British, and the Proclamation of 1763 resulted. While the Proclamation "angered the colonists," most texts omit information about its effect on the financial interests of George Washington and other wealthy colonists—an effect that, in part, led to their anger with Britain. Large plantation owners, like Washington, were frequently in debt to British merchants and often speculated in western (Native American) lands to make quick profits. Thus, the Proclamation was a major irritant to these speculators.

Washington was paid for his services in the French and Indian War with thousands of acres of Native land beyond the Appalachians. And, immediately before the Proclamation of 1763, he had invested heavily—along with Patrick Henry, Benjamin Franklin and other businessmen—in land speculation schemes involving millions of acres of that now forbidden Native American territory. It is clear that he had a pressing personal stake because he hired his own surveyor to locate additional lands in that legally untouchable territory. The surveyor had written instructions to maintain the utmost secrecy. Washington, at the time of his death, "owned" over 40,000 acres of those disputed Native American lands west of the Alleghenies.

The American Revolution 1763-1783, Herbert Aptheker. See pp. 29-30 discussing plantation owners, land speculation and the Proclamation.

An Economic Interpretation of the Constitution of the United States, Charles A. Beard. See pp. 144-145 discussing Washington.

Chronicles of American Indian Protest. See pp. 36-48 for discussion of land speculation and Proclamation of 1763.

"The Revolution and the American Indian Frontier," Steve Talbot, in *WASSAJA.* August, 1976, p. 9.

QUOTATION	COMMENT	REFERENCE

11. Native nations fought the invaders to maintain their communities and lands.

The Old Southwest had everything—a rich soil, a mild climate, and plenty of wild animals. There were Indians, too, and other dangers. But what were dangers compared with opportunities? *East and West Florida were now American territory. But trouble with the Indians slowed down the process of settlement.* America: Its People and Values, pp. 287 & 292 *Traders and pioneers who crossed the plains on their way to California and the Pacific Northwest reported that much of the plains country was good for settlement. But a tremendous obstacle to settlement remained—the Plains Indians.* Rise of the American Nation, p. 440	While many Euro American settlers did view Native Americans as "obstacles," creating "dangers" that "slowed down" settlement, it is Eurocentric for textbooks to present this one perspective as fact. It is not sufficient remedy for the newer books to state—in one section—that Native people were fighting for their lands and way of life, if—in another section—Native people are still characterized as "trouble," "dangers," or "obstacles." Textbooks should include information on the reactions of Native people within various nations to the threat of invasion. Such information would offer an alternative perspective and provide the human dimension necessary to counteract the objectified image of "the Indian."	*Bury My Heart At Wounded Knee.* *Chronicles of American Indian Protest.* *To Serve the Devil, Vol. I: Natives and Slaves.* *The Patriot Chiefs.* *The American Indian Wars.* *This Country Was Ours.* *Red Man's Land, White Man's Law.* *Who's The Savage?*

12. Land has a special significance to Native Americans and has been the central issue of conflict with the U.S.

As the settlers pushed inland, they found the Indians living in the areas the settlers wanted. The Indians did not understand the settlers' idea of land ownership. They thought the land belonged to all people who needed to use it.... America: Its People and Values, p. 564	This quote reflects a textbook tendency to "blame" Native Americans for not understanding European concepts of land ownership. It does not discuss the failure of Europeans to respect the Native American concept of communally using—but not individually owning—land, just as people use—but do not own—air. It should be noted, however, that Native nations did have defined territorial areas for their peoples' use. The Euro American "respect" for land ownership is applied with a double-standard. Even when Native title to land is clearly defined by legal treaty, Euro Americans have no compunction about disregarding "ownership" or about taking over the land of others.	*Of Utmost Good Faith.* Vine Deloria, Jr. *This Country Was Ours.* *Red Man's Land, White Man's Law.*

13. It is Eurocentric to categorize Native Americans as either "friendly" or "unfriendly."

A friendly Indian named Squanto helped the colonists. He showed them how to plant corn and how to live on the edge of the wilderness. A soldier, Captain Miles Standish, taught the Pilgrims how to defend themselves against unfriendly Indians. America: Its People and Values, p. 73	Sacajawea, Squanto and other Native Americans are portrayed as "friendly" because they assisted the invaders, while Metacom ("King Philip"), Goyathlay (Geronimo) and other Native Americans are often portrayed as "unfriendly" because they attempted to defend their communities. All nations define a "patriot" as one whose allegiance is toward his or her own people. Consequently, true Native American heroes are those who fought to preserve and protect their people's freedom and land.	*Bury My Heart At Wounded Knee.* *The Patriot Chiefs.*

QUOTATION	COMMENT	REFERENCE

14. U.S. policies toward Native Americans reflect many political and economic factors within U.S. society.

How Did Jackson Deal with the Indians? As a westerner Jackson knew what it meant to fight Indians. His Indian policy as President is a dark chapter in his administration. Under Jackson it became the official policy of the administration to remove the Indians from any and all lands east of the Mississippi. The Removal Act of 1830 gave the administration the right to force the Indians to move from their homelands to tracts of land set aside for them in the far West. . . . In Georgia, the people of that state were eager to have the lands on which the Cherokee Indians lived.

The Pageant of American History, p. 174

If events related to the relations between the U.S. and specific Native nations are discussed, they are usually presented in a void, often labelled "trouble with the Indians." Texts describe all the interest groups, ideologies and political considerations associated with Jackson's actions regarding the Bank of the United States, but provide no more than simplistic reasons for his removal policies toward Native peoples. Jackson's policies were not merely a "dark chapter" in his administration but a consistent part of the ongoing U.S. policies toward Native Americans. These policies are an integral part of the political and economic dynamics within U.S. society at any given time, and need to be discussed within that context. For example, the long and enormously expensive U.S. war against the Seminoles was fought, in large part, because slaveholding interests, heavily represented in the national government, wanted to destroy the sanctuary that the Seminoles provided for escaped slaves.

Chronicles of American Indian Protest.
See pp. 110-152 and 153-161.

Removal of the Choctaw Indians. A.H. DeRosier, Jr.

The Black West. William Katz. Black involvement in Seminole War.

This Country Was Ours.
See pp. 107-136 for Jackson and removal.

Redskins, Ruffled Shirts and Rednecks. Mary E. Young. Socio-political background of Jackson's policies.

15. Textbook terminology is Eurocentric, ignoring Native American presence and perspectives.

The purchase of the Louisiana Territory was one of the greatest real-estate bargains in history. The vast and empty territory . . . was mostly unexplored.

The Challenge of America, p. 230

Daniel Boone in Kentucky. Among the first men to make their way through the Appalachian Mountains and look longingly at the land to the west was Daniel Boone. . . . But he did not start the first settlement there. James Harrod did that . . . in 1774. . . . Thanks to the efforts of Daniel Boone and others like him, Kentucky soon became safe for settlement.

America: Its People and Values, p. 289

In 1889 Oklahoma—once supposed to be preserved as Indian Territory—was opened to homesteading. . . . Overnight, Oklahoma got a population and tent-and-shack towns. . . .

The Impact of Our Past, p. 451

Native Americans are often relegated to special sections of textbooks and ignored outside of those sections. This invisibility is often accomplished through use of specific terminology. Areas outside European settlements were not *"empty"* or *"unexplored"* but were inhabited for centuries by Native peoples. Boone may have been among the first *"white people"* to enter the Appalachian Mountains, but was certainly not among the first *"men."* From a Native American perspective—particularly those who were settled there long before 1774—Boone's exploits cannot be thanked for making Kentucky *"safe for settlement."* Similarly, the territory that became Oklahoma got a *"white"* population in 1889. It already was home to a large Native American population (both those indigenous to the area and others forced into the area from their homelands east of the Mississippi).

QUOTATION	COMMENT	REFERENCE

16. Legally binding treaties are central to the relations between Native nations and the U.S.

The government policy toward the Indian was a confused one, to say the least. Few people in authority understood the Indian and his way of life. The Indians, in their turn, did not understand the terms of the treaties or agreements that the tribes had made with the government.

The Pageant of American History, p. 315

With the reservation system, the Indians became wards of the United States government. The tribes were no longer to be treated as nations with whom the United States would make treaties.

America: Its People and Values, p. 505

Most textbooks do not take the treaties seriously, discussing them as unimportant curiosities of the past or omitting any reference to them. There is no basis to the frequent claim that Native Americans "did not understand the terms of the treaties," for the treaties were generally quite specific. It has been the U.S. government that has consistently reneged on these documents.

Article III of the United States Constitution states: " . . . all treaties made, or which shall be made, under the authority of the United States, shall be the supreme law of the land. . . . " Treaties with Native American nations are of equal legal standing as are treaties with European nations. This interpretation has been repeatedly confirmed by federal courts, most importantly by the 1832 Supreme Court decision of *Worcester vs. Georgia*. They are U.S. law and are binding under international law.

In 1871, the period the second quote refers to, Congress passed the Indian Appropriation Act which stated: "No Indian nation or tribe within the territory of the United States shall be acknowledged or recognized as an independent nation, tribe or power with whom the United States may contract by treaty. . . . " However, since 372 legally ratified treaties previously existed, the Act also stated: " . . . but no obligation of any treaty lawfully made and ratified with any such Indian nation or tribe prior to March 3, 1871 shall be hereby invalidated or impaired." While a few documents concluded after that date were called "treaties," most were called "agreements" and were ratified by both houses of the U.S. Congress and not just the Senate.

Handbook of Federal Indian Law. Felix Cohen.

Behind the Trail of Broken Treaties. Vine Deloria, Jr.

Indian Affairs, Laws and Treaties. Charles Kappler.

This Country Was Ours.
See pp. 124-132 for text of Worcester vs. Georgia. See pp. 162-165 for text and discussion of 1871 Act.

17. The 1881 Dawes Act resulted in the loss of three-quarters of the remaining land of Native Americans.

The [Dawes] act grew out of a growing concern by many that America's policy toward the Indian was unjust. . . . [It] tried to improve Indian life. One of its basic provisions in policy matters was that of treating Indians as individuals rather than as tribal nations. It provided that land be distributed to individual families.

The Pageant of American History, pp. 317-318

U.S. President Arthur proposed the Dawes Act in 1881 to provide allotments of land "to such Indians . . . as desire it," but Congress made allotments compulsory. The stated intent of the Act was to "civilize" Native Americans by making them private property owners—a concept contrary to Native beliefs and practices. In reality, the Act was designed to take away "excess" Native lands, and it resulted in the loss of more than three-quarters of the remaining land held by Native Americans at that time. This "surplus" land was sold or given to white homesteaders, industrialists and ranchers.

Behind The Trail of Broken Treaties.
100 Million Acres. Kirke Kickingbird and Karen Duchenau.
The American Indian Today. Stuart Levine and Nan O. Lurie (eds).
This Country Was Ours.
See pp. 174-181

QUOTATION	COMMENT	REFERENCE

17. (Continued)

A Native American head of household was allotted 160 acres. While provision was made for lesser allotments to single people and orphaned children, no provision was made for descendants to receive additional land. Native Americans were usually allotted the poorest parcels. Some boycotted the allotment procedures to protest the Act, and the government used troops to force them to take an allotment. The Act provided that Native Americans who received allotments could gain citizenship if they farmed the land for 25 years and adopted "the habits of civilized life."

The Dawes Act was illegal, given the Constitutional status of treaties which had guaranteed the lands to Native nations, rather than to individuals within those nations.

18. The Citizenship Act of 1924 was not a benevolent action.

A turn for the better in the Indians' lives came after 1910. . . . In 1924, Congress declared that all Indians were full citizens of the United States.

America: Its People and Values, p. 507

This 1924 action was, in part, a recognition of the numbers of Native Americans who fought in WW I. It did not confer "full citizenship" rights upon Native Americans because existing laws and practices denied many such privileges.

Eight Native nations protested to Congress that the Act was illegal and, when no relief was forthcoming, took their appeal to the League of Nations. The Act was part of federal policy to "Americanize" and "civilize" Native people by assimilation into white society. As part of this policy, Bureau of Indian Affairs' officials and federal troops forcibly cut the long hair of Native American men.

This Country Was Ours. See pp. 194-195.

19. The Reorganization Act of 1934 heightened Native American alienation and powerlessness.

Congress made another shift in policy by passing the Indian Reorganization Act in 1934. The main purpose of this act was to allow Indians to use their own culture. . . . it encouraged tribes to set up self-governing constitutions on their reservations . . . [and] made funds available for loans to the tribal governments and for Indians' education. Surplus government lands were returned to the tribes, to be used for conservation purposes. . . . [The Act] guaranteed freedom of religion to the

The Reorganization Act of 1934 was the only major government act with a benevolent intent. Yet many Native Americans view it as one of the most disastrous laws ever passed regarding Native Americans.

Prior to 1934, most Native Americans were not allowed to openly practice their religions, speak their languages or hold meetings of more than three people (although the latter restriction was relaxed in the 1920's). Although traditional governments had no legal standing, they nevertheless functioned, providing secret religious ceremonies and secret teaching of their own languages. The Act imposed an alien form of government based on U.S. practice—an elected "tribal

Our Brother's Keeper: The Indian in White America. Edgar S. Cahn.

Behind the Trail of Broken Treaties.

A Pictorial History of the American Indian.

This Country Was Ours.

QUOTATION	**COMMENT**	**REFERENCE**

19. (Continued)

Indians. Under the Indian Reorganization Act, tribal governments were formed. Indian leaders gained confidence as they gained experience.

Man In America, p. 546

chairman" and elected "tribal council." Traditional forms of government are almost always more democratic, with leaders chosen by consensus—not by majority rule or election. Because it is an alien system, most Native Americans do not vote in the tribal elections.

The 1934 law reversed the Dawes Act and allowed Native Americans to own land communally and—as "tribes"—to reaccumulate land that had been lost, but only through purchase rather than recognition that it was rightfully theirs. The Act strengthened control by the Bureau of Indian Affairs and gave the Secretary of the Interior extraordinary power. The BIA maintains trusteeship of the land and exercises total veto power over any decisions that the chairpersons or councils make. Native people are forced to deal with this white bureaucracy because the U.S. channels health, education and welfare funds through it.

To say that "Indian leaders gained confidence as they gained experience" is paternalistic and condescending. It implies that Native Americans did not govern themselves prior to the 1934 Act and had no confidence in governing themselves until given permission.

The Way. Shirley Hill Witt and Stan Steiner.
Discusses traditional government.

---

20. The termination policy of the 1950's resulted in the loss of more land and the abrogation of treaties

. . . in the 1950's, Congress announced a policy of "termination," that is, ending government support for certain reservations. Termination caused hardship for some tribes. Among them were the Paiutes in Utah and the Menominees in Wisconsin.

Man In America, p. 546

Six nations were terminated, each by a specific act of Congress. While the policy as a whole was subsequently dropped, the six acts remained in force. Termination was not simply the ending of "government support for . . . reservations." A "terminated" nation no longer legally existed and the nation's land became federal or state land. The Menominees were the first to be terminated and their land became a county of Wisconsin. Thus, they no longer "owned" the land, land that they had been allotted individually through the Dawes Act and had then reaccumulated communally after the Reorganization Act.

The Menominee immediately incorporated to run their land as a company, but local and state taxes forced them into bankruptcy. While terminated, the Menominee sued the U.S for not honoring treaty provisions concerning hunting rights. The Supreme Court ruled that the treaty was valid, but dealt only with hunting rights, and skirted the issue of termination. After years of litigation, the Menominee were re-established as a reservation in 1973, but the new lands were smaller and poorer than those held before 1953.

Our Brother's Keeper.

This Country Was Ours.

Who's The Savage?

QUOTATION	**COMMENT**	**REFERENCE**

21. The BIA is a corrupt and inefficient bureaucracy controlling the affairs of one million people.

QUOTATION	COMMENT	REFERENCE
Today, the Bureau [of Indian Affairs] *is trying to help the Indians to build new ways of life that they themselves want.* America: Its People and Values, p. 565	The Bureau of Indian Affairs has a history of Congressional politicking, mismanagement, internal corruption, and general non-responsiveness to Native people's concerns. Numerous Congressional studies over the years have condemned the BIA for inefficiency and outright cruelty. For example, BIA schools are notorious for their failure to educate Native American youth. The schools frequently exclude Native languages, values and customs from the curriculum and over-emphasize Euro American values and customs. Teachers' lack of knowledge of Native American values and heritage combined with teacher prejudice and textbook bias drive large numbers of students out of the schools. The BIA is a bureaucracy that controls the affairs of a million people. No other group of people in the U.S. have a special bureau controlling their affairs. Until such time as the people control their own lives, the BIA must be held responsible for the dismal living conditions of Native Americans today.	*Our Brother's Keeper.* Documented information that exposes the BIA's policies and practices. *Behind the Trail of Broken Treaties.* *Indian Education: A National Tragedy—A National Challenge.* U.S. Senate. Most condemning report ever issued on the education of Native Americans. Gov't Printing Office claims out of print. Can be obtained through office of **Senator Edward Kennedy.** *This Country Was Ours.* See especially pp. 233-238.

22. Oppressive conditions lead to proportionately lower population increase for Native Americans.

QUOTATION	COMMENT	REFERENCE
No one today is certain of how many Indians there are in the United States. Vine Deloria . . . estimates the number at about one million. If so, this is close to the number that lived here when Columbus landed in America. For centuries the number of Indians decreased, but now the Indian population is increasing. Man In America, p. 546	There are approximately one million Native Americans in the U.S. today. While the Native American population has risen since the turn of the century, it was—and still is—rising much more slowly than the population as a whole. Native Americans have a life expectancy of 64 years compared to 71 for whites. Twice as many Native American infants die during their first year as do infants as a whole. Native Americans suffer the highest incidence of suicide, TB, and alcoholism of any group in the U.S. And an estimated 25-35 percent of all Native children are removed from their families and placed in foster or adoptive homes or institutions. These figures are symptoms of the oppressive conditions under which Native Americans exist.	*Our Brother's Keeper.* *Fact Sheet on Institutional Racism.* Foundation for Change. *Indian Family Defense.* Association on American Indian Affairs. This quarterly newsletter demonstrates the national scope of the Indian child-welfare crisis.

23. Reservations represent a paradox for Native Americans.

QUOTATION	COMMENT	REFERENCE
Today, Indians may choose whether or not they want to live and work on reservations. However, most of them still live there. . . . Indian reservations are now owned by the Indians who live on them. America: Its People and Values, p. 565	On the one hand, reservations are perceived as concentration camps and are a constant reminder of the loss of land and of sovereignty. Yet reservations—as bad as they are—represent the only land Native Americans have left. Land is an integral aspect of Native American cultures, and, despite widespread poverty, reservations provide Native Americans with a sense of community and attachment to the earth.	

QUOTATION	COMMENT	REFERENCE

23. (Continued)

Fewer than half the Indians in the United States live on reservations. Those who do may leave if they wish. Today they are as free to move about as other Americans.

Man In America, p. 546

Traditional Native American communities are communal, non-competitive and non-alienating. Outside these communities, Native Americans are forced to participate in a competitive system that discriminates against them and denies them necessary skills and education. The resources of reservations are exploited by white ranchers and corporations, with little or no profit to Native people, many of whom are forced to seek jobs off the reservations. Many return whenever possible and consider the reservation to be "home." Less than 20 percent live outside the reservations permanently.

Given Native American legal and cultural ties to the land, it is misleading for textbooks to state that Native people are as "free to move as other Americans." It is also misleading to state that "Indian reservations are now owned by the Indians who live on them" without discussing other factors. Native American do, in fact, own reservation land as well as vast other areas of the country under legal treaties. But the BIA maintains control over their land and Native Americans cannot make decisions without BIA approval.

Indians of the Americas.

Our Brother's Keeper.

Behind the Trail of Broken Treaties.

The Way.

A Pictorial History of the American Indian.

---

24. Treaty rights, sovereignty, self-determination and the return of land are the major goals of Native Americans.

. . . the Indians are increasingly demanding their rights as American citizens.

The Pageant of American History, p. 318

Dramatic confrontations against the white establishment . . . brought concerted action and support from tribes across the country. Yet Indian nationalism is essentially tribal nationalism, with each tribe having separate needs. Disputes between tribes and between young and old leaders within tribes have characterized Native American development.

The American Experience, pp. 642-643

While there have been minor disputes between Native nations, Native American "development" has been mainly "characterized" by disputes with the U.S. Each reservation has been confronted by specific hostile actions of federal or state governments. Although the "needs" of each reservation are thus defined by its particular struggle, major Native American organizations are united on the over-all need to redress the cause of oppression through treaty rights, sovereignty, self-determination and the return of land. These—and not rights as American citizens—are the central goals of the modern Native American movement.

Native Americans do not all share the same viewpoints, but there has never been a "generation gap." A basic characteristic of Native American cultures is strong cross-generational ties and respect. The occupation of Wounded Knee was an example of the involvement of people of all ages in the struggle for self-determination.

Akwesasne Notes.

Chronicles of Indian Protest.

Behind the Trail of Broken Treaties.

The American Indian Today.

WASSAJA

The Way.

QUOTATION	COMMENT	REFERENCE

25. The struggle to maintain land continues today.

A long, and often bloody, conflict began over the land. It did not end until the settlers had spread their farms and ranches and cities from coast to coast and from Canada to Mexico.

America: Its People and Values, p. 564

Much of the land in the Last West is public domain; that is, it is owned either by the national government or by a state government. Millions of acres are still held as reservations for Indians. Valuable timber, coal, oil and natural gas resources lie on or under parts of these lands. Who shall decide how they will be used?

Man In America, pp. 373-374

Textbooks frequently imply that the conflict over land ended long ago. Native Americans continue to struggle to regain lost land that legally still belongs to them. And land continues to be taken from them. Federal, state, local and corporate efforts to take over and/or exploit the resources of Native American lands are a constant source of concern and struggle.

Reservations contain almost all of the known reserves of uranium, huge oil and gas reserves, and 1/3 of the low-sulphur coal within the U.S. According to the Federal Energy Administration, over $2.7 billion of oil and gas; $187 million of coal; $349 million of uranium and $434 million of non-energy mineral resources have been produced from Native lands through 1974. Additionally, there are important fresh water reserves, timber and other resources. Yet the exploitation of these resources by private corporations, through arrangements with the BIA, has resulted in high profits for the corporations and very low return of revenue to Native peoples.

The second quote gratuitously asks who shall decide how the land will be used—continuing the long tradition of ignoring Native American treaty rights and sovereignty.

Akwesasne Notes, Vol. 8, No. 1, Early Spring, 1976. See pp. 22-23.

100 Million Acres.

The American Indian Today.

This Country was Ours. See pp. 214-233.

U.S. News and World Report, August 2, 1976, pp. 29-30.

WASSAJA, October, 1976, p. 8.

26. There is a relationship between the past experiences and the present reality of Native Americans.

In the spring of 1973, the second Battle of Wounded Knee broke out. AIM took over the town of Wounded Knee on the Pine Ridge Indian reservation in South Dakota. They held the town for several weeks. There was occasional gunfire and some people were wounded. Buildings were burned in Wounded Knee and other damage was done. Arrests were made after the AIM Indians gave up Wounded Knee and left town.

History of the American People, pp. 400-401

Still another hazard to white settlement on the Plains was the Indians. . . . They attacked isolated settlements, seeking to protect their land. They fought pitched battles with soldiers

Each of these three quotes from the same textbook refers to the Sioux Nation. No connection is made between the discovery of gold in the sacred Black Hills of the Lakota Nation (the richest gold strike in U.S. history) and the invasion of U.S. troops (including Custer). This invasion was not to protect white settlements but to force the Lakota to give up the Black Hills which had been guaranteed to them in the 1868 Fort Laramie Treaty. The text provides no information on the terms of the Treaty and the repeated actions of the U.S. which directly contravened the Treaty—such as the application of the Dawes Act to the Lakota in 1902 or the imposition of an alien form of government in 1934.

Without such background information, students have little chance of understanding the reasons for the occupation of Wounded Knee in 1973 (which was initiated by traditional Lakota residents of the reservation, lasted for 71 days, and resulted in the death of two Native Americans). The book does not mention the demands that reflected the grievances of the Lakota: a U.S. Presidential Treaty

Akwesasne Notes, Vol. 5, No. 6, Early Winter, 1973. See pp. 10 and 11 for discussion of provisions of 1868 Fort Laramie Treaty.

Voices From Wounded Knee, 1973. Akwesasne Notes. Excellent discussion of the background and events of the 1973 occupation of Wounded Knee.

Bury My Heart At Wounded Knee. See particularly pp. 102-142, 264-296 and 390-418 for discussion of the history of Sioux-U.S. relations up to the massacre at Wounded Knee, 1890.

QUOTATION	COMMENT	REFERENCE

26. (Continued)

sent West to help white settlers. Sometimes the Indians won. The Sioux massacred Colonel George Armstrong Custer and over two hundred men at the Battle of the Little Big Horn, in Montana, in 1876. But usually the Indians lost. Farther and farther west they were pushed, and herded onto reservations.

History of the American People, p. 221

Gold discoveries opened other areas to Americans . . . gold strikes were made in the Black Hills of South Dakota. Once again the rush was on.

History of the American People, p. 210

Commission to discuss treaty rights and abuses; an investigation of the BIA and of the corrupt "tribal" government; and the establishment of a traditional government for the Lakota Nation. Without a cohesive presentation of the experiences of Native Americans, students can develop little understanding of their history or of their present reality.

Chronicles of American Indian Protest.
See pp. 209-233 for historical background.

NATIVE AMERICAN TEXTBOOK CHECKLIST

Title _____

Publisher _____ **Year** _____ **Grade Level** _____

There are 26 criteria to be scored. The highest possible rating is +52.
The lowest is –52. This text scores _____ .

	Incorrect Information −2	No Information −1	Omits This Period 0	Limited Information +1	Full Information +2
1. Native Americans are the original inhabitants of North America.					
2. Pre-Columbian Native American societies reflected great diversity and complexity.					
3. The myth of "discovery" is blatantly Eurocentric.					
4. At least ten to twelve million Native peoples may have lived in what later became the U.S.					
5. "Advanced culture" is an ethnocentric concept and does not explain or justify European conquest.					
6. War and violence were not characteristic of Native nations.					
7. Native American technology and knowledge were achievements in their own right.					
8. Missionary activities were an integral part of European conquest.					
9. Native nations made alliances with European nations for their own strategic purposes.					
10. Conflicting European and colonial economic interests in Native lands helped trigger the US. Revolution.					
11. Native nations fought the invaders to maintain their communities and lands.					
12. Land has a special significance to Native Americans and has been the central issue of conflict with the U.S.					
13. It is Eurocentric to categorize Native Americans as either "friendly" or "unfriendly."					
14. U.S. policies toward Native Americans reflect many political and economic factors within U.S. society.					
15. Textbook terminology is Eurocentric, ignoring Native American presence and perspectives.					
16. Legally binding treaties are central to the relations between Native nations and the U.S.					
17. The 1881 Dawes Act resulted in the loss of three-quarters of the remaining land of Native Americans.					
18. The Citizenship Act of 1924 was not a benevolent action.					
19. The Reorganization Act of 1934 heightened Native American alienation and powerlessness.					
20. The termination policy of the 1950's resulted in the loss of more land and the abrogation of treaties.					

	−2	−1	0	+1	+2
21. The BIA is a corrupt and inefficient bureaucracy controlling the affairs of one million people.					
22. Oppressive conditions lead to proportionately lower population increase for Native Americans.					
23. Reservations represent a paradox for Native Americans.					
24. Treaty rights, sovereignty, self-determination and the return of land are the major goals of Native Americans.					
25. The struggle to maintain land continues today.					
26. There is a relationship between the past experiences and the present reality of Native Americans.					
Total					
Textbook Final Score					

PUERTO RICANS

Puerto Rico's original name was Boriquen and the Native people of the Island were the Taino. The country has endured foreign domination since 1509, when Spanish settlement began. Four hundred and eighty years later, in 1973, 104 nations in the United Nations voted to reaffirm "The inalienable right of the people of Puerto Rico to self-determination and independence." That vote was considered to be a rebuke of the U.S. for its role in the continued domination of Puerto Rico.

STRUGGLE AGAINST SPAIN

In the early 1500's the Taino fought against the Spanish invaders. While most were killed by the Spaniards, or by European-introduced diseases, some intermarried with Spanish settlers and—later on—with African slaves. It is that basic blend of three peoples and cultures which formed the Puerto Rican nation.

The long struggle for independence from Spain was highlighted by the 1868 Proclamation of the Republic of Puerto Rico. Spain crushed the Republic, but resistance continued. In the 1890's the Puerto Rican people forced major concessions from Spain. However, the U.S. take-over of the Island in 1898 turned the clock backwards for Puerto Rican self-government.

U.S. STEPS IN

The 1898 military invasion was the culmination of almost 80 years of U.S. interest in controlling Puerto Rico. In 1822 President Monroe wrote: "Cuba and Puerto Rico are natural appendices of the United States." In 1869 the U.S. offered 150 million dollars to Spain for the two countries. In 1876 Secretary of State, Arthur E. Blaine, said: "I believe there are three non-continental places of enough value to be taken by the United States. One is Hawaii; the others are Cuba and Puerto Rico."

Little or none of this background appears in textbooks. Nor are students told much about the U.S. role in Puerto Rico after "winning" the Island from Spain. The U.S. was interested in Puerto Rico both as a source of sugar and as a strategic military site. After the take-over, four large U.S. sugar corporations stepped in and began to amass large amounts of land for sugar plantations. In the process, thousands of small farm-owning families were displaced, creating a ready source of low-paid labor for the cane fields and sugar mills.

While Spain had conceded some powers of self-government to Puerto Rico in 1897, the U.S. abolished most of these as being "not compatible with American methods and progress." One U.S. commander wrote: "I am getting in touch with the people and trying to educate them to the idea that they must help themselves, giving them kindergarten instruction in controlling themselves without allowing them too much liberty."

"AMERICANIZATION"

The U.S., in addition to assuming economic and governmental control of Puerto Rico, attempted to "Americanize" it, culturally. English was made the official language for schools and government, although the vast majority of people spoke only Spanish. President Theodore Roosevelt said it was the intent of the U.S. "to remodel all Puerto Ricans so that they should become similar in language, habits and thoughts to continental Americans."

As a result of Puerto Rican resistance to these measures, the U.S. gradually adopted more sophisticated means of control. A "commonwealth" government was established in 1952, changing the form, but not the substance, of U.S. domination. The major change brought about by the commonwealth was to permit Puerto Ricans to elect their own governor, rather than having the governor appointed by the U.S. President. But the basic power relations remained unchanged, and to this day the U.S. Congress retains almost total control over the commonwealth government. U.S. laws, judicial rulings and administrative regulations continue to affect the Puerto Rican people in a myriad of ways. In matters of trade, foreign relations, justice, immigration, communications, labor relations, and numerous other areas, Puerto Rico is controlled by the U.S.

OPERATION BOOTSTRAP

The famed industrialization under "Operation Bootstrap" intensified U.S. control of the Puerto Rican economy after WWII. This provided U.S. businesses with low-paid Puerto Rican labor and, in addition, exempted them from paying taxes to Puerto Rico or to the U.S. Today, almost half of the U.S. $23 billion investment in Latin America is in Puerto Rico. U.S. interests control 85 percent of Puerto Rican industry, and the extraordinarily high profits created by the labor and resources of Puerto Rico are returned to the U.S., rather than reinvested in Puerto Rico to meet the needs of the people.

The results of U.S. colonialism have been summed up by Adalberto Lopez and James Petras in *Puerto Rico and Puerto Ricans:*

> ". . . development through dependency misdevelops and distorts the economy, whether it be through foreign-owned sugar plantations, manufactures or tourist plants: An agrarian society becomes an importer of food; an industrial society an exporter of labor; an island resort—a distant memory to hundreds of thousands enclosed in tenement jungles and mazes of dilapidated shacks. Dependency results in the misallocation of land, labor and public resources to meet foreign needs at the expense of the Puerto Rican people. Dependency means control of development decisions from the outside. And outside decision-makers, corporate executives, U.S. government officials and bankers, calculate costs and benefits of investments and loans according to the criteria relevant to the larger needs of their firms—the profit margins. . . . Exploitation in all its manifestations has been the result of dependency: unemployment, migratory labor, low income for the laboring classes and wealth and luxury for the rich, especially the foreign rich and local *politicos* (pp. 121-122)."

No textbook we examined provides even a hint of the above analysis. In varying degrees, every text portrays Puerto Rico as an Island liberated from Spain by a benevolent U.S. Through a slow but steady process, the U.S. is said to have taught Puerto Ricans how to govern themselves and to have progressively allowed them more self-government. Finally, in 1952, say the textbooks, Puerto Rico became a "free" or "independent" commonwealth, affiliated with the U.S. by "bonds of friendship" and "favorable trade and defense" relationships.

All the textbooks make the same claim: Puerto Rico has benefitted greatly from its relationship with the U.S.—economically and politically. To substantiate that claim, textbooks make a favorable comparison between Puerto Rico's standard of living and conditions in Latin America. A more honest evaluation, since Puerto Rico has been under U.S. control for 78 years, would be to compare conditions in Puerto Rico and the U.S. Such a comparison would show that, in 1940, Puerto Rico's per capita income was 80 percent lower than that of Mississippi, the poorest state. Thirty years later, in 1970, Puerto Rico's per capita income was 81 percent lower than Mississippi's.

Textbooks do not report that, during the period of intensive industrialization, unemployment in Puerto Rico never fell below an official rate of 10 percent, and today it is higher than before "Operation Bootstrap" began. While the wages of Puerto Rican workers rose during that period, they remain 1/2 to 1/3 of U.S. wages, while the cost of living is 25 percent higher.

OVERPOPULATION

To be sure, most texts do state that Puerto Rico still suffers from poverty—but poverty is invariably said to result from overpopulation. "Overpopulation" is a term that is relative to the productive base of any nation—for instance, the well-to-do Netherlands has a population density comparable to Puerto Rico's. Textbooks never suggest that it is the export of profit which puts unbearable pressure on the population, rather than the population which strains the economy.

The dislocation of the Puerto Rican economy has created vast numbers of Puerto Ricans unable to find productive work. The existence of this large pool of "excess" labor has led to two shockingly destructive consequences: the massive sterilization of 35 percent of Puerto Rican women of child-bearing age, and the forced migration of a third of the population to the U.S. This lowering of the birth rate and the migration of so many Puerto Ricans acts as a safety valve for the economic system by somewhat reducing the build-up of labor's frustration and anger. The migration also provides a source of exceptionally low-paid workers for industrial and agricultural interests in the U.S.

COMMONWEALTH, STATEHOOD, INDEPENDENCE

Since textbooks ignore these facts, it is hardly surprising that they do not treat the struggle for Puerto Rican independence seriously. Throughout the years of U.S. domination, nationalists and independentistas—reflecting varying ideologies, strategies, and objectives—have worked for the same goal of independence for Puerto Rico. While many texts do mention the two plebiscites which favored commonwealth status, they do not mention the many challenges raised by "independentistas" to the validity of those two votes. And because textbooks portray Puerto Rico as "free," "independent," or "self-governing," they fail to note that, whatever status the Puerto Rican people choose, the U.S. Congress still lays claim to decide their future.

Whether Puerto Ricans favor independence, statehood or commonwealth status, whether they live in Puerto Rico or in the U.S., they all share a common national oppression. And the status of the 2 million Puerto Ricans in the U.S.—like the status of the 3.3 million in Puerto Rico—remains an unsettled and volatile issue.

TERMINOLOGY

Unlike many immigrants to the U.S., Puerto Ricans who migrated here have not severed their ties to their country. In the U.S. today they face economic exploitation and cultural oppression similar to that faced by other third world peoples. That is one reason that—even though four of every ten Puerto Ricans in the U.S. today were born here—most Puerto Ricans identify themselves as *Puertorriqueños* (Puerto Ricans). Their frame of reference remains their Island nation—*la patria*—and many, if not most, hope to return sooner or later. Thus a term rarely, if ever, used by Puerto Ricans themselves is "Puerto Rican American."

The most common alternate for *Puertorriqueño* is *Boricua,* which is based on the ancient Taino name for the Island—Borinquen. Some second-generation persons may describe themselves as "Ricans," "Neo-Ricans" or "Neyoricans" (the latter refers to New York, the residence of approximately 60 percent of Puerto Ricans in the U.S.). However, "neo-Rican" and "Neyoricans" are terms disliked by most Puerto Ricans living in the U.S.

Because so many Puerto Ricans feel that the term "mainland"—to describe the U.S.—implies that one land is "main" (the U.S.) and the other is secondary or less important (Puerto Rico), we have avoided the use of "mainland" and referred either to the "U.S." or "North America"—the latter being the term frequently used by Puerto Ricans to describe the U.S.

Textbooks and Puerto Ricans

QUOTATION	COMMENT	REFERENCE

1. The histories of Taino and African peoples are important in understanding Puerto Rican history.

In the years following Columbus' first voyage, the Spanish quickly conquered and colonized Puerto Rico, Jamaica, Cuba, Hispaniola, and other islands. . . . They raised cattle and grew sugar and cotton. Most of the Spanish colonists were unemployed soldiers. . . . They became overseers and forced the Indians to work as laborers on the land.

Man In America, p. 68

Texts provide little or no information on the non-Spanish history and heritage of Puerto Rico before the U.S. take-over. Puerto Rico was a flourishing center of Taino (a Native people of the Caribbean) culture, and they called their country Borinquen. The Tainos were an agricultural people who worked communally to satisfy their people's needs. The Tainos possessed a well organized social system and a complex religion. At first the Taino welcomed Columbus, but resistance was organized as they learned of Spanish intentions from the people of Dominica, where the Spanish had first colonized. Most of the Taino people were killed, or died of disease, but some escaped to remote mountain areas and later intermarried with European settlers and African slaves. While there is no longer a distinct Taino culture in Puerto Rico, the Taino left a striking racial and cultural imprint.

The Spanish brought African slaves to Puerto Rico. Unlike the case of other islands in the Caribbean, where slaves outnumbered Europeans, they never exceeded 14 percent of the population in Puerto Rico. Nonetheless, there is evidence of at least 14 slave revolts during Spanish rule (slavery was formally abolished in 1873). The African influence is strongly reflected in the music, language, diet, and forms of religious practice of Puerto Ricans.

Taller de Cultura. (Spanish and English). Centro de Estudios Puertorriqueños—C.U.N.Y.

Historia de la Esclavitud Negra en Puerto Rico. Luis M. Diaz Soler.

Historia de la Cultura de Puerto Rico (1493-1960). Eugenio Fernandéz Mendéz.

2. Puerto Ricans have a long history of striving for independence.

During most of the 18th and 19th centuries, Puerto Rico had a rather sleepy economy based on coffee, sugar, and tobacco plantations. Slavery and the extreme poverty of the many existed side by side with the great wealth of the very few. The American Civil War and the uprisings in Cuba touched it somewhat. The heavy hand of Spain held Puerto Rico firmly in its grip. Nevertheless, a small rebellion, which was put down, served notice on Spain that the

Both of these quotes are misleading. There was a long history of resistance to Spanish control, ranging from peaceful efforts to liberalize colonialism, to boycotts of Spanish firms, to armed insurrection by secret revolutionary societies. Rather than being "touched" by uprisings in Cuba, Puerto Rican and Cuban revolutionaries collaborated closely. The Comite Revolucionario de Neuva York worked in the U.S. for the liberation of both Puerto Rico and Cuba.

QUOTATION	COMMENT	REFERENCE

2. (Continued)

islanders were discontent. In 1873 slavery was finally abolished. Through the efforts of Louis Muñoz-Rivera, Spain allowed Puerto Rico some limited self-government in 1898.

The Pageant of American History, p. 363

There had never been a very active anti-Spanish movement in Puerto Rico. . . .

The Free and the Brave, p. 551

The "small rebellion" was the 1868 Lares uprising (Grito de Lares), led by the great patriot Ramón Emeterio Betances. The town of Lares was liberated and the Republic of Puerto Rico declared. That insurrection failed, as did the 1897 uprising at Yauco. But those actions, along with the weakened condition of the Spanish empire, had as much to do with winning concessions from Spain as did the actions of Muñoz Rivera. For a text to discuss Muñoz Rivera, and not Betances, is to distort the Puerto Rican people's desire for self-determination.

Puerto Rico and Puerto Ricans: Studies in History and Society. Adalberto López and James Petras. pp. 66-82.

Puerto Rico: A Socio-Historic Interpretation. Manuel Maldonado-Denis. pp. 22-51.

We, The Puerto Rican People: A Story of Oppression and Resistance. Juan Angel Silén. pp. 30-33.

---

3. The U.S. declared war on Spain in order to establish its own hegemony in this hemisphere.

The United States entered the [Spanish-American] *war with the argument that it was fighting merely to free the oppressed Cubans. It ended the war with an empire on its hands.*

Rise of the American Nation, p. 579

Throughout the 19th century, officials of the U.S. had expressed the desire to control Puerto Rico and Cuba for economic and military reasons. Even before the military invasion, Puerto Rico's economy had been increasingly oriented toward production of sugar for the U.S. (and the monopolization of sugar production and concentration of land by four major U.S. sugar corporations became the major orientation of the economy up to 1940, with devastating results on Puerto Rican land ownership and employment). The Spanish-American War was the first major step to be taken by the U.S. as a world imperialist power, giving it possession of the Philippines and Puerto Rico and almost absolute control over Cuba. In none of these new possessions did the U.S. establish institutions for self-government. The former Spanish colonies remained colonies, but under the U.S. flag. This policy was often justified by the racist myth of Manifest Destiny, which claimed the responsibility of the "superior" Anglo-Saxon race to guide "inferior" people who were "incapable" of self-government.

To Serve The Devil Vol. II: Colonials and Sojourners. Paul Jacobs, et al. See pp. 317-355 for brief discussion of racism and Manifest Destiny.

Puerto Rico and Puerto Ricans, p. 83.

Puerto Rico: A Socio-Historic Interpretation. See pp. 54-56 for early U.S. interest in acquiring Puerto Rico and pp. 65-72 for U.S. imperialism.

Taller De Migracion. (English and Spanish) Centro De Estudios Puertorriqueños-C.U.N.Y., pp. 102-146. U.S. interests in Puerto Rican sugar production.

---

4. Puerto Ricans had mixed reactions to the U.S. take-over of their country.

. . . the American troops were warmly welcomed. . . . A leading citizen may have expressed the feelings of his people when he said

Most Puerto Ricans were united in their dislike of Spanish domination and many felt that the U.S. had come to help liberate them from Spanish control. Some (los macheteros) offered armed resistance to the U.S., and well-known patriots, like Betances, opposed U.S. intervention. On the other hand, a small elite of

Puerto Rico and Puerto Ricans, pp. 83-84.

Puerto Rico: A Socio-Historic Interpretation, pp. 50-51 and 57-62.

QUOTATION	COMMENT	REFERENCE

4. (Continued)

simply, "We are glad that the United States is to be our country."

The Free and the Brave, p. 551

Spanish and Puerto Rican businessmen favored U.S. annexation of the Island. The majority of the people, however, "accepted" the U.S. take-over in the same way that small nations everywhere "accept" invasion by a strong, seemingly invincible, foreign power.

5. Puerto Rico had greater autonomy under Spanish rule than it has today under the U.S.

The Treaty of Paris, which ended the Spanish-American War, gave Puerto Rico to the United States. A new era began for the island.

The Pageant of American History, p. 363

Before the war, in the Royal Decree of November 25, 1897, Spain granted Puerto Ricans universal suffrage and 16 representatives in the Spanish Cortes (Congress). Puerto Rico was granted the power to ratify commercial treaties with any nation and to set tariffs, as well as the right to be consulted in pertinent legislative matters. Spain continued responsibility for the military defense of the Island, but Puerto Ricans had their own citizenship and were not obliged to enter into military service in the Spanish army.

The U.S. revoked these gains and took complete control through the Treaty of Paris, an agreement between Spain and the U.S. in which Puerto Rico had no voice. Albizu Campos, an independence leader, stated: "The Treaty of Paris was not negotiated by Puerto Rican plenipotentiaries and was never submitted to our parliament for ratification. It is null and void as far as Puerto Rico is concerned."

The "new era" began with the Island reverting to complete colonial status. The U.S. abolished the Puerto Rican provincial assembly and insular cabinet as "not compatible with American methods and progress." English became the official language, in a country where 99 percent of the people spoke Spanish. The U.S. took absolute control of Puerto Rico's foreign affairs. Puerto Ricans had no vote in the U.S. Congress. Their economy was monopolized by the U.S., and exploitation of Puerto Rican low-paid labor by U.S. corporations began. To this day, most of the rights Spain had granted to Puerto Rico have been withheld by the U.S.

Puerto Rico and Puerto Ricans. See pp. 82-83 and 123-133 for discussion of Charter of Autonomy. See pp. 103-110 and 214-220 for discussion of U.S. monopolization of economy.

Puerto Rico: A Socio-Historic Interpretation, pp. 48 and 72-78.

6. The Foraker Act formalized U.S. domination of Puerto Rico.

In 1900, with the Foraker Act, Congress provided for the government of Puerto Rico. The new government consisted of a governor and an executive council appointed by the

All 15 governors appointed between 1900 and 1947 were from the U.S. The executive council had six mandated positions for North Americans and five for Puerto Ricans. The laws passed by the elected House of Delegates were subject to U.S. veto. Judicial affairs were under the control of the Circuit Court of Boston, commerce was subject to U.S. laws, the U.S. dollar was imposed as the currency of the country, and U.S. laws became the laws of Puerto Rico.

Puerto Rico and Puerto Ricans, pp. 128-129.

Puerto Rico: A Socio-Historic Interpretation, pp. 83-92 and 95.

QUOTATION	COMMENT	REFERENCE

6. (Continued)

President of the United States, and a lower house elected by the Puerto Ricans.

Rise of the American Nation, p. 590

To protest U.S. control, the House of Delegates, in 1909, refused to approve any further legislation, including the government's budget for the coming year. It sent a memorandum to the U.S. President and Congress complaining of "the unjust law which makes it impossible for the people's representatives to pass the laws they desire." The U.S. Congress reponded by passing the Olmstead Act, requiring the previous year's budget to be carried over to the new year.

---

7. U.S. citizenship was imposed on Puerto Ricans despite their protests.

In 1917, the Puerto Ricans were granted citizenship. As American citizens, Puerto Ricans could migrate freely from Puerto Rico to the mainland of the United States and back again whenever they chose to do so.

The Pageant of American History, p. 417

Citizenship was imposed by an act of the U.S. Congress. Puerto Rico's elected resident commissioner in Washington pleaded that a referendum be held to determine the people's wishes on the issue, but he was ignored. In 1913 the only Puerto Rican-elected legislature had unanimously refused U.S. citizenship, stating: "We firmly and loyally oppose our being declared, against our express will or without our express consent, citizens of any other than our own beloved country. . . . "

Many believe that the U.S. forced citizenship on Puerto Rico for reasons of national security—the action took place just one month before the U.S. entered WW I. By granting citizenship to its colonial subjects, the U.S. strengthened its strategic presence in the Caribbean, making the Island a more permanent part of its hegemony. The action also enabled President Wilson to order, on June 27, 1917, the induction of Puerto Ricans into the U.S. military. Over 20,000 were drafted. Yet in 1922 the U.S. Supreme Court ruled that the Jones Act did not extend the full protection of the Constitution to Puerto Ricans. Puerto Ricans could refuse U.S. citizenship as individuals by signing special documents, but doing this deprived them of legal rights and made them aliens in their own country.

Congressional Record. 64th Congress, 1st Session, 1916, LIII, p. 73.
Speech by Luis Muñoz Rivera to Congress on citizenship issue.

The Independent, LXX, February 16, 1911, pp. 356-359.
Article by Puerto Rico's resident commissioner in Washington.

Puerto Rico and Puerto Ricans, p. 129.

Puerto Rico: A Socio-Historic Interpretation, pp. 103-110.

We, The Puerto Rican People, pp. 55-60.

---

8. The U.S. established an educational system designed to "Americanize" Puerto Rico.

Puerto Rico, unlike Cuba, remained a possession of the United States. Under American guidance, improvements were made in the . . . education . . . of the Puerto Rican people.

Man In America, p. 464

Spanish-controlled education in the late 19th century was based on the schooling of a small elite, so any change could be regarded as improvement. The U.S. did introduce a more egalitarian approach to education, but it was largely motivated by the desire to "Americanize" the populace and to provide more disciplined laborers who could speak a little English. English became the language of instruction, though the vast majority of the teachers were unable to speak it. In

The Remaking of a Culture: Life and Education in Puerto Rico. Theodore Brameld.

Bulletin, Council on Interracial Books for Children, Vol. 4, Nos. 1&2.
Contains articles related to education in Puerto Rico.

QUOTATION	**COMMENT**	**REFERENCE**

8. (Continued)

| | 1948 Spanish was reestablished as the basic language for classroom teaching, with English as a required second language. Puerto Rican children were taught more about the history of the U.S. than of their own country. Education in Puerto Rico continues to instill the values and perspectives of the U.S. government, and denies Puerto Rican youth their national heritage. | *Puerto Rico and Puerto Ricans*, pp. 132-133 and 175-192.

Americanization in Puerto Rico and the Public School System 1900-1930. Aida Montilla de Negron.

"Children's Books as a Liberating Force," Dr. Luis Nieves Falcón, in the *Bulletin*, Vol. 7, No. 1.

To Serve The Devil, pp. 283-285.

We, The Puerto Rican People, pp. 93-102. |

9. Commonwealth status retained all significant aspects of U.S. control of Puerto Rico.

| *In 1952, the island adopted a constitution and became the free Commonwealth of Puerto Rico. As a* commonwealth, *or free republic, Puerto Rico today governs itself, but receives military and tariff protection from the United States.*

America: Its People and Values, p. 683

As a commonwealth, Puerto Rico is self-governing. It makes its own laws and controls its own finances.

Rise of the American Nation, p. 590 | Commonwealth status has allowed greater Puerto Rican involvement in the Island's local affairs, but the commonwealth government often serves U.S. interests rather than the needs of the Puerto Rican people. Before approving the new constitution, the U.S. Congress insisted on adding an amendment stating that: "Any amendment or revision of this constitution shall be consistent with the resolution enacted by the Congress of the United States approving this constitution, with the applicable provisions of the Constitution of the United States, with the Puerto Rico Federal Relations Act, and with Public Law 600." This means that ultimate power over the Puerto Rican people remains in Washington, D.C.
Hundreds of U.S. laws and thousands of U.S. administrative and judicial rules and regulations govern the Puerto Rican people. The U.S. still controls the Island's external and trade affairs, operates the Post Office and Customs Service, licenses radio and TV stations and continues jurisdiction of the legal structure through the Circuit Court in Boston. All U.S. labor laws apply to Puerto Rico, including the Taft-Hartley Law which gives the U.S. National Labor Relations Board jurisdiction over labor disputes in Puerto Rico. Puerto Rico cannot engage in commercial agreements with foreign countries without the authorization of the U.S., and the U.S. controls Puerto Rico's participation in international bodies, foreign trade, relations with other countries and immigration. The U.S. maintains 50,000 military personnel on bases which occupy 13 percent of the arable land of Puerto Rico. | *Puerto Rico and Puerto Ricans*, pp. 153-157.

Puerto Rico: A Socio-Historic Interpretation, pp. 189-209.

Memorandum Supporting the Petition of the Puerto Rico Independence Party and The Puerto Rico Socialist Party in Relation to the Colonial Case of Puerto Rico, Puerto Rican Independence Party and Socialist Party of Puerto Rico, pp. 9-27.

Puerto Rico: A Colony of the United States. Puerto Rican Youth Movement. |

QUOTATION	COMMENT	REFERENCE

10. Despite severe repression, the struggle for Puerto Rican independence continues.

In 1967, the Puerto Ricans held a vote to decide whether they wanted their island to become an independent nation, to become a state . . . or to remain a commonwealth. They voted to remain a commonwealth. As a commonwealth, the people of Puerto Rico govern themselves, and they are free to decide what their relationship to the United States will be in the future. Meanwhile, in the words of one of the island's leading statesmen, Puerto Rico is "associated with the American Union by bonds of affection, common citizenship, and free choice."

America: Its People and Values, p. 684

Most texts ignore the existence of the independence movement in Puerto Rico. Some texts mention the 1951 and 1967 referenda in Puerto Rico which favored commonwealth status. They fail to mention that the 1951 vote offered only the choice between accepting or rejecting "commonwealth" status, which for the most part merely formalized existing U.S. domination of the country. They also fail to mention that "independentistas" boycotted those votes. In the 1967 plebiscite 50 percent of qualified citizens abstained from voting, while more than 60,000 North Americans residing in Puerto Rico were allowed to vote. "Independentistas" denounce the legitimacy of any vote held in a country occupied by foreign troops and carried out without international supervision. Independence advocates also point out that they have faced continuous repression when they attempt to advocate their viewpoint. And the U.S. government admitted, in May of 1975, that Puerto Rican independence groups were a major target of the FBI's illegal COINTELPRO operation, designed to disrupt and destroy those groups.

The 1935 police killings of pro-independence demonstrators at Rio Piedras, a similar occurrence in 1937 at Ponce, the 1948 repression of university students and faculty in San Juan, and the 1950 nationalist uprising at Jayuya, are highlights of the contemporary struggle for independence. The 1950 attacks on Blair House and the House of Representatives in Washington, D.C., were further attempts by nationalists to call world attention to their campaign for independence. Labor organizing is also an important aspect of the independence movement, as workers increasingly feel that U.S. economic exploitation is harmful to their own and their country's interests. In 1973 the General Assembly of the United Nations voted (104 to 5, with 10 abstentions) a resolution that, in effect, recognized Puerto Rico as a U.S. colony and reaffirmed the "inalienable right of the people of Puerto Rico to self-determination."

"Independence Movement Wins Victory At UN," *Puerto Rico Libre,* December-January 1973-74.

To Serve The Devil, pp. 305-316.

Puerto Rico and Puerto Ricans, pp. 133-162 and 296-307. Discussion of labor and independence struggles during U.S. rule.

Memorandum Supporting the Petition of the Puerto Rico Independence Party and the Puerto Rico Socialist Party in Relation to the Colonial Case of Puerto Rico, pp. 28-60.

11. Operation Bootstrap led to the industrialization of Puerto Rico for the benefit of U.S. capital.

After Puerto Rico became a free commonwealth, conditions improved greatly. The Puerto Rican government set about developing new industries and improving the lives of its people.

"Operation Bootstrap" was begun by the Puerto Rican government in the 1940's. More than 1,800 manufacturing plants were opened, helping to convert Puerto Rico from an agricultural land to a mainly industrialized society. However, Puerto Ricans have not been

QUOTATION	COMMENT	REFERENCE

11. (Continued)

The island began to prosper. Today, Puerto Rico has a democratic government and flourishing businesses and industries.

America: Its People and Values, p. 684

One way the United States has helped Puerto Ricans in their efforts to raise living standards is through free trade. There are no tariff barriers between the United States and Puerto Rico.

Rise of the American Nation, p. 832

the principal beneficiaries of this plan.

Puerto Rico's relationship with the U.S. represents classic colonialism. It is a source of cheap labor and raw materials as well as a captive market for surplus U.S. goods. Puerto Rico is highly industrialized, yet its economy is based on processing imported intermediary and raw materials for export. Almost 98 percent of all food, raw materials and manufactured goods consumed must be imported from the U.S. Puerto Rico is the largest per capita purchaser of U.S. goods in the world and, in absolute terms, is among the five largest importers of U.S. goods. By U.S. law, all goods carried between Puerto Rico and the U.S. must be transported by the U.S. merchant marine, the most costly available. And U.S. tariff laws deny Puerto Rico access to cheaper foreign products.

Eighty-five percent of industries in Puerto Rico are owned by U.S. interests. They do not have to pay Island taxes for 10 to 25 years. This, along with lower wages than those they pay in the U.S., has allowed U.S. industries to average 20 percent profit per year, far higher than comparative profits in the U.S. When profits are threatened—for instance by a wage raise—many plants move to countries paying still lower wages. The ultimate effect of Operation Bootstrap has been to assure complete U.S. control of the Puerto Rican economy, as well as to increase social dislocation and economic inequality.

Puerto Rico: Freedom and Power in the Caribbean. Gordon K. Lewis. Traces impact of Operation Bootstrap in economics, family life and community. Analyzes problem of economic dependency between Puerto Rico and U.S.

Puerto Rico and Puerto Ricans, pp. 221-248.

Puerto Rico: A Socio-Historic Interpretation, pp. 151-188.

Taller De Migracion, pp. 148-183.

We, The Puerto Rican People, pp. 87-93 and 116-117.

12. Operation Bootstrap has not changed Puerto Rico's relative economic position vis-à-vis the U.S.

Today . . . Puerto Ricans enjoy a per capita income higher than that of any other Latin-American country with the single exception of oil-rich Venezuela.

Rise of the American Nation, p. 832

While Puerto Rico is in a better comparative position than most Latin American countries, the Island has been part of the U.S. since 1898 and its people have been U.S. citizens since 1917. Thus, comparisons must be made with the U.S., not with Latin America. Puerto Rico—which would rank 26th in population with the 50 U.S. states—is far poorer than any state. In 1940, Puerto Rico had a per capita income 80 percent lower than Mississippi's, the poorest state; in 1970, after 30 years of "Operation Bootstrap," Puerto Rico's per capita income was 81 percent lower than Mississippi's. The average wage in Puerto Rico is 1/2 to 1/3 that paid U.S. workers, while the cost of living is 25 percent higher. The size of the workforce in proportion to the population has remained stationary and official

Puerto Rico Libre. Publication of The Committee for Puerto Rican Decolonization is an excellent source for current information on Puerto Rico and the independence struggle.

"Puerto Rico Seeks Way Out As Economic Woes Mount," *New York Times,* October 15, 1975.

Taller De Migracion.

12. (Continued)

unemployment has remained at double digit levels for the last three decades—official unemployment today is more than double that in the U.S. More than six out of every ten Puerto Ricans live below the federal poverty standard and 71 percent depend on food stamps. While the overall standard of living in Puerto Rico did rise during the period of industrialization, the effect would have been negligible without massive migration to the U.S.

---

13. Puerto Rican women face a double oppression.

During the 1950's Puerto Ricans poured their energies into a program to improve their standard of living. This program became known as "Operation Bootstrap." The Puerto Rican government encouraged new industries, better agriculture, and tourism. Income from these projects was put to work improving housing, schools, and medical facilities. . . . Despite progress, many Puerto Ricans remained poor, partly because the island is overpopulated. [Emphasis added]

The Challenge of America, p. 727

To deal with so-called "overpopulation" the government established a priority program for birth control which has resulted in the sterilization of 35 percent of all Puerto Rican women between the ages of 20-49 (92 percent of these are under the age of 35). This represents the highest incidence of sterilization in the world. While medical care is inadequate for the population as a whole, 18 free sterilization centers (funded by the U.S. through HEW) were opened in 1974. These centers are capable of performing 1,000 sterilizations a month. Puerto Rican women also suffer from experimental drug testing by U.S. drug firms. A 1957 experimental study of the birth control pill on 838 Puerto Rican women led to five deaths.

These genocidal programs most directly affect the lives and health of women, who also endure sexist discrimination in the workforce. Women comprise 35 percent of the Puerto Rican labor force, but they earn 17.4 percent less than do men in the same jobs.

Textbooks never point out another reality about Puerto Rican women. They are actively involved in current labor and independence struggles, continuing a long tradition highlighted by patriots such as Mariana Bracetti, Lola Rogriguez de Tió, Blanca Canales and Lolita Lebrón.

"Puertorriqueñas In The United States," Lourdes Miranda King, in *Civil Rights Digest*, Spring 1974. Discusses birth control pill experiment.

Puerto Rico Libre, Vol. III, No. 1, August 1975. Special issue on Puerto Rican women.

"Sterilization Abuse of Women: The Facts," *Health/PAC Bulletin*, No. 62, January/February 1975.

Sterilization & Fertility Decline in Puerto Rico. Harriet Presser.

"35% Puerto Rican Women Sterilized," *Puerto Rico Libre*, Vol. 2, No. 5, December, 1974.

---

14. Extensive migration was caused by U.S. exploitation of the country.

Operation Bootstrap did not solve all problems. Dramatic as the increase in wealth was, the per capita income of Puerto Ricans was less than half that in the United States. Unemployment was high. But the most persistent problem was overcrowding. The Puerto Rican death rate

Textbooks uniformly laud the "new prosperity" of Operation Bootstrap and explain migration to the U.S. as due to "overcrowding." No textbook even implies that economic development in Puerto Rico (before and after Operation Bootstrap) was designed to profit North American capital rather than to make Puerto Rico self-sufficient and capable of meeting the needs of the Puerto Rican

QUOTATION	COMMENT	REFERENCE

14. (Continued)

dropped more rapidly than its birth rate, with resulting heavy density of population (over 600 per square mile). Free migration to the United States offered an apparent safety valve, and there was an exodus in the 1950's of nearly a million people to the United States . . . 500,000 Puerto Ricans live in New York City alone.

A Free People, p. 477

Since 1946 many [Puerto Ricans] have come to the mainland, adding their unique culture to others in the United States.

Man In America, p. 464

people. The resulting distortion of Puerto Rico's economy has led to what has been called "the geographic dismemberment of the Puerto Rican nation."

Approximately 2 million Puerto Ricans now live in the U.S. while 3.3 million live in Puerto Rico. Migration long predated 1946—between 1898-1944 (while U.S. sugar corporations were consolidating their landholdings) 90,000 people left Puerto Rico. In 1944, it became official policy to encourage migration of people whose excess labor was not needed in Puerto Rico.

The U.S.—and not the Puerto Rican government—controls immigration into Puerto Rico and has allowed 70,000 non-U.S. foreigners (about half of whom are Cuban refugees) and approximately 90,000 foreigners of North American origin (excluding military) to enter and reside in this supposedly "overpopulated" country. It might also be noted that while Puerto Rico had a population density of 618 persons per square mile in the 1940's (over 900 per square mile today), 90 percent of Puerto Ricans who migrated at that time came to New York City, which has a population density of 90,000 persons per square mile.

Puerto Rico: A Socio-Historic Interpretation, pp. 302-324.

Taller De Migracion, pp. 102-251

---

15. Puerto Rican migrants in the U.S. face national and racial oppression not experienced by white immigrants.

Puerto Rican newcomers have served in important government positions in New York City and in New York State. Puerto Ricans have made important contributions to American life as artists, entertainers, and athletes, as well as doctors, social workers and lawyers. . . . [They] have now begun to move up the ladder of opportunity climbed in earlier times by so many generations of immigrants to America. But, like earlier immigrants, they, too, face many difficulties. Discrimination and prejudice often are especially serious to these newcomers. They also must face the problems of low income, poor housing, and lack of job skills and training.

America: Its People and Values, pp. 561-562

While it is unusual and positive for a text to note the achievements of some Puerto Ricans, this text mistakes the problems facing Puerto Ricans in the U.S. and understates the results of their oppression.

Puerto Ricans face a different reality from that of earlier immigrants, who arrived when there were great demands for unskilled labor. In addition, Puerto Ricans face racial oppression and national oppression caused by U.S. domination of their country. It is the distortion of the economy of Puerto Rico for the profit of U.S. capital which has forced 1/3 of the Puerto Rican nation to move to the U.S. and accept low-paid menial and service occupations.

(Continued)

QUOTATION	COMMENT	REFERENCE

15. (Continued)

As of March, 1975, while 11.6 percent of all U.S. families were below the low-income level, the figure for Puerto Ricans living in the U.S. was 32.6 percent. (For Chicanos it was 24 percent.) The incidence of both poverty and unemployment among Puerto Ricans is more severe than that of virtually any other ethnic group in the U.S., and the incidence of poverty has been *rising* since 1970. Accounting for these statistics, according to the U.S. Commission on Civil Rights, is "Official insensitivity, coupled with private and public acts of discrimination. . . ." Despite all this, 75 percent of Puerto Rican families in the U.S. are self-sufficient and do not require any public assistance.

Puerto Rico and Puerto Ricans, pp. 313-416.

Puerto Rico: A Socio-Historic Interpretation, pp. 302-324.

Taller De Migracion, Unit 2 pp. 1-19, Unit 3 pp. 1-55.

Puerto Ricans in the Continental United States: An Uncertain Future, U.S. Commission on Civil Rights.

---

16. Puerto Rican life in the U.S. is characterized by circular migration to the homeland.

Other non-white minorities are also entrenched residents of American cities. Maintaining a close identity with others of their ethnic backgrounds, groups such as the Puerto Ricans in New York City . . . form additional urban sub-populations which keep the nation's cities seething with discontent and conflict. Urban problems increase in magnitude as a result of the tensions generated by inter-group conflict. In large metropolitan cities it is not unusual for "rumbles" among youth gangs claiming to be the "protectors of a territory" to characterize slum life. The gang warfare between different ethnic and racial groups as reflected in the musical West Side Story is not atypical.

The American Experience, p. 646

Puerto Ricans are not "entrenched" in U.S. cities. There is great back and forth movement, and many plan, or hope, to return to their own country at some point. It is estimated that, in the 1960's, 283,000 returned to Puerto Rico, and the rate is higher in the 1970's, with figures for 1973, 1974, and 1975 showing more Puerto Ricans returning to Puerto Rico than arriving in the U.S. The 1970 census showed that one out of twenty residents of Puerto Rico had been born in the U.S.

By presenting only this one image of Puerto Ricans this textbook stereotypes a whole people as keeping cities "seething with discontent and conflict" and as violent "gang" people. Gangs have always been symptomatic of slum life and are by no means peculiar to Puerto Ricans. The text would do better to include more information about how Puerto Ricans are forced to cope with economic and cultural oppression.

Return Migration to Puerto Rico. José Hernández Alvarez.

Puerto Ricans in the Continental United States: An Uncertain Future.

---

17. Institutional racism results in the miseducation of Puerto Rican students in the U.S.

The lot of young Puerto Ricans was especially difficult. In school they were handicapped by unfamiliarity with English and embittered by the antagonism they often met from other children.

Rise of the American Nation, p. 831

Textbooks frequently blame Puerto Ricans for their oppressed situation because they are "unfamiliar with English." This rationale is particularly used to explain the widespread miseducation of Puerto Rican children in U.S. schools. This text places additional blame on antagonism from "other" students. Like most texts it avoids discussion of the institutionalized racism in education which subordinates *all* third world students. That Puerto Ricans have the

Bilingual/Bicultural Education: A Privilege or a Right? U.S. Civil Rights Commission. Miseducation of Puerto Rican students in Chicago.

QUOTATION	**COMMENT**	**REFERENCE**

17. (Continued)

| | highest drop-out rate in New York City schools is not a result of their language. It is the failure of the schools to provide bilingual/bicultural instruction and materials, to hire adequate numbers of Puerto Rican staff, to involve the parents in development of educational programs to serve the community, and to provide curriculum relevant to the needs and struggles of the students. Disproportionate numbers of Puerto Rican students thus join the pool of surplus labor, trained for nothing more than the lowest-paid work.

While most Puerto Ricans recognize the need to learn English in order to survive in the U.S., it is their national right, as well as their democratic right, to speak their own country's language and to have the governmental institutions that are supposed to "serve" them respect that language. | *Badges and Indices of Slavery,* Antonia Pantoja, pp. 89-95.

"New Study Confirms Educational Slaugher of Puerto Rican Children," *Bulletin of Interracial Books for Children,* Vol. 4 Nos. 1 & 2.

Schools Against Children: The Case for Community Control. Annettee T. Rubinstein, ed, pp. 93-126.

A Better Chance to Learn: Bilingual-Bicultural Education. U.S. Civil Rights Commission. |

18. Puerto Rican culture is a synthesis of Taino, African and Spanish cultures.

| *Many of New York's million Puerto Ricans were becoming proud of their culture and taking part in festivals and celebrations that stressed their Spanish past. This search for cultural identity was coupled with political demands for a voice in running educational and medical programs in Puerto Rican neighborhoods. These activities were denounced by many Americans— including some members of such minority groups—who believed the special strength of the United States lay in keeping different peoples peaceably together. A degree of conformity, they argued, was a price worth paying for so rare an achievement.*

The Impact of Our Past, p. 739 | This is a derogatory quote suggesting that Puerto Ricans are recently "becoming proud of their culture." In fact, they have *always* been proud of their unique culture, which is not a reflection of a "Spanish past." Rather it reflects a synthesis of Taino, African and Spanish cultures.

The quote also suggests that pride in culture and control over institutions (schools and hospitals) which daily affect people's lives is antithetical to different people living peacefully together. This negates the potential for a pluralistic society. It suggests that "peaceful" assimilation is desirable and it ignores the long history of third world oppression in the U.S. | *Taller De Cultura.* A comprehensive discussion of Puerto Rican culture. |

19. Migrant farm workers from Puerto Rico are exploited by U.S. agribusiness.

| *Among the poor were many migrant farm workers, that is, workers who migrated or moved around the country to pick fruit and vegetables. The poor also included farmers who* | This is one of the few texts to mention—though indirectly—an important aspect of Puerto Rican migration. In 1973 there were 14,000 contract and at least 70,000 non-contract migrant farm workers from Puerto Rico in the U.S. Conditions under which | |

QUOTATION	COMMENT	REFERENCE

19. (Continued)

worked for low wages or for part of the crops they grew. . . . These groups were often made up of minorities—Mexican-Americans, black Americans, Puerto Ricans, and Indians.

America: Its People and Values, pp. 793-794

contract workers labor are negotiated by the Puerto Rican government (which wants to encourage the migration of unemployed labor) and U.S. agricultural interests. These contracts do not provide for grievance procedures, standards for feeding or housing workers, or overtime pay. The dreadful living conditions and astounding exploitation of such workers has been well documented.

What has not been well documented is the way the living standards of U.S. agricultural workers are related to the economy and living standards of Puerto Rico. The ATA (Asociasión Trabajadores Agricolas) began organizaing Puerto Rican migrant labor in the Northeast during the 1960's and recently affiliated with the UFW (United Farm Workers). Multi-racial unity of all farm workers across the country will be necessary to counter racial divisions which have always been encouraged by agribusiness. The need for unity is highlighted by the effort of Florida growers to block a unionizing drive by the UFW among Florida's predominantly Black farm workers. The growers are contracting for Puerto Rican labor in an attempt to keep farm wages down. Future textbooks should help students to understand such links between economic conditions in the U.S. and in Puerto Rico.

Taller De Migracion, Unit 4 pp. 2-43.

Discussion of migrant farm workers, reprint of the commonwealth contract, and comparison of UFW, Teamster and commonwealth contracts.

PUERTO RICAN TEXTBOOK CHECKLIST

Title _____

Publisher _____ Year _____ Grade Level _____

There are 19 criteria to be scored. The highest possible rating is +38.
The lowest is –38. This text scores _____ .

	Incorrect Information −2	No Information −1	Omits This Period 0	Limited Information +1	Full Information +2
1. The histories of Taino and African peoples are important in understanding Puerto Rican history.					
2. Puerto Ricans have a long history of striving for independence.					
3. The U.S. declared war on Spain in order to establish its own hegemony in this hemisphere.					
4. Puerto Ricans had mixed reactions to the U.S. take-over of their country.					
5. Puerto Rico had greater autonomy under Spanish rule than it has today under the U.S.					
6. The Foraker Act formalized U.S. domination of Puerto Rico.					
7. U.S. citizenship was imposed on Puerto Ricans despite their protests.					
8. The U.S. established an educational system designed to "Americanize" Puerto Rico.					
9. Commonwealth status retained all significant aspects of U.S. control of Puerto Rico.					
10. Despite severe repression, the struggle for Puerto Rican independence continues.					
11. Operation Bootstrap led to the industrialization of Puerto Rico for the benefit of U.S. capital.					
12. Operation Bootstrap has not changed Puerto Rico's relative economic position vis-á-vis the U.S.					
13. Puerto Rican women face a double oppression.					
14. Extensive migration was caused by U.S. exploitation of the country.					
15. Puerto Rican migrants in the U.S. face national and racial oppression not experienced by white immigrants.					
16. Puerto Rican life in the U.S. is characterized by circular migration to the homeland.					
17. Institutional racism results in the miseducation of Puerto Rican students in the U.S.					
18. Puerto Rican culture is a synthesis of Taino, African, and Spanish cultures.					
19. Migrant farm workers from Puerto Rico are exploited by U.S. agribusiness.					
Total					
Textbook Final Score					

WOMEN

U.S. history textbooks are often guilty of stereotyping women, often guilty of distorting women's experiences, but they are always—without exception—guilty of omitting almost all relevant information about half of our population. To quote historian Gerda Lerner, "Men have defined their experiences as history and have left women out."

THE INVISIBLE HALF

Not one history text gives visibility to womankind. This widespread omission of women is not attributable solely to the sex bias of male publishers, historians and editors. The reasons are more complex. Historians of both sexes have been trained to examine the past through a traditional, male perspective which views history as a chronology of momentous wars, treaties, explorations, elections, and so forth. Such a perspective automatically excludes women as they never were generals, diplomats, explorers or presidents.

Another reason for the omission of women is the constant use of the male pronoun to represent all of humanity. This standard usage has a double consequence. On the one hand it effectively eliminates the reality of women's involvement in events being described and, on the other, it leads the reader to infer that women's historical experience was the same as men's. In the latter case the generic use of the male pronoun implies that women have shared the same opportunities and oppressions, the same hopes and glories, the same work and rewards, the same education and concerns, as men. But in a society long stratified along sexual lines, such a conclusion is clearly false.

UPDATED TEXTBOOKS

Studies of U.S. history textbooks published prior to the 1970's (conducted by Janice Law Trecker and by other feminists) cited this invisibility of women. Newer textbooks show small improvement. Women are still rarely included. Both new and old books enter the names of a few women under "Witch Trials," "Women's Rights," and "Reform Movements." The newer texts also carry a few paragraphs about "Women's Liberation," emphasizing the aspirations of some middle-class, professional women, while for the most part ignoring the aspirations of the millions of working-class women.

At best, updated versions of older texts have inserted a few paragraphs of compensatory history about individual women who were "first" in some endeavor, women who married "important" men, or women reformers who attempted to influence the society in which they lived. These insertions are glaringly obvious, often consisting of a full-page illustrated biography of a woman who is not mentioned elsewhere in the body of the text.

WOMEN'S EXPERIENCE

Some of the newest history texts attempt to respond to feminist criticism, but even these fail to delineate the similarities and the differences between the male and the female experience. The reality was that women shared similar work experiences with men on farms, plantations, and in factories—in addition to carrying the extra burden of traditional women's work. This reality is generally ignored in textbooks. While childbearing, childrearing and "women's work" in the home have never been a male experience, textbooks neglect to analyze the essential importance of these activities to community building. And on the issue of birth control and abortion—an issue of transcendent importance to women—textbooks are for the most part silent. The effect on women's lives of such factors as law, education, pay scale, sexual attitudes and absence of day-care are generally considered unimportant as topics for textbook treatment.

All textbooks contain an index entry titled "Women." The listings under that entry have changed little in the newer texts. They still consistently total less than one half of one percent of the number of pages in the book. The male perspective and the one-sided assumptions of textbooks are highlighted when one considers that they never include an index listing for "Men."

WHAT IS HISTORY

Recognition that women have been as essential to history as to life itself—in more ways than biologically reproducing the workforce—will require a radically different perspective for judging what is, and what is not, important in our past. The deeds of those few, upper-class, white males who molded and controlled the institutions of our society will then comprise but one segment of our total history.

To arrive at an approximation of historical truth regarding women, the roles played by *all* women must be recognized. The experiences and interests of upper-class, white women are often totally different from the experiences and interests of poor women, working-class women and third world women. Textbooks must recognize and analyze these differences.

Women's history can no more be defined solely by the life experience of a southern "belle" or of a northern "lady" than by the life experience of an African woman held in slavery, a New England mill girl sweating in a factory or a Cherokee grandmother exiled on the "Trail of Tears." Rather, women's history must encompass all such diverse lives. It must include an analysis of the oppression *some* women encounter because of their race and class in addition to an analysis of the sexual oppression faced by *all* women. Finally, it must include the reality of women's resistance to these various oppressions.

OMISSIONS CHEAT STUDENTS

Young women of today have been cheated by these textbook omissions. Women of the U.S. have had among them many wise and brave leaders. The suffrage struggle alone gave us Susan B. Anthony, Charlotte Perkins Gilman, Sojourner Truth, Alice Paul and dozens more whose courageous words and deeds offer bold inspiration for young women of today. But how are the young to know of these women? How are they to benefit from the lessons learned by women of yesterday? By neglecting to tell about women who have thought about, and acted upon, many problems similar to those faced by women of

today, textbooks limit the information and the role models available to the young. In this way they seriously limit the struggle for change.

To ask for an inclusion of women in history is to ask for a redefinition of *all* history. This will require innovative and extensive research conducted along uncharted paths. It will encounter determined opposition from traditionalists clinging to the "Great Man" approach. But we hope it will encourage young people to appreciate the role played by ordinary women and men in shaping our past. And it will strengthen young people for the role they themselves must play in reshaping our future and improving the quality of human life for all.

Textbooks and Women

QUOTATION	COMMENT	REFERENCE

---

1. The original American women, Native Americans, wielded considerable power within their own societies.

Political life among the North American Indians was quite varied. The least common political system was a monarchy *(rule by a single leader). When the nobles of a tribe held the real power, even though there was one recognized leader in nearly every tribe, the political system was an* aristocracy. *Within some tribes a* democracy *(rule by common consent) existed that allowed both men and women to have their say.*

The Impact of Our Past, p. 44

There were over 500 different Native American societies when Europeans first arrived. Most of the larger ones had a matrilineal structure, with property inherited through the mother. The Judeo-Christian concept of woman being made from man's rib, and consequently being considered inferior, was unknown to any Native culture, all of which venerated the Earth Mother. Since religion, politics and culture were intertwined in Native American life, women in most Native nations held property, could divorce, and could fully participate in societal decision making. Women were particularly powerful in the Iroquois Confederacy, yet the second book quoted, like many, makes no reference to that fact.

"A justifiable conclusion seems to be that in the vast majority of the hundreds of prehistoric American Indian tribes, whether their social structure was patrilineal, matrilineal, or bilateral, women not only enjoyed well-defined prerogatives, but among a very large number wielded considerable social, religious, and political powers." *Indian Women of the Western Morning,* John U. and Donna M. Terrell

Founding Mothers: Women in the Revolutionary Era. Linda Grant DePauw.

Women in American Life. Anne Firor Scott.

Indian Women of the Western Morning. John Upton Terrell and Donna M. Terrell.

Demeter's Daughters: The Women Who Founded America. Selma R. Williams.

The Tuscaroras. Shirley Hill Witt.

The Iroquois League was set up a little before the time Columbus arrived in America. It had a constitution (passed along by word of mouth). It also had a council of chiefs with a set number of members from each tribe. . . . At home, Iroquois women grew corn, beans, and squash on small patches of cleared land. . . . The deer the men hunted provided food and a number of other things as well.

Man In America, p. 36

---

2. Native women were not the overworked "drudges" described by many white observers.

The men [Eastern Woodland Indians] hunted and fished; the women tended the fields and gathered fruit.

The Challenge of America, p. 11

Native American people did have roles assigned on the basis of sex. Roles varied according to the lifestyles of each society. The common European description of a Native woman was "drudge" or "work mule." Women frequently carried heavy packs and in some societies farmed the land without male participation. But Native women were

QUOTATION	COMMENT	REFERENCE

2. (Continued)

Woman's role. All Indian women worked steadily at a series of daily tasks. They cooked meat or dried it for later use. They cured the skins and made clothing. They served meals and cared for the children. Indian women did most of the home building, and when the tribe moved they carried their share of the baggage. They gathered wood and built the fires. In most tribes each family tended a small garden. This was considered to be women's work in most of North America.

Man In America, p. 38

trained for such labor in their youth. They were generally reported to be stronger, healthier, physically cleaner—most practiced year-round daily bathing which was unheard of in colonial families or in Europe—and had less difficulty in childbirth than did European women of that period. White women who lived among Native Americans reported that Native women's work did not seem as difficult as white women's and seemed to be more appreciated by their society.

In many societies the essential male role was hunting. Men kept in shape for hunting by exercise and games, practices which were often misunderstood by whites as mere laziness or play.

Despite sex role differences, some Native women were warriors, some were the equivalent of "medicine men" and many were leaders of their societies. Because Europeans insisted on negotiating only with males, women gradually became less and less associated with political leadership as European domination increased.

Founding Mothers: Women in the Revolutionary Era.

Women in American Life.

Indian Women of the Western Morning.

Demeter's Daughters: The Women Who Founded America.

The Tuscaroras.

---

3. Pocahontas and Sacajawea were not typical of Native American women.

Living with these Indians was a young woman by the name of Sacajawea. . . . When the [Lewis and Clark] expedition set out again, in the spring of 1805, Sacajawea agreed to go along and act as guide and interpreter. Her husband, a French fur trapper, agreed to help guide the expedition.

America: Its People and Values, pp. 260-261

If texts make *any* mention of individual Native American women, it is inevitably of Pocahantas, Sacajawea, Nancy Ward or Mary Brant . . . women who, in some way, aided Europeans.

The vast majority of Native women—who learned that their own interests were opposed to European interests and who suffered greatly, along with their people, when they fought to defend their homelands—are not discussed in textbooks.

---

4. The early European settlers included many women.

The dangers the immigrant suffered in coming to America make one wonder why he *came.* (emphasis added)

The Pageant of American History, p. 20

A woman was part of De Soto's early 1500's expedition, and Spanish women helped settle St. Augustine, Florida, in 1565. Chicana women were settlers of Santa Fe in 1609. Dutch women arrived in New York in 1621. Other European women, of many nations and religions, arrived with the initial settlers from their countries. All of these women endured the same hardships as did men, plus the added burden of frequent pregnancies. Throughout the colonial period, one birth in five resulted in the mother's death.

Women's Life and Work in the Southern Colonies. Julia Cherry Spruill.

Demeter's Daughters: The Women Who Founded America.

QUOTATION	**COMMENT**	**REFERENCE**

---

5. Textbook use of the English language obscures women's lack of human rights in colonial days and in the present.

So they drew up a plan of government called the Mayflower Compact, which all of the men *signed. According to the Mayflower Compact, all the* people *would share in setting up a government for the new colony. (emphasis added)*

America: Its People and Values, p. 73

This textbook does not clarify that women were "people" too, yet were not allowed to sign the Compact or to share in "setting up a government." Nor does any textbook seriously question the fact that our "government" always has basically excluded women.

Womanhood in America: From Colonial Times to the Present. Mary P. Ryan.

Herstory: A Woman's View of American History. June Sochen.

---

6. Ann Hutchinson and other women challenged the male monopoly of religious leadership.

The Narragansett Bay area received more settlers when Anne Hutchinson, also driven from Massachusetts Bay for her religious views, formed a new colony of her friends at Portsmouth.

The Pageant of American History, p. 29

While some texts fail to mention Hutchinson at all, this text provides only this brief passage.

Denied participation in governmental affairs, Puritan women were encouraged to become pious wives and mothers. They were welcomed into religious observations, but were not permitted to train for the ministry or to become active in church affairs. Anne Hutchinson created a serious controversy when she challenged church authorities by interpreting the Bible and forming groups of women for discussion and prayer. She was exiled not only as a heretic, but for "acting the part" of a "husband rather than a wife" and conducting herself in a manner "not fitting for your sex." (She had fourteen children at that time.)

Other women played leading roles in founding the Methodist Church (Barbara Ruckle Heck), the first synagogue (Bilhah Abigail Franks), the first southern Quaker mission (Elizabeth Harris) and the Shaker community (Ann Lee Standerin). As the colonies grew, women increasingly participated in church affairs, but men continued to control the ministry and the decision-making positions.

The Woman in American History. Gerda Lerner.

Womanhood in America: From Colonial Times to the Present.

Herstory: A Woman's View of American History.

Demeter's Daughters: The Women Who Founded America.

---

7. Women were imported to the colonies by London investors because their work and presence were profitable to business.

A second reason for the success of Jamestown was that the owners of the London Company began to realize that a colony should include more than just men and boys. It must be a settlement of families. The owners of the company began to search for families to settle in

The London Company, and other businesses establishing colonies for profit, quickly learned that survival of their ventures required the full-time work of women and children, as well as men. They recruited— often kidnapped—poor women to be sold as wives or as indentured servants. For many years this activity profited shipping interests and London investors anxious to develop the colonies.

Women in American Life.

Herstory: A Woman's View of American History.

QUOTATION	COMMENT	REFERENCE

7. (Continued)

QUOTATION	COMMENT	REFERENCE
Jamestown and other parts of Virginia. They also persuaded young women to go to Virginia and marry the men already there. America: Its People and Values, p. 70	Without the presence of women, men often went to Virginia for quick riches and returned to England—rich or poor—without making a permanent commitment to the growth of the colony. The investing companies correctly assumed that women would force men to devote more time and energy to creating homes, farms and surplus goods, thus contributing to the financial success of the colony.	*Women's Life and Work in the Southern Colonies.* *Demeter's Daughters: The Women Who Founded America.*

8. As indentured servants imported as cheap labor by wealthier colonists, women were doubly oppressed.

QUOTATION	COMMENT	REFERENCE
A poor person who wanted to go to America signed a contract called an indenture. He agreed to work without pay for a certain number of years for any person who paid the cost of his trip. At the end of his period of service— anywhere from three to seven years—the indentured servant became a free man. *(emphasis added)* America: Its People and Values, p. 69 *When the period of servitude was over, the servant might be given free land or money. He certainly was given the chance to be a free* man *and a free worker. (emphasis added)* The Pageant of American History, p. 39	There were 80,000 women among the 250,000 white indentured servants who came to the colonies from England. Some were former convicts, others chose to leave England to increase their chances for a successful life. Some were tricked or kidnapped onto ships. There were especially severe restrictions on the hardworking female indentured servants. They were prohibited from marrying without their owner's consent. Most colonies required them to serve an extra year if they became pregnant (the father was not subjected to penalty). Once their term of service was over, women did not receive land, as did men, and only rarely were given money.	*Founding Mothers: Women in the Revolutionary Era.* *Demeter's Daughters: The Women Who Founded America.*

9. Most non-enslaved women enjoyed a greater degree of economic and social freedom than did European women of that time.

QUOTATION	COMMENT	REFERENCE
Everyone worked hard: the womenfolk at their pots, pans, spinning wheels, and needles and the men in the barns, fields, and stables. The Impact of Our Past, p. 113	Early colonial women's work included: keeping the homes cleaned and heated; making soap and the wax for candles; planting; harvesting; cooking and preserving food; growing and spinning flax and making it into clothes; sewing and washing clothes; making splints and ointments; brewing herbs, lancing wounds; delivering babies; tending livestock and seeing to the education of the children. In addition to their "women's work," a number of colonial women participated in community commerce. Women—some of whom were free Blacks—ran businesses, shops, newspapers, schools and farms, often while their husbands were away, less frequently on their own. They were also involved in shipping, trading and the practice of law and were barbers, blacksmiths and printers.	*The Woman in American History.* *Founding Mothers: Women in the Revolutionary Era.* *Demeter's Daughters: The Women Who Founded America.*

QUOTATION	COMMENT	REFERENCE

10. Women played a key role in the Revolution.

Members of the Sons of Liberty, an organization formed soon after passage of the Stamp Act, expressed their anti-British attitudes by encouraging non-importation, tarring and feathering loyalists and British tax agents, destroying property, and threatening British officials with bodily harm.

The American Experience, p. 37

The first of many women's organizations was formed in New Jersey in 1681. Most such groups later concentrated on political discussion about the need for independence from England. In the years prior to the Revolution, the boycotting of English imports was organized primarily by women. This became an important method of economic warfare. Women organized and participated in demonstrations against the British and against colonists cooperating with the British. Much of this was done through the "Daughters of Liberty." It is thought by some historians that the famed Committees of Correspondence were actually initiated by Mercy Otis Warren—a well-known propagandist, author and historian—but credited to her husband, as only a male signature would be taken seriously.

The Woman in American History.

Demeter's Daughters: The Women Who Founded America.

11. After the Revolution, women's options and freedoms were curtailed.

A new nation is full of opportunities for bright young men.*(emphasis added)*

The Impact of Our Past, p. 221

Not one text notes that, after the Revolution, the "opportunites" for bright young women were even more restricted than in earlier days. The increasingly populous and productive society made women's work in the home less essential. When that critical need abated, the previous flexibility some women had enjoyed to participate in the economic life of their communities declined. Legal equality never existed, despite pleas such as Abigail Adams' to her husband that, ". . . in the new Code of Laws which I suppose it will be necessary for you to make I desire you would remember the Ladies, and be more generous and favourable to them than your ancestors."

Legally, at that time and for almost a hundred years to come, a husband had custody over his wife's person, sole ownership of all her property, sole control over their children, and exclusive right to the products of her labor. The wife had no legal role in choice of residence, could not sue or be sued in her own name, could not serve on juries, sign a contract or make a will.

Two days before the Declaration of Independence, New Jersey adopted a constitution which said that "All inhabitants of this Colony, of full age, who are worth fifty pounds . . . Shall be entitled to vote." Married women could not legally own money or property. But single women worth 50 pounds realized that they *could* vote (though it is not clear whether this was the intention of the men who adopted the constitution). They voted until 1807, when the lawmakers amended the state constitution to prohibit women from voting.

Founding Mothers: Women in the Revolutionary Era.

The Woman in American History.

Womanhood in America: From Colonial Times to the Present.

QUOTATION	COMMENT	REFERENCE

12. Differences also sharpened between the lives of ordinary, and of rich, women.

QUOTATION	COMMENT	REFERENCE
By the time Washington's second administration ended, in 1797, the United States was prospering. The Challenge of America, p. 219	Textbooks tend to report U.S. prosperity as though it affected all people. But at that time—as now—"prosperity" was the state of a few while financial hardships were faced by the many. A small number of newly rich (white) women of that period became "ladies," concentrating on self-decoration. Most women, being poor, continued work in homes and on farms. Starting about 1770, some began to find work outside the home in the new mills and factories.	*The Woman in American History.* *Womanhood in America: From Colonial Times to the Present.*

13. From the earliest industrial era, women's labor was especially exploited.

QUOTATION	COMMENT	REFERENCE
The early New England mills were small and crude. But many men, women and children were eager to work in them. New England farmers often found it hard to make a living from the poor New England soil. Thus the mills drew most of their labor from the poor farm families in nearby areas. The Challenge of America, p. 286	What textbooks don't tell is that the industrialization of spinning and weaving was the single greatest factor affecting young women's lives at that time. Because their work was no longer essential in their parents' households, and because of poverty at home, they left for, or were sent to, the new mills. Women and children in the mills outnumbered men by seven to one. Fourteen or more hours a day was not uncommon, and pay, little as it was for men, was less than half as much for women. Many of the early "mill girls" viewed their jobs as temporary and were consequently reluctant to do anything to challenge unsafe and inadequate work conditions. Even so, large numbers of women working in the new industries did organize and strike. The Lowell Strikes of the 1830's and 1840's were largely strikes by women workers. Women and children in states outside of New England and in non-textile industries also organized and struck, conducting very militant campaigns. In the long-run, the women workers of this period were defeated because 1) their long working days, plus their household duties left little time for organizing; 2) the newly arriving immigrants were hungry and desperate and had to accept any wages offered; and 3) the government sided with business against labor.	"Women, Work, and The Family: Female Operatives in the Lowell Mills, 1830-1860," Thomas Dublin. *The Golden Thread: New England Mill Girls and Magnates.* Hannah Josephson. *Womanhood in America: From Colonial Times to the Present.* *Women and Work in America.* Robert Smuts.

14. Women's right to education, like all extensions of human rights, was achieved through a determined struggle.

QUOTATION	COMMENT	REFERENCE
. . . provisions for the education of women was limited and meager. In time, America would be the first country to establish an educational	Support for women's education was a cause of wealthier women, or those of the middle class. In the early 1800's there were 40 high schools in the country, but few admitted females. Oberlin, in 1833, was the first college to admit women and, eleven years later, to permit them to take the same courses as men. Lucy Stone, one of its graduates, and later a suffragist leader, refused to write a	

QUOTATION	COMMENT	REFERENCE

14. (Continued)

system available to all. During the post-revolutionary period, however, there was no widespread acceptance or support for such a system.

The Pageant of American History, pp. 129-130

commencement essay because the college insisted that only males could read essays to the audience. She educated and trained herself as a public speaker because, "I expect to plead not for the slave only, but for . . . the elevation of my sex."

Many middle-class women—notably Emma Willard, Mary Lyon and Catherine Beecher—as well as a few men, participated in lengthy struggles to provide more and improved schools, colleges and universities for women. The advancement of education for women led to new independence for many middle-class women who became school teachers. Elementary school teaching became an acceptable alternative for unmarried women who previously depended on male relatives for support.

In spite of education's increasing accessibility to white middle-class women, Black women had almost no opportunity to learn to read and write. In the South, educating slaves was illegal, although some did manage to learn. In the North, racism prevented Black children from receiving an education.

The Woman in American History.

Growing Up Female in America: Ten Lives. Eve Merriam.

Women in American Life.

---

15. Women reformers accomplished major changes in U.S. society.

The movement for better treatment of the mentally ill was led by Dorothea Dix, a Massachusetts schoolteacher. One March day in 1841, a friend asked her to teach a Sunday school class at a women's prison near Boston. She was horrified to find among the prisoners several insane women who were locked in a dark room without heat.

The Challenge of America, p. 315

Most of the newer textbooks give a page or two to reform movements and include Dorothea Dix. Few ever mention Elizabeth Blackwell, the first woman doctor and a crusader for better medical care for, and by, women. What textbooks don't make clear is that these two women, and many other reformers, had greater impact on human life than many a "statesman" who is accorded page after page in the same history texts.

Dorothea Dix (1802-1889) single-handedly affected reform in the penal system and in the care of the mentally ill. Before her campaign, there were 13 "insane" institutions. By 1880, due to her efforts, there were 123 such institutions. She had personally designed, and planned 35 of these. Training schools for the feeble-minded, nursing schools, prisons, poorhouses and county jails also adopted her reforms. Her remarkable accomplishments alleviated much human misery.

The Woman in American History.

Growing Up Female in America: Ten Lives.

Women in American Life.

QUOTATION	COMMENT	REFERENCE

16. Many advocates of abolition—a cause in which women activists predominated—were also advocates of women's rights.

QUOTATION	COMMENT	REFERENCE
In 1840 an anti-slavery convention was held in London. Among the delegates from many nations were eight American women. Because they were women, they were denied admission. Thus, the anti-slavery movement and the women's rights movement were joined. Usually the same people took part in both. The Pageant of American History, p. 194	This text tells us of the flagrant sexism in the abolitionist movement. It does not make clear that this sexism did not pervade the entire movement, nor does it mention that the majority of anti-slavery activists were women. In fact, the leading female abolitionists were also committed to the cause of women's rights, as were Frederick Douglass, William Lloyd Garrison and many of their followers. Angelina and Sarah Grimke, Lucretia Mott, Elizabeth Cady Stanton, Susan B. Anthony, and the ex-slave and brilliant orator, Sojourner Truth, deserve much credit for creating the reform environment which led to improvement in the status of women and Blacks during the mid-nineteenth century. Students are not told, in any text, that female anti-slavery societies outnumbered male and that most of the movement's funds were raised by women.	*Century of Struggle.* Eleanor Flexner. *Black Women in White America: A Documentary History.* Gerda Lerner. *Womanhood in America: From Colonial Times to the Present.* *Women in American Life.*

17. The 1848 Seneca Falls Convention signified the historic start of the suffrage movement.

QUOTATION	COMMENT	REFERENCE
This movement for women's suffrage grew out of the abolition movement, before the Civil War. . . . But these reformers were not always taken seriously, even by abolitionist men. . . . In 1838, women held a convention at Seneca Falls, New York, to do something about this discrimination. The Challenge of America, p. 793	Though it is not typical for textbooks to err in dates (the Seneca Falls convention was in 1848, not 1838) it *is* typical for "new" editions of old texts to acknowledge the existence of females by inserting a few paragraphs—as this one did—about a momentous historical event. (Such "editing in" always proves to be ineffective, "band-aid" treatment of the deeper manifestations of sexism.) Lucretia Mott and Elizabeth Cady Stanton assembled over 100 women and men at Seneca Falls. They issued a Declaration, modeled after the Declaration of Independence, demanding that men give political, social, religious and economic equality to women. This became an important ideological basis for further activities.	*Century of Struggle.* *Up From the Pedestal.* Aileen S. Kraditor. *Everyone Was Brave.* William O'Neill.

18. Because women lacked legal rights, alcoholism posed a greater threat to them than it did to men.

QUOTATION	COMMENT	REFERENCE
A fifth type of reform was aimed at raising the moral tone of all society by getting people to change habits that the reformers thought were bad. The move for temperance (prohibition or strict control over the drinking of liquor) was one of these. The Impact of Our Past, p. 321	The movement against "Demon Rum" is often belittled. The temperance movement aimed at much more than "raising the moral tone." Women and children suffered, without legal recourse, when their husbands and fathers drank. Women could not leave or divorce their husbands, or legally protect themselves from physical abuse. Law made women responsible for their husbands debts and did not force men to support their families. Many temperance leaders later became active in the women's rights movement.	*The Woman in American History.* *Womanhood in America: From Colonial Times to the Present.* *Herstory: A Woman's View of American History.*

QUOTATION	COMMENT	REFERENCE

19. Enslaved Black women struggled against sexual, as well as racial, oppression.

A slave who sought to escape in this way did so under cover of night. A conductor on the Underground Railroad helped him. (emphasis added)

The Pageant of American History, p. 193

Black women, as well as white, are obliterated by textbook use of the male pronoun. Textbooks also generally refuse to deal with the extra burden of sexual oppression faced by female slaves. Not only were they helpless before their master's sexual desires, but they were forced to bear children who became marketable property of the slaveowner. There are endless examples of advertisements for women who are described as "Prime Breeders." The slave population doubled between 1790 and 1850, largely because the women were forced to have seven to eight babies all-the-while working from dawn to dark in the fields. Nevertheless enslaved women were active in revolts, were frequent runaways and participated in innumerable resistance actions.

"Reflections on the Black Woman's Role in the Community of Slaves," Angela Davis, in *Black Scholar.* December, 1971.

Black Women in White America: A Documentary History.

Herstory: A Woman's View of American History.

The lives of slave women and house slaves were usually better.

The Challenge of America, p. 332

Harriet Tubman is an outstanding example of just such a woman. Her exploits as a union spy commander during the Civil War deserve more credit than is generally given in textbooks.

20. Black women also resisted oppressive laws.

The slaves could not learn of other places and other people from travel or books. . . . it was against the law for slaves to learn to read or write.

The Challenge of America, p. 335

While education of slaves by white people was illegal, many people held in bondage did manage to learn. Textbooks generally tell us of Frederick Douglass, but no text tells the incredible story of Milla Granson who was taught to read by her owner's children. Later, when sold to a different owner, she secretly taught 12 people at a time, from 11 p.m. until 2 a.m. each night, for seven years. She graduated hundreds of students, many of whom later escaped to Canada. The legislature of Louisiana, learning of her work, debated the legality of a slave teaching slaves. Milla Granson was just one of many, many slave women who did whatever they could to subvert the control of the slaveholder.

Black Women in White America: A Documentary History.

Though Sojourner Truth's work for abolition and women's suffrage is mentioned in some texts, her successful legal struggle to free one of her 14 children, and her remarkable battle against Jim Crow seating in trolley cars, are never included.

21. Women played a significant role in the Civil War.

Elizabeth Blackwell, the first woman doctor in the United States, was refused by eight medical colleges before a ninth one accepted her. When

It is a rare textbook that even mentions Dr. Blackwell. Yet even this text omits her Civil War role, as well as the war roles of thousands of other women.

QUOTATION	COMMENT	REFERENCE

21. (Continued)

she opened her own hospital in New York City, in 1857, she was laughed at by many people. America: Its People and Values, p. 387	At the start of the Civil War, the Union Army had one hospital, 40 beds and no trained staff. Dr. Blackwell, in April 1861, organized 3,000 women into the Women's Central Association for Relief. They initially trained 100 army nurses. Mary Bickerdyke, known as "Mother," was a legendary army nurse. She served in General Sherman's army and "became the terror of any inefficient, lazy, or drunken staff doctor or employee." Clara Barton worked without an appointment for the Sanitary Commission. She was aware of the need for helping the wounded as soon as possible after injury. At Antietam, she arrived with an oxcart laden with medical supplies in the thick of the battle. She later made her greatest contribution by organizing the training of nurses and the American Red Cross. At least 3,200 women worked as nurses on both sides in the Civil War, saving thousands of lives. They had great difficulty in gaining official recognition for their services, and not until 1892 did the Congress grant Civil War nurses a pension of $12 a month.	*The Woman in American History.* *Growing Up Female in America: Ten Lives.* *The Southern Lady: From Pedestal to Politics, 1830-1930.* Anne Firor Scott.

22. Women were essential to the "settlement" of the West.

The hunters, trappers, and fur traders were the first occupants of the frontier. These were followed by ranchers and by farmers. Where the farmer or rancher was secure, there the frontier vanished. The Pageant of American History, p. 219	Textbooks rarely explain how much "women's work" was required to make the "farmer or rancher secure." In addition to all the domestic chores, women participated in planting, harvesting and animal care. Most reports concur that women worked longer and harder than did men, and with frequent childbearing "a thirty-year-old woman was already worn out." The women, like the men, were intruders on Native American land and became involved in the struggle over that land. Some were killed and some were killers in such skirmishes. Due to the hardships of frontier life, women remained in short supply and therefore were granted some privileges they did not enjoy in the East. Wives were granted the right to hold their own land. Single women in Oregon were given 320 acres as an inducement to migrate.	*The Woman in American History.* *Womanhood in America: From Colonial Times to the Present.* *Herstory: A Woman's View of American History.*

23. Wyoming and other western states granted women rights when it benefited the states to do so.

Feminists soon became enraged, however, when male legislators showed no sign of extending equality and voting rights to women. The	This heartwarming message makes it sound as though males in Wyoming were genuinely interested in female equality. In 1869, Wyoming had 8,000 males and 2,000 females. By permitting women	

QUOTATION	COMMENT	REFERENCE

23. (Continued)

repudiation was lessened somewhat by the action of Wyoming lawmakers who extended voting rights to women in the territory in 1869. When congress threatened to detain Wyoming's admission to the Union until it abolished women's suffrage, the Wyoming legislature responded quickly. "We will remain out of the Union a hundred years rather than come in without the women."

The American Experience, pp. 687-688

to vote, Wyoming advanced its own petition for statehood and hoped to attract more women settlers. Thus, what was advantageous to men turned out to be advantageous to women as well.

Everyone Was Brave.

Herstory: A Woman's View of American History.

24. Many Black women were active social reformers in the late 1800's and early 1900's.

Settlement house workers like Jane Addams were among those most interested in the special problems of blacks. . . . Few national leaders or reformers took much notice of blacks.

The Challenge of America, p. 517

Textbooks omit mention of Black women who were social reformers in the late 1800's and early 1900's. Mary Church Terrell organized the National Association of Colored Women in 1896. It had over 100,000 members in 26 states within four years. They organized schools and hospitals. Terrell was a prominent speaker and writer, devoting her life to racial justice. Lucy Laney, born a slave, graduated from Atlanta University in 1886 and started a school which had 1,000 pupils. Fannie Williams founded the first nursing school for Black women. Charlotte Forten, an upper-middle-class Black woman from Philadelphia, was active in teaching newly freed slaves during the Civil War.

Another heroic Black woman, Ida B. Wells, campaigned against lynching, printing her own anti-lynching newspaper. She spoke in England and all over the U.S. She sometimes carried two guns to defend herself against white mobs which frequently gathered.

In later years, a Black leader, Mary McLeod Bethune, accomplished wonders against the odds of poverty and racism to open up educational opportunities for Black children, especially Black girls.

Black Women in White America: A Documentary History.

Herstory: A Woman's View of American History.

25. Women social reformers had significant impact upon aspects of urban life.

A second effort to examine and to do something about the urban poor was the "settlememt house" movement. The best known, if not the first settlement house in America, was Jane

Jane Addams and a group of college friends organized Hull House in Chicago and inspired a network of 400 settlement houses. They not only set up programs for the urban immigrants, mainly women and children, but they were basically responsible for establishing the

QUOTATION	COMMENT	REFERENCE

---

25. (Continued)

Addams' Hull House.

The Pageant of American History, p. 454

social service profession. They contributed substantially to the elimination of child labor. They also established a new lifestyle for concerned middle-class women who would live and work together. Jane Addams helped found the National Association for the Advancement of Colored People and, like another settlement house leader, Lillian Wald, worked with labor and pacifist movements.

Up From the Pedestal.

These middle-class women reformers did not fundamentally challenge the economic system but acted as "social housekeepers." As Professor Mary P. Ryan writes, "They tidied up the man's world, removing the most unsightly evidence of corrupt politics, smoothing over the ugly clash between the rich and the poor and cleaning up around the slums." Though they did not attack the root-cause of poverty, they eased many of life's hardships for hundreds of thousands of families.

Womanhood in America: From Colonial Times to the Present.

Women and Work in America.

---

26. In the early 1900's women workers were especially exploited. Some organized, despite lack of union interest in their conditions.

Women's rights became a crucial issue in the early 1900's. One reason for this was the increasing number of women in the work force.

The Challenge of America, p. 624

Women's rights had been a "crucial issue" long before the 1900's. It was not the increasing number of working women, but a combination of militant feminists and rather conservative, middle-class, political women who succeeded in forcing legislators to enfranchise women. Around 1900, five million women were in the labor force. About one and one half million were domestics, working 16 hour days, seven days a week. A slightly lesser number were in heavy industry, earning one fourth to one third of men's wages for a 10-hour-day, six days a week. (Of children 10 to 15 years old, 25 percent of boys and 19 percent of girls were working 10 to 12 hours a day.) For women who had families, work included still more hours for home and child care.

Liberating Women's History. Berenice Carroll.

The American Woman: Her Changing Social, Economic and Political Roles, 1920-1970. William H. Chafe.

Understandably, the effort for suffrage meant little to most of these women. Their grim lives held other priorities. Some of the women who spoke to those priorities were "Mother Jones" (1830-1930) who, after losing her miner husband and four children to a yellow fever epidemic, spent 50 years organizing workers. Another was Elizabeth Gurley Flynn (1890-1964), who began labor organizing at age 15 for the Industrial Workers of the World (Wobblies). She, too, had a long career, in and out of jails, leading women and men on picket lines.

The Woman in American History.

Women and Work in America.

An example of women's militancy occurred in 1909. A general strike of shirtwaist workers involved 20,000 people, 80 percent of whom were women, as was most of the strike leadership.

QUOTATION	COMMENT	REFERENCE

26. (Continued)

It is important to note that leaders in the major labor unions made few efforts to organize women or to allow them to assume union leadership. In fact, many of the unions actively excluded women, claiming that, as workers, women were transient and uncommitted to their jobs. (What union leaders ignored was the fact that women seldom had anyone to perform their household duties so they were unable to attend union meetings.) Union leaders also feared that women would take jobs "belonging" to men.

---

27. The 1920 victory for women's suffrage represented years of costly sacrifice.

This quote not only underestimates the amount of effort required of women in the struggle to win the vote, but also derisively stereotypes them as having "pestered congressmen" (men lobby, women "pester").

To bring their cause to America's attention, women paraded in the streets. They pestered Congressmen. They formed groups and gave speeches.

American History for Today, pp. 366 & 368

When a suffrage leader, Carrie Chapman Catt tried to figure the cost of the 19th Amendment, she found that winning the vote took 52 years of continuous campaigning. During that time they were forced to conduct 56 campaigns of referenda to male voters; 480 campaigns to get legislatures to submit suffrage amendments to voters; 47 campaigns to get woman suffrage into state constitutions; 277 campaigns to get woman suffrage planks in state party platforms; and 19 campaigns with 19 successive Congresses. Catt's list did not include speeches, fund drive petitions, campaign marches, jailings, hunger strikes and forced feeding in jail, and many of the other actions that were prerequisites to winning the vote.

Century of Struggle.

Up From the Pedestal.

Everyone Was Brave.

Womanhood in America: From Colonial Times to the Present.

Not until 1920 did the Constitution give all American women the right to vote. (emphasis added)

The Challenge of America, p. 624

Women *won* the vote; after a long struggle; it was not *given*. Also, *all* women did *not* get the right to vote in 1920. Textbooks ignore the fact that Black women in the South, like Black men, were effectively prevented from voting, and most Native American women were not citizens before 1924.

---

28. Suffrage did not succeed in making women equal to men.

For 100 years before the 1920's women had been winning larger opportunities in political, economic and social affairs. But their greatest gains came in the 1920's. With the adoption of the Nineteenth Amendment in 1920, women won

The textbook implies undue optimism about women's "gains." The 19th Amendment merely prohibited the denial of formal, electoral equality because of sex. It failed to affect the inferior economic position of most women, both third world and white. It did not challenge the prevailing social and sexual prejudices against women.

Womanhood in America: From Colonial Times to the Present.

Herstory: A Woman's View of American History.

QUOTATION	COMMENT	REFERENCE

28. (Continued)

the right to vote in national elections. This was a landmark in women's long struggle to win equality with men. Rise of the American Nation, p. 661	And it didn't really grant political equality, since "politics" in the U.S. is based on much more than the right to vote.	

29. The availability of birth control information was, perhaps, more important to women than suffrage.

No quote was available.	Birth control is one of the most important historical factors to change women's lives, health and hopes. Yet, textbooks do not discuss Margaret Sanger and the struggle to legalize birth control. Margaret Sanger, a nurse, worked among poor women. She saw how desperate they were made by numerous pregnancies they could not afford. She saw how many lives were lost in attempts at abortion, so she studied about contraception in Europe, introduced the phrase, "birth control," and opened the first clinic in 1916. She spoke, wrote, pamphleteered, organized conferences and was often jailed until—finally—in 1937, dissemination of birth control information by doctors was legalized. Yet, despite Sanger's efforts, it is unlikely that male legislators would have legalized birth control were it not that, by 1937, large families and a larger labor force were no longer an economic necessity. Margaret Sanger understood that the availability of birth control was, in many ways, a class issue. By the early 20th century, many middle- and upper-class women had the information they needed to prevent unwanted births. Sanger sought to make such information widely available to poor women, against the wishes of religious groups and legislators.	*Liberating Women's History.* *The American Woman: Her Changing Social, Economic and Political Roles, 1920-1970.* *The Woman in American History.* *Margaret Sanger: An Autobiography.* Margaret Sanger.

30. The 1920's "flapper" era did not significantly liberate women.

The nineteenth-century pioneers of women's rights would not recognize this short-skirted, short-haired "new woman" of 1926. The Impact of Our Past, p. 613	Charlotte Perkins Gilman, an important feminist leader and writer, was disappointed in the "flapper," "new woman" era, even though she was a strong believer in sexual liberation. She said flappers were, ". . . as much the slaves of fashion as before." She realized that there is no freedom for women in becoming fashion consumers or in concentrating on sexuality. The "flappers," like today's fashion-first women, were a minority. Even so, the 1920's made work outside the home increasingly acceptable for middle-class women. It was also a period of considerable upward mobility for working-class women,	

QUOTATION	COMMENT	REFERENCE

30.   (Continued)

A change in women's clothing typified the new American female. Instead of heavy, concealing clothing, styles began to emphasize comfort and physical allure. Skirts became shorter and bathing suits skimpier. Girls began using cosmetics such as "kissproof" lipstick and rouge to enhance their physical charms. They also began cutting their hair in "boyish bobs," which brought them into one of the last male refuges— the barbershop.

The American Experience, p. 419

who began to work as secretaries, telephone operators, and at other white-collar jobs. Women continued to be paid much less than men, and the jobs that they were permitted to take were increasingly sex-segregated. The wearing of make-up, which does little more than make profits for cosmetics manufacturers, is also a dubious sign of progress. Texts too frequently judge women's advancement by superficial factors rather than by examining economic, sexual and social perspectives.

The Woman in American History.

Womanhood in America: From Colonial Times to the Present.

Herstory: A Woman's View of American History.

---

31.   White ethnic immigrants had greater chances for upward mobility than did Black women and men.

In the 1920's, laws were passed severely reducing the number of immigrants who could enter the United States. Those who were here learned new skills. They moved upward from the lowest paying jobs. These jobs were increasingly left for blacks to fill.

The Pageant of American History, p. 424

The textbook—unlike many others we have seen—does not deny the existence of racism. Even in the 1920's, there were few jobs for Black men in the South. Men and women eked out a meager existence as sharecroppers, working together to stay alive. Many Blacks migrated north to urban areas, where Black women discovered that they could often find jobs more easily than their husbands. They took the jobs that immigrant women had abandoned, and became house-cleaners, cooks, nursemaids, and laundry workers. Even today, Black women find that low-paid and low-status work is primarily what is available to them.

Black Women in White America: A Documentary History.

Herstory: A Woman's View of American History.

---

32.   The great labor struggles of the 1930's actively involved women of all colors.

Labor's most important gains came in the 1930's under President Franklin D. Roosevelt. Two examples of these gains were (1) social security and unemployment benefits for workers who lost their jobs or retired, and (2) the creation of the National Labor Relations Board. . . . by the 1950's organized labor had won out.

In Search of America, p. 112-C

This quote is misleading on many scores. Labor as a whole has not "won out." Most workers—particularly women—remain unorganized and underpaid. Also omitted from most books is the vital participation of women in many strikes. Coal miners' wives in 1933 were beaten and gassed by police, shot by government militia, arrested and jailed. The famous auto plant "sit-ins" needed and received women's support to make them effective. Asian American, Chicano, Black and white women, were all militantly involved in major strikes, often as active leaders. For Black women in the South, this could mean defying the Ku Klux Klan.

Nevertheless, large unions have always kept women out of leadership, accepted contracts giving them lower pay, and failed to support their seniority.

Liberating Women's History.

Black Women in White America: A Documentary History.

Herstory: A Woman's View of American History.

QUOTATION   **COMMENT**   **REFERENCE**

---

33. Women's labor has often been recruited, abused and discarded by business interests.

The millions of women who answered the nation's call [during WW II] in industrial jobs were an advance guard of liberated women. Yet the change pulled up an important social anchor. The question of how family duties were shared between working husbands and wives remained unanswered. It was one of many such problems that would linger on to become important in postwar American life.

The Impact of Our Past, p. 706

How family duties are shared is important, but it is not the primary feminist concern. Instead, many modern feminists are concerned with ending all sex, race and class oppression. Day care and equal pay are more essential to working women than is a husband's cooperation in household duties. This textbook is also misleading in not exploring what happens to women after a labor shortage ends.

Millions of women, like third world people generally, did get jobs, previously closed to them, during the WW II labor shortage. But white women's consciousness at that time did not lead them to believe they had a right to keep such jobs. After the war, most willingly returned to their homes. Others were forced there by the rhetoric of the 1950's which claimed that women's happiness rested in the home. It took a later surge of feminism—the Women's Liberation Movement—to awaken women to their right to all kinds of work.

When new laws about equal pay and equal hiring rights for women were passed in the early 1970's, militant efforts by feminists sometimes led to friction with third world men who found women a threat to their own, still-limited opportunities. Employers, who had always played third world workers against white, began to pit third world men against women for jobs and promotions.

In the 1975-76 recession, still more serious friction arose about job seniority and lay-offs. As third world people and white women were the last hired, they were the first fired. This destroyed their hard won gains of recent years. The unions took no action to protect them. Thus, the power of industry to use, discard and abuse the labor of women has still to be successfully addressed.

Liberating Women's History.

Women in Sexist Society. Vivian Gornick and Barbara Moran.

The Woman in American History.

---

34. Poor third world women face triple oppression today.

The census showed that 9.1 percent of all white families were headed by women. Women were the heads of 28.3 percent of black families. Why are families headed by women likely to be poor?

Man In America, p. 628

Though the textbook is asking good questions, it does not begin to present students with the dimensions of the problem facing third world women today. While all women, as a group, earn 57 percent of what men earn, third world women earn even less than do white women. They are *over*represented in low status, low paying jobs, in the unemployment lines, as single heads of households, among those living below the poverty level, and in jails and reform schools. They receive less education than white women, and suffer poorer health conditions, shorter life spans and vastly more forced sterilizations than their white counterparts. In addition to sexism, they are

Black Women in White America: A Documentary History.

Herstory: A Woman's View of American History.

"Sexism and Racism: Feminist Perspectives," U.S. Commission on Civil Rights, *Civil Rights Digest,* Spring, 1974.

QUOTATION	COMMENT	REFERENCE

34. (Continued)

oppressed by racism. And those third world women who are poor—the vast majority—also suffer from classism. This is the triple oppression third world feminists strive to overcome.

---

35. Institutional change, not mere passage of the Equal Rights Amendment, is necessary to improve the status of U.S. women.

As with the 14th Amendment, which gave equality to blacks on paper, the proposed women's rights amendment [E.R.A.] will not bestow instant equality on women. Equality will have to be supported and tested by the courts, by all levels of government, and by men as well as women.

The Pageant of American History, p. 679

Since the textbook admits that—since the XIV Amendment—one hundred years have passed without Blacks receiving more than paper equality, the logical question the book should pose is: Will our present capitalist system—controlled by upper-class, white men—ever voluntarily "support and test" equality for minorities or women?

Textbooks dodge that question as well as dodging an examination of the basic institutions of our society. No textbook reports that:

—*In the church* . . . Women are a majority of the participants but a handful of the leadership.

—*In education* . . . Women are a majortiy of the lower-paid practitioners while white males control the vast majority of top-paying, decision-making posts.

—*In business* . . . The nation's wealth is controlled, as far as decision-making, by a small number of white males. Women are not represented in those top echelons. Women *are* represented in the work force, where they earn 43 percent less than men.

—*In unions* . . . Women are 25 percent of membership but only 4 percent of leadership.

—*In health institutions* . . . Low-paid staff is female and/or third world, and high-paid doctors and pharmaceutical firm officers are white males. Feminists charge that medical practice—from sterilization forced upon poor third world women, to unneeded surgery performed on millions of women—is shockingly racist and sexist.

—*In government* . . . Since the founding of this nation wealthy white males have controlled all, or almost all, of the executive, legislative and judicial branches of our national, state and local offices.

Fact Sheets on Institutional Sexism. Contains statistics.

WOMEN TEXTBOOK CHECKLIST

Title _____

Publisher _____ Year _____ Grade Level _____

There are 35 criteria to be scored. The highest possible rating is +70.
The lowest is –70. This text scores _____ .

	Incorrect Information −2	No Information −1	Omits This Period 0	Limited Information +1	Full Information +2
1. The original American women, Native Americans, wielded considerable power within their own societies.					
2. Native women were not the overworked "drudges" described by many white observers.					
3. Pocahontas and Sacajawea were not typical of Native American women.					
4. The early European settlers included many women.					
5. Textbook use of the English language obscures women's lack of human rights in colonial days and in the present.					
6. Ann Hutchinson and other women challenged the male monopoly of religious leadership.					
7. Women were imported to the colonies by London investors because their work and presence were profitable to business.					
8. As indentured servants imported as cheap labor by wealthier colonists, women were doubly oppressed.					
9. Most non-enslaved women enjoyed a greater degree of economic and social freedom than did European women of that time.					
10. Women played a key role in the Revolution.					
11. After the Revolution, women's options and freedoms were curtailed.					
12. Differences also sharpened between the lives of ordinary, and of rich, women.					
13. From the earliest industrial era, women's labor was especially exploited.					
14. Women's right to education, like all extensions of human rights, was achieved through a determined struggle.					
15. Women reformers accomplished major changes in U.S. society.					
16. Many advocates of abolition—a cause in which women activists predominated—were also advocates of women's rights.					
17. The 1848 Seneca Falls Convention signified the historic start of the suffrage movement.					
18. Because women lacked legal rights, alcoholism posed a greater threat to them than it did to men.					

	−2	−1	0	+1	+2
19. Enslaved Black women struggled against sexual, as well as racial, oppression.					
20. Black women also resisted oppressive laws.					
21. Women played a significant role in the Civil War.					
22. Women were essential to the "settlement" of the West.					
23. Wyoming and other western states granted women rights when it benefited the states to do so.					
24. Many Black women were active social reformers in the late 1800's and early 1900's.					
25. Women social reformers had significant impact upon aspects of urban life.					
26. In the early 1900's women workers were especially exploited. Some organized, despite lack of union interest in their conditions.					
27. The 1920 victory for women's suffrage represented years of costly sacrifice.					
28. Suffrage did not succeed in making women equal to men.					
29. The availability of birth control information was, perhaps, more important to women than suffrage.					
30. The 1920's "flapper" era did not significantly liberate women.					
31. White ethnic immigrants had greater chances for upward mobility than did Black women and men.					
32. The great labor struggles of the 1930's actively involved women of all colors.					
33. Women's labor has often been recruited, abused and discarded by business interests.					
34. Poor third world women face triple oppression today.					
35. Institutional change, not mere passage of the Equal Rights Amendment, is necessary to improve the status of U.S. women.					
Total					
Textbook Final Score					

OBSERVATIONS ABOUT NEW TEXTBOOKS

Before 1965, Chicanos, Puerto Ricans and Asian Americans were nearly invisible in U.S. history textbooks. Women, Afro American and Native American people were mentioned, though usually misrepresented through stereotyping, biased reporting or omission of important information.

In today's textbooks, the groups previously invisible are granted a few more paragraphs than heretofore. Blacks and Native Americans are receiving more "sympathetic" treatment. A bit more attention is being paid to other third world groups and to women as well.

However, heightened visibility, we found, does not necessarily assure an accurate depiction of reality. Our survey has led to a number of observations about the way current textbooks present U.S. history. These observations fall into three general categories: Perspective, Methods of Including Third World People and Women, and The Underlying Assumptions.

PERSPECTIVE

A basic problem with history textbooks is perspective, or point of view. The perspective dominating textbooks has always been white, upper-class and male. Generations of young people have been taught that the U.S. is a white country and that the prime architects of U.S. life and history are white males. This perspective continues in near ubiquity. *The American Experience, A Free People, The Pageant of American History, Man in America,* are all current texts with titles that do not reflect reality. There has always been more than one "American Experience"; people in the U.S. are "Free" to very different degrees; history, for many people,

has not been a glorious "Pageant," and "America" is populated by more than "Man." Although new textbooks include some information that was previously omitted, too frequently the information is a porthole view *about* a people, but not *from the perspective of* the people described. In other instances, the information is set apart from the rest of the text which continues to reflect one viewpoint only.

SINGLE PERSPECTIVE

Numerous examples of this restricted perspective were found in each of the books surveyed. In the midst of several pages devoted to slavery and the life of "the slave," a statement like the following appears: "To live in the South was to live in daily fear of slave violence." Clearly, this statement speaks only for white people, as does, "Alone in the wilderness, the frontier family had to protect itself from wild animals and unfriendly Indians." Had the books represented other perspectives, these quotations might have read: "To live in the South was to live in the daily hope of a successful rebellion against slave-owners." or "While the people were trying to live, farm, and hunt peacefully in their homelands, they had to constantly be on guard against marauding and invading whites."

From book titles to chapter headings to text commentary, all of the textbooks depict U.S. history through the eyes of society's white majority—in particular, through the eyes of its more privileged members. Though these eyes are more sensitive to the presence of others than they have previously been, they are nevertheless *particular,* not universal, eyes.

NARROW PERSPECTIVE

Because events are viewed through the eyes of the privileged, textbooks do not indicate that the lives and the aspirations of the average white citizens are linked to the lives and the interests of third world people. This limitation is exemplified in a quotation like: "This 1896 ruling *[Plessy v. Ferguson]* by the Supreme Court was a serious blow to the efforts of black Americans to improve their lives."

Surely it was a "serious blow" to the efforts of Blacks, but by re-legalizing segregation, the decision had profoundly adverse effects on whites, too. By viewing *Plessy* as a Black problem the textbook subtly places the onus for overcoming obstacles onto the backs of Black people alone. A broader perspective would demonstrate that others, besides Black people, have an interest in and responsibility for ending segregation; others, besides Native Americans, in ending the tragedy exemplified by the *Trail of Tears;* and others, not only Asian Americans, in protesting the internment of Japanese Americans during WW II; as does everyone, in overcoming the oppression of women today. These issues affect *all* people in our society. A defeat for one group has repercussions on all, and results in prolonging the racist and sexist aspects of U.S. society.

EUROCENTRIC PERSPECTIVE

As with their older counterparts, there is a wide disparity between the way new textbooks report on the origins of U.S. third world cultures, compared to their treatment of the origins of the European colonists and immigrants. While Black reaction to white-imposed slavery is discussed, information about life in African countries is scant. Hence, students gain no sense of who African Americans were before they were brought to these shores and no insights into the values, beliefs, cultures and skills they brought with them. Similarly, Chicano life and culture prior to the U.S. annexation of their land is omitted. The heritages brought to the U.S. by Chinese, Japanese and Pilipino laborers remain obscure. And Puerto Rican culture, if discussed, is written off solely as being "Spanish."

The one exception, space-wise, is coverage of Native American cultures. Most textbook descriptions, however, are reserved for pre-Columbian societies and are too superficial and generalized to be of value. The continuity between pre-Columbian and present-day Native values and beliefs is not described.

This one-sided, Eurocentric perspective emphasizes the importance of white roots and European backgrounds. It conveys the impression that third world people in the U.S. lack a cultural heritage, are definable *only* in terms of their relationship to white people, and are, therefore, inferior to whites.

METHODS OF INCLUSION

We observed that inclusion of third world people and women in textbooks takes three major forms: as "greats," as "contributors" and as "protestors."

INCLUSION AS "GREATS"

Basically, textbooks still recount history according to the "Great Man" approach, interpreting the past to be the activities and accomplishments of a relatively few statesmen, generals, inventors and merchants—almost invariably white and male. In the newer texts, one finds that a few "Great Minorities" and "Great Women" have been added to the limited cast of characters.

While the inclusion of a few individual achievers from previously excluded groups is a positive improvement, a cautionary note must be sounded. Writing in *The Black Scholar* of March 1976, James Oliver Horton points out that the inclusion of such individuals "usually amounts to no more than spot appearances . . . in the dramatic production of the great American epic." Moreover, serious scrutiny of the communities from which these individuals came and from which they drew their strength "brings confrontation with the American myth. . . . The black experience, much like that of women, Indians and some other minorities, is distinctly 'un-American'" (that is, un-Euro-male-American). While the exceptional careers of a few individuals reinforce the Horatio Alger myth-pattern, the group experiences of the peoples, as a whole, illustrate, the grave failures of the U.S. system.

Inevitably, by regarding a few individuals as the moving force in human history, and by under-representing the activities of working people, textbooks ignore the skills, concerns and struggles of the average citizens who have played a primary role in creating and shaping events. Reading these books, female, third world and poor students especially, must feel like powerless cogs unable to play any vital role.

Whether or not one adheres to the "Great Man" interpretation of history, there is no denying that textbooks create role models for young people when they select, for description, certain historical personages. It is interesting that older texts routinely preferred Booker T. Washington's "moderation" over W.E.B. DuBois' anti-establishment activities. They extolled the non-violent methods of Martin Luther King and ignored or deplored the angrier style of Malcolm X. John Brown was unfailingly described as a fanatic, while Abraham Lincoln's view—"If I could save the Union without freeing any slave I would do it"—was never criticized.

Newer texts still retain all the traditional white, male heroes, but their wider cast of characters now includes a few alternative role models. But what if textbooks were to select heroes through the eyes of different perspectives? Might they then praise Chicanos such as Joaquin Murieta and Juan Cortina who led resistance to the U.S. take-over of their lands after the war of conquest with Mexico? Might they admire Tatanka Iotanka (Sitting Bull) and Tashunka Witko (Crazy Horse) who led their people in the defeat of Custer? Honor the actions of Sojourner Truth, Mother Jones and Margaret Sanger? Describe Albizu Campos and Lolita Lebrón as Puerto Rican patriots and martyrs? Report approvingly of the Japanese Americans who resisted incarceration during WW II?

Such suppositions may seem very far-fetched. But, in fact, they coincide with the perspectives of a significant number of third world people, feminists and historians. Were textbooks to aim for a truly pluralistic scope, they would grant the legitimacy of resistance to white or male oppression and give it some page-space, along with the traditional heroes and role models they now present to students.

INCLUSION AS "CONTRIBUTORS"

A frequent method of including third world people is by listing their "contributions": Native Americans gave "us" corn; African Americans gave "us" jazz; and Chinese Americans helped to build "our" railroads. The implication is that third world people, and their achievements, are valuable only insofar as they prove useful to "us." (In the case of Native Americans, their development of corn stands as a major scientific and agricultural achievement, important to their own societies and having global significance.) Overall the achievements of women and third world people are minimized. They frequently are isolated in special sections and paragraphs, tangential to the central tale of the "Great White Men" who "forged this nation" and are presumably "us."

The "contributions" approach also overlooks the fact that the "contributors" have not benefited much from their contributions. For example, a new textbook will cite the military service of tens of thousands of Blacks during WW I, but will ignore discrimination in the armed forces and the segregation and racism to which Black veterans returned. Or when discussing the bounty of the U.S. corn belt, texts never note that Native Americans fail to share in the national wealth made possible by their development of corn and their "contribution" of the land upon which it is grown.

Textbooks would be more informative if they explained that the unpaid, underpaid and/or unheralded work of third world people and women, plus the land expropriated from Native Americans, Chicanos and Puerto Ricans, were usually *coerced contributions* which have primarily benefited the white community. Textbooks should also convey to students that *all* of the people who make up the U.S. population share claim to the benefits which have evolved out of the labor and skill of many groups. Not to do so is to reinforce the idea that white people are "us"—and third world people are "other." This fosters alienation and resentment in third world students and it also fosters an unrealistic sense of superiority in white students.

INCLUSION AS PROTESTORS

A good deal of the expanded treatment of third world people and women in the newer texts focuses on the liberation movements of the 1960's and 1970's. Unfortunately for students, these movements are not placed in any sort of historical context that might show them as part of a long continuum of social and political protest. Some books imply by omission, and others state outright, that political protest and self-liberation efforts are but recent developments. In this way, textbooks doom new generations to act blindly, instead of building on a careful study of the thoughts and actions, the successes and mistakes of those who struggled in the past. Denied knowledge of these details of their history, young people are forced today to reinvent the wheel.

Today's textbook writers also fail to connect the present struggles of third world people in the U.S. with liberation movements around the globe and are vague as to which groups, or what circumstances, stand in opposition to such efforts.

INCLUSION OF CHOSEN PROTESTORS

With the little information presented on current liberation struggles, textbook emphasize intra- and inter-group *divisions,* and tend to ignore intra- and inter-group *unity.* On the other hand, textbooks tend to avoid any serious consideration of the variety of goals and methods which characterize liberation movements. For instance, some feminists view the opportunity to become highly paid, decision-making executives as a liberating goal, yet others feel that the revamping of the basic economic and patriarchal structure must be the primary focus. Similar differences in aims exist within all third world groups. However, the textbooks seriously discuss only those organizations and individuals who want a larger "piece of the pie," that is, reform within the present social and economic system. They scarcely recognize those groups who want truly basic change, be it social, political, or economic.

Although the U.S. was born in violent revolution, a new text states "Americans throughout our history have believed that all men must obey the law if democracy is to continue. . . No man can put himself above the law. . . . Most Americans still believe freedom is based on government by law." Most textbooks imply that only legal protest is legitimate, rather than indicating that progress has been achieved through active and passive resistance, violent and non-violent tactics, legal and extra-legal methods. On the whole, textbooks present neither the limitations of electoral and legal reforms, nor the viability (and often necessity) of other options.

THE UNDERLYING ASSUMPTIONS

Implicit in all of the textbooks surveyed is the assumption that U.S. society is a true democracy, by virtue of its electoral system in which citizens can vote for the leader of their choice. Democracy is never defined as people controlling the institutions which daily affect them and their families: workplace, schools, courts, and so on. Furthermore, it is assumed that a democratic government like ours is the best of all possible governments. Perhaps it really *is* best, but the textbooks describe "communist" and "socialist" nations by their economic systems, while rarely describing U.S. society in terms of its capitalist economic system. This muddies comparisons of both economies and governments. The distortion which results is serious, for by calling both our government and economic system "democratic," the textbooks deny the realities of capitalism and all that goes with it—classes, conflicting class interests and the ongoing struggle between those few who control wealth and those many who are trying to share the wealth.

Stemming from this refusal to recognize the conflict of class interests is the refusal to link sexism and racism to economic exploitation. While the newer books have broadened previous descriptions of poverty and economic hardship and are now more "sympathetic" towards third world people and women, the resulting picture has no depth of composition. No group, no institution, no system seems to bear responsibility for these conditions. There are victims, but no victimizers; exploited, but no exploiters. Those who benefit from the system, and their profit motivations, are not explored.

The situation of farmworkers may be described as deplorable, but the combination of agribusiness, government officials and the leadership of the Teamster's Union who are fighting the United Farm Workers' Union today, and have fought decent working and living conditions for farmworkers for years, is neither named, described, nor condemned. Ghettos also are pictured as deplorable. But no connection is made to a competitive profit system and its supportive institutions which perpetuate institutional racism. Women may be said to be paid lower wages, but no mention is made of who profits from the savings in pay differentials. Discrimination, racism, and sexism are never analyzed as structures which profit some people at the expense of others.

BLAMING THE VICTIM

Students might well conclude that women and third world people are unsuccessful by nature, heredity, or inclination. The presentations in the texts would not dissuade them. Frequently, moreover, the texts would encourage such assumptions, for even the new texts tend to "blame the victims" for their own oppressed circumstances. Native Americans were dispossessed of their land because they "did not understand the concept of private land ownership;" Asian workers received low wages because they were "willing to work for very little;" Blacks could not find good urban jobs because they "were unskilled and uneducated;" Chicanos face problems because "they were not fluent in English;" Pilipinos and Puerto Ricans were colonized because they were "not ready for self-government;" and women "lack sufficient physical strength" and were "too frequently pregnant" to be an important part of the workforce.

Texts may imply that individual bigots, or groups of ignorant and prejudiced people, are to blame for some unfortunate situations, while ignoring a society that manipulates and encourages working-class divisions. Or texts may imply that poverty is a temporary condition which people will leave behind as they increase their education and skills. Because the economic system is not held accountable, students are led to believe that education and greater tolerance will eliminate societal flaws, and that 300 years of institutional racism against third world people and patriarchal repression against women will gradually wither away.

By defining the U.S. only as a democracy, and ignoring its role as an imperialist power, the presentation by these texts of U.S. foreign policy is also distorted. The take-over of the Philippines and Puerto Rico become almost accidental occurrences. U.S. administration of these possessions is presented as "teaching the people how to govern themselves"—democratically, of course. The profit motive, and the desire for raw materials, cheap labor, and captive markets for finished goods, are ignored.

SUMMARY

To the extent that discrimination, racism, and sexism are dealt with in textbooks, they are treated as aberrations, as isolated mistakes of the past. Since oppression is rarely examined from the perspective of its victims, these brief inclusions appear as footnotes to a grander, happier story. Yet even these isolated "mistakes" are treated in a simplistic, casual manner which downplays their significance. The internment of 110,000 Japanese in concentration camps was not an isolated "mistake" when seen in the light of the systematic mistreatment of, and hostility towards, Japanese and other Asians working and living in this country. The *Trails of Tears* of the Cherokee, Choctaw, Chickasaw, Seminole, and Creek nations were not aberrations, but elements of systematic and continuous national policy that led to the extermination of millions. The adoption of a pro-slavery constitution was not a "temporary" compromise; rather it was a logical result of 150 years of enslaving African people as free labor to profit white people. The effects of that compromise were not "temporary," but still exist today. Racism, sexism, and economic exploitation are not occasional aberrations of the U.S. system, but deeply ingrained mechanisms of the national social and economic structure. By isolating specific events from the overall context of a people's historical experiences, their histories are fragmented and downplayed. By failing to compare the experiences of different peoples (e.g. reservations for Native Americans, concentration camps for Japanese), the evolution of recurrent, basic themes is lost.

The role of economic gain for the overgroup is a solid pillar in the development and play of U.S. history, from the days of exploration and settlement to the separation from Britain, from the opening of the interior and the building of railroads to the concentration of capital and the industrial and technological revolutions. In a sense, the faulty and idealistic transmission of U.S. history has contributed to keeping working women and men ignorant of the forces which limit their options and frustrate their goals. An honest, pluralistic presentation of the history of all peoples in these United States would go some distance to helping each student achieve greater control in directing their own, and their country's, future.

GLOSSARY

PERSPECTIVE—All textbooks reflect—consciously or unconsciously—the interpretations of their authors. Authors usually present information from the experiences and viewpoints of certain groups and ignore the experiences and viewpoints of other groups. Unless we view an event from the varying perspectives of all of the groups involved, we achieve only a partial understanding of the event itself.

Example: *To live in the South was to live in daily fear of slave violence.*
The Pageant of American History, p. 211

Example: *Woodrow Wilson had gained national prominence as a foe of privilege and as a person with extraordinary powers of leadership. . . . a scholar who knew the past as well as the present, Wilson was able to see public questions in perspective. . . . He approached public questions with high idealism. Wilson's inauguration, like that of Jefferson or of Jackson, represented a peaceful revolution on behalf of the common people.*
A Free People, p. 125

Discussion: Both quotes reflect a white perspective and ignore the experiences and views of Black people.

MYTH—A myth is an ill-founded belief that is perpetuated in the face of contrary facts. Textbooks frequently perpetuate myths which support the status quo.

Example: *Americans throughout our history have believed that all men must obey the law if democracy is to continue. If a law is wrong, the constitution provides ways of changing the law. No man need break it. No man can put himself above the law.*

American History for Today, p. 193

Discussion: The U.S. itself was born in violent revolution, and throughout our history, people have agitated and struggled against injustice. Abolitionism, women's suffrage, civil rights, union organizing and anti-war activities are among the struggles which have utilized extra-legal tactics of boycotts, passive resistance, civil disobedience and breaking of law. Changes in the law to correct injustice have often resulted *because* of extra-legal types of agitation.

STEREOTYPE—An untruth or oversimplification about the traits and behaviors common to an entire people is a stereotype. The stereotype is applied to each member of the group, without regard to that person's individual character. Authors, like other people, often believe stereotypes common within their own culture. Such stereotypes then distort what they report about particular groups of people.

Example: [Ku Klux Klan] *members dressed in grotesque robes and hoods. These costumes were supposed to frighten the superstitious "darkies." They also made the white wearers feel self-important, just as the ritual paint and feathers did that were worn by Indian braves.*

The Impact of Our Past, p. 403

Discussion: This text puts "darkies" in quotes, but leaves "superstitious" without quotation marks. This suggests that Black people were (are) superstitious. It also perpetuates the stereotype of Native American males wearing paint and feathers, a cultural practice of a few Native nations that white society has applied as a stereotype to all "Indians." Finally, the quote applies the stereotyped term "braves" to Native American men.

CHARACTERIZATION—Many words and descriptions are commonly used to create negative images of groups of people. The use of such characterization reinforces stereotypes. Examples of such words are: savage, lazy, massacre, primitive, warlike, squaw, crafty, inscrutable, scatterbrained, greasy, gossipy.

Example: *In San Francisco the historically* compliant *Chinese aggressively resisted attempts to bus their children to schools outside of Chinatown.* (Emphasis added)

The American Experience, p. 832

Example: *To bring their cause to America's attention, women paraded in the streets. They* pestered *Congressmen. They formed groups and gave speeches.* (Emphasis added)

American History for Today, pp. 366-368

Discussion: The first quote refers to Chinese as compliant, perpetuating the stereotype of a submissive, passive people. This characterization ignores the long history of struggle by Chinese working people. The second quote states that women "pestered" legislators. "Pester" is defined as "to harass with petty irritations." The characterization of women "pestering" is similar to those of women "bickering" or "gossiping." By contrast, men would be said to have "lobbied" Congress.

DISTORTION—Textbooks can twist the meaning of history by slanting their presentation of facts, resulting in a distorted view of history. Distortion can also occur by the omission of information that would alter the viewpoint being presented.

Example: *Today . . . Puerto Ricans enjoy a per capita income higher than that of any other Latin-American country with the single exception of oil-rich Venezuela.*

Rise of the American Nation, p. 832

Example: *. . . three and a half million blacks became free men. Many southerners did not know how to live without slaves. Many former slaves did not know how to live without their former masters. The law had made them free but had left them helpless.*

The Pageant of American History, p. 281

Discussion: While both quotes present some true information, they distort the truth. The first is distorted by omission, because Puerto Rico has been controlled by the U.S. since 1898, and its per capita income should also be compared with per capita income in the U.S.—a comparison in which Puerto Rico would rank below any U.S. state. The second quote distorts the meaning of "free men" (not to mention the fact that half of them were free women). Perhaps *white* Southerners did not *like* to live without slaves (the textbook forgets that the slaves were also Southerners), but the skilled Black farmworkers and artisans knew full well how to live without their former masters, provided they were given some way in which to earn a living. Calling them "helpless" is a gross distortion.

OMISSION—One way of distorting history and maintaining myths is to omit certain information and viewpoints which do not support the author's views. Such omissions seriously distort a reader's understanding of events.

Example: *Included among those who served [in WW I] were tens of thousands of black Americans. Most served in laboring jobs, but a number of individuals and units won fame in battle against the Germans. American Negroes fought especially well as parts of larger French units.*

American History for Today, p. 398

Example: *A new nation is full of opportunity for bright young men.*

The Impact of Our Past, p. 221

Discussion:This first book omits information on the discrimination faced by Black troops, the paradox of Black troops fighting "to make the world safe for democracy," and the racism they faced when they returned to the U.S. All of those were critical realities to the Blacks, and their omission distorts the understanding that students receive of U.S. society. The second quote was accurate for *some* young white men but readers never are led to suspect that the period referred to—post-Revolutionary U.S.—witnessed the loss of social and economic opportunities previously open to women.

ETHNOCENTRISM—People often feel that their own group's values, culture and standards are superior to all others. They develop a perspective which judges other people's culture and customs as different from, and therefore inferior to, their own. Authors, historians and students can try to develop an understanding of other viewpoints, values and customs and recognize that all have legitimacy on their own terms. Judging other cultures by the standards of one's own culture is ethnocentric.

Example: *The Spaniards had established a capital city at Monterey, in 1769. And, led by a remarkable Franciscan leader, Junipero Serra, these Spaniards began building a series of missions. . . . The work of the missions was successful. Many of the California Indians were converted to the Roman Catholic religion. Except for these Spanish mission settlements, and a few outposts, most of California was unsettled land.*

America: Its People & Values, p. 408

Discussion: This quote is ethnocentric because it implies that converting Native Americans to Christianity is positive, all the while ignoring the functional and legitimate religious practices and beliefs of Native people. The presumption is that Christianity was superior to Native American religions. The quote also ignores the fact that Native Americans were living throughout the area of California.

EUROCENTRISM—Presenting information from the perspective of Euro Americans on this continent, authors often ignore the experiences, motivations, aspirations and views of people of color. To interpret the experiences and actions both of Euro Americans and of people of color only from the perspective of Euro Americans and not give similar space and legitimacy to the other perspectives, is Eurocentric.

Example: *In reality, Columbus "rediscovered" the new world. Other Europeans had explored there many years before. . . . Other Europeans may also have "discovered" the New World before Columbus. . . . However, after Columbus' voyage the Americas stayed discovered.*

Rise of the American Nation; p. 10

Example: *As the settlers pushed inland, they found the Indians living in areas the settlers wanted. The Indians did not understand the settlers' idea of land ownership. They thought the land belongs to all people who needed it.*

America: Its People & Values, p. 564

Discussion:To state—as the first quote does—that Europeans discovered a hemisphere occupied and utilized by some 50 to 100 million people is totally Eurocentric, for it presents history only from the perspective of Europeans. Native Americans were well aware that the hemisphere existed, and evidence also suggests that African and Chinese travellers had travelled to the Americas before Europeans. The second quote assumes that private ownership of land is more natural or legitimate than communal use of land. It places responsibility on Native Americans for not understanding the European concept of land ownership. Not only was the cultural relationship of Native Americans to the land legitimate, but since it was *their* land in the first place, it was the European settlers who failed to understand the Native American viewpoint.

SEXISM—Sexism is any attitude, action or institutional structure which subordinates a person or group because of their sex. (Since most authors, editors and historians are, and have been, male, and all have been reared in a patriarchal society, they reflect the perspective that male activity is most important and that the viewpoints and actions of females are of little consequence.) U.S. institutions have always been controlled by males and have been run for the advantage of males.

Example: *There are times in the lives of* men *and of nations when the world seems to stand still. April, 1865, was such a time. After years of work and hardships, the American people were at peace. Everywhere,* men *tried to understand the meaning of what had happened.* (Emphasis added)
America: Its People & Values, p. 476

Example: *In the 1830's and 1840's some workers began to join trade unions. These were associations which united* workingmen *to improve their wages and working conditions. The unions led strikes to force employers to grant their demands.* (Emphasis added)
The Impact of Our Past, p. 320

Example: *The lives of slave women and house slaves were usually better. Many women were allowed to look after their own children.*
The Challenge of America, p. 332

Discussion: By use of the term "men," the first quote ignores the fact that women were over half the population, and the second quote ignores the fact that women were active in union organizing and strikes during that period. The third quote ignores the fact that Black women held in slavery were required to do most of the same work required of men, in addition to regular "women's work." They also were exploited sexually for the slave owner's pleasure, or to reproduce wealth in the form of saleable children.

RACISM—Racism is any attitude, action or institutional practice which functions to subordinate a person or group because of their color. In the U.S., the institutions which compose our society (education, business, unions, banks, government, etc.) are controlled by whites. Thus, because white society exercises institutional power to oppress third world people, we refer to white racism when we use the term racism. The control of institutional power distinguishes racism from individual prejudice. All people in our society can hold prejudiced attitudes and beliefs.

Example: *Under the Indian Reorganization Act* [1934], *tribal governments were formed. Indian leaders gained confidence as they gained experience.*
Man In America, p. 546

Example: [The Pilipinos] *were weak and defenseless. They had no experience in governing themselves. . . . President McKinley and Congress finally accepted responsibility for governing the islands of the Philippines. . . . The United States tried to help the Filipinos to develop their land into a democratic nation. Step by step, the Filipinos learned to govern themselves.*
America: Its People & Values, p. 683

Discussion: Each of these quotes suggests that people of color are unable to govern themselves without the paternalistic guidance of the U.S. Such implications perpetuate the racism of "manifest destiny" and the "white man's burden." No textbook presents similar assumptions when discussing the settlement of Europeans in the Americas and the development of their governmental practices.

AFRICAN AMERICAN

BIBLIOGRAPHY

Adams, Russell L., *Great Negroes Past and Present*. David P. Ross, Jr., ed. Chicago: Afro-Am Publishing Company, 1969.

Allen, Robert L. *Reluctant Reformers: Racism and Social Reform Movements in the United States*. New York: Anchor Press, 1975.

Aptheker, Herbert. *American Negro Slave Revolts*. New York: International Publishers Co., Inc., 1952.

_____. *The American Revolution*. New York: International Publishers Co., Inc., 1967.

_____, ed. *A Documentary History of the Negro People in the United States*, Volume II. Secaucus, NJ: The Citadel Press, 1964.

_____. *To Be Free: Studies in American Negro History*. New York: International Publishers Co., Inc., 1958.

Bailey, James. *The God-Kings and the Titans*. New York: St. Martins Press, 1973.

Bennett, Lerone, Jr. *Before the Mayflower: A History of the Negro in America*. Baltimore: Penguin Books, 1966.

_____. *Black Power USA: The Human Side of Reconstruction*. Chicago: Johnson Publications, 1967.

_____. *Pioneers in Protest*. Baltimore: Penguin Books, 1969.

_____. *The Shaping of Black America*. Chicago: Johnson Publications, 1975.

Berlin, Ira. *Slaves Without Masters: The Free Negro in the Ante-Bellum South*. New York: Pantheon Books, 1974.

"Black Prosperity Image Found to be Superficial." *New York Times*, May 31, 1976.

"Blacks Have Made Political Gains But Signs of Frustration are Widespread." *New York Times*, June 1, 1976.

Blassingame, John W. *The Slave Community: Plantation Life in the Ante-Bellum South*. New York: Oxford University Press, 1972.

Bracey, John M., August Meier and Elliot Rudwick. *American Slavery: The Question of Resistance*. Belmont, CA: Wadsworth Publishing Company, 1971.

Bryce, Herrington J. "Are Most Blacks In the Middle Class?" *Black Scholar*, February 1975.

Buckmaster, Henrietta. *Let My People Go: The Story of the Underground Railroad and the Growth of the Abolition Movement*. Boston: Beacon Press, 1941.

Burt, Olive W. *Negroes in the Early West*. New York: Julian Messner, 1969.

Campbell, Stanley W. *The Slave Catchers: Enforcement of the Fugitive Slave Law, 1850-1860*. Chapel Hill: University of North Carolina Press, 1968.

Carmichael, Stokely and Charles V. Hamilton. *Black Power: The Politics of Liberation in America*. New York: Random House, 1967.

Chu, Daniel and Elliott Skinner. *A Glorious Age in Africa: The Story of Three Great African Empires*. New York: Doubleday, 1965.

Clarke, John Henrik and Vincent Harding, eds. *Slave Trade and Slavery*. New York: Holt Rinehart and Winston, 1970.

Davidson, Basil. *The African Slave Trade: Precolonial History, 1450-1850*. Boston: Atlantic, Little and Brown, 1961.

_____. *A Guide to African History*. New York: Doubleday, 1969.

Dobler, Lavinia and William A. Brown. *Great Rulers of the African Past.* New York: Doubleday, 1965.

DuBois, W.E.B. *Black Reconstruction in America, 1860-1880.* New York: Atheneum, 1962.

———. *The World and Africa.* New York: International Publishers, 1947.

Durham, Philip and Everett L. Jones. *The Negro Cowboys.* New York: Dodd, Mead and Co., 1965.

Fact Sheets on Institutional Racism. New York: Foundation for Change, 1975.

Fierce, Milfred. "Black Struggle for Land During Reconstruction." *Black Scholar,* February 1974.

Franklin, John Hope. *From Slavery to Freedom.* New York: Alfred A. Knopf, 1967.

———. *Reconstruction After the Civil War.* Chicago: University of Chicago Press, 1961.

Friedman, Lawrence J. *The White Savage: Racial Fantasies in the Postbellum South.* Englewood Cliffs, NJ: Prentice-Hall, 1970.

Genovese, Eugene D. *The World the Slaveholders Made.* New York: Vintage, 1971.

Goldman, Peter. *Civil Rights: The Challenge of the Fourteenth Amendment.* New York: Coward-McCann, Inc., 1965.

Grant, Joanne. *Black Protest: History, Documents and Analysis, 1619 to the Present.* New York: Fawcett, 1974.

Gratus, Jack. *The Great White Lie: Slavery, Emancipation, and Changing Racial Attitudes.* New York: Monthly Review Press, 1973.

Greene, Lorenzo Johnston. *The Negro in Colonial New England 1620-1776.* Port Washington, NY: Kennikat Press, 1966.

Heard, Norman J. *The Black Frontiersman.* New York: John Day, Co., 1969.

Hill, Herbert. "The Racial Practices of Organized Labor—The Age of Gompers and After." *Employment, Race & Poverty.* Arthur M. Ross and Herbert Hill, eds. New York: Harcourt, Brace and World, 1967.

Hughes, Langston and Milton Meltzer. *A Pictorial History of the Negro in America.* New York: Crown Publishers, 1963.

Jackson, John G. *Introduction to African Civilizations.* Secaucus, NJ: Citadel Press, 1970.

Katz, William. *The Black West.* New York: Doubleday, 1971.

———. *Eyewitness: The Negro in American History.* New York: Pitman Publishing Company, 1968.

Knowles, Louis L. and Kenneth Prewitt. *Institutional Racism in America.* Englewood Cliffs, NJ: Prentice-Hall, 1969.

Litwack, Leon F. *North of Slavery.* Chicago: University of Chicago Press, 1961.

Loewen, James and Charles Sallis, eds. *Mississippi: Conflict and Change.* New York: Pantheon Books, 1974.

Logan, Rayford W. *The Betrayal of the Negro.* New York: Collier Books, 1965.

Lynd, Staughton. *Class Conflict, Slavery and the United States Constitution.* Indianapolis: Bobbs-Merrill, 1967.

Malvin, John. *North Into Freedom.* Allan Peskon, ed. Cleveland: Western Reserve University Press, 1966.

Mannix, Daniel P. *Black Cargoes: A History of the African Slave Trade, 1518-1865.* New York: Viking Press, 1962.

McManus, Edgar J. *Black Bondage in the North.* Syracuse: Syracuse University Press, 1973.

Mellon, Matthew. *Early American Views on Negro Slavery*. New York: The New American Library, 1969.

Nelson, Truman, ed. *Documents of Upheaval: Selections from William Lloyd Garrison's The Liberator, 1831-1865*. New York: Hill and Wang, 1966.

Olsen, Otto H. *The Thin Disguise: Turning Point in Negro History, Plessy v. Ferguson—A Documentary Presentation (1864-1896)*. Atlantic Highlands, NJ: Humanities Press, 1967.

Quarles, Benjamin. *The Black Abolitionists*. New York: Oxford University Press, 1969.

————. *The Black American*. Glenview, IL: Scott, Foresman and Co., 1970.

————. *Lincoln and the Negro*. New York: Oxford University Press, 1962.

————. *The Negro in the American Revolution*. Chapel Hill: University of North Carolina Press, 1961.

Report of the National Advisory Commission on Civil Disorders. New York: Bantam Books, 1968.

Rogin, Michael Paul. *Fathers and Children*. New York: Alfred A. Knopf, 1975.

Ryan, William. *Blaming the Victim*. New York: Vintage Books, 1971.

Stampp, Kenneth. *The Era of Reconstruction*. New York: Alfred A. Knopf, 1966.

————. *The Peculiar Institution*. New York: Vintage Books, 1956.

Sterling, Dorothy. *Forever Free*. New York: Doubleday, 1963.

Turnbull, Colin. *The Peoples of Africa*. Cleveland: World Publishing Co., 1962.

Van Sertima, Ivan. *They Came Before Columbus*. New York: Random House, 1976.

Weld, Theodore. *American Slavery As It Is*. New York: Arno Press, 1968.

Wells, Ida B. *Crusade For Justice: The Autobiography of Ida B. Wells*. Chicago: University of Chicago Press, 1970.

Williams, Eric. *Capitalism and Slavery*. New York: Capricorn Books, 1966.

Woodward, C. Van. *The Strange Career of Jim Crow*. New York: Oxford University Press, 1957.

ASIAN AMERICAN BIBLIOGRAPHY

Note: All citations in column three for *Asian Women, Contacts and Conflicts: The Asian Immigration Experience, Letters in Exile,* and *Roots: An Asian American Reader* are listed in the Asian American bibliography under "Asian American Studies Center."

Asian American Studies Center. *Asian Women*. Los Angeles: University of California, October 1975.

————. *Contacts and Conflicts: The Asian Immigration Experience*. Los Angeles: University of California, 1975.

————. *Letters in Exile*. Los Angeles: University of California, 1976.

————. *Roots: An Asian American Reader*. Los Angeles: University of California, 1971.

Bulasan, Carlos. *America Is in the Heart*. Seattle: State University of Washington, 1974.

Canillo, Alex, et al., eds. *Pinoy Know Yourself: An Introduction to the Filipino American Experience*. Santa Cruz: Third World Teaching Resource Center, Merrill College, University of California, 1975.

Chernow, Ron. "Chinatown, Their Chinatown: The Truth Behind the Facade." *New York Magazine,* June 11, 1973.

Conrat, Maisie and Richard Conrat. *Executive Order 9066*. San Francisco: California Historical Society, 1972.

Conroy, Hilary and Scott Miyakawa, eds. *East Across the Pacific*. American Bibliographical Center, CLIO Press, Santa Barbara, CA: 1972.

Corporate Information Center, National Council of Churches. "The Philippines: American Corporations, Martial Law and Under-development." *IDOC,* No. 57, November 1973.

Daniels, Roger. *Concentration Camps USA: Japanese Americans and WW II*. New York: Dryden Press (Holt, Rinehart & Winston), 1971.

_____. *The Politics of Prejudice: The Anti-Japanese Movement in California and the Struggle for Japanese Land Exclusion*. Berkeley: University of California Press, 1962.

Dinnerstein, Leonard and David Reimers. *Ethnic Americans—A History of Immigration and Assimilation*. New York: Dodd, Mead & Co., 1975.

Elliott, Charles B. *The Philippines to the End of the Military Regime*. Indianapolis: Bobbs, Merrill, 1917.

Fong, Patricia. "The 1938 National Dollar Strike." *Asian American Review,* Vol. 2, No. 1, 1975.

Fuchs, Lawrence. *Hawaii Pono: A Social History*. New York: Harcourt Brace, 1961.

Hill, Herbert. "Anti-Oriental Agitation and the Rise of Working Class Racism." *Society,* January 1973.

Ichioka, Yugi. "Early Issei Socialists and the Japanese Community." *Amerasia Journal,* UCLA Asian American Studies Center, July 1971.

Isaacs, Harold. *Images of Asia: American Views of China and India*. New York: Capricorn Books, 1962.

Jacobs, Paul, Saul Landau and Eve Pell. *To Serve the Devil: Vol. II—Colonials and Sojourners*. New York: Vintage Books, 1971.

Kalaw, T.M. *The Philippine Revolution*. Philippines: Jose B. Vargas Filipiniana Foundation, 1969.

Kitano, Harry. *Japanese Americans: The Evolution of a Subculture*. Englewood Cliffs, NJ: Prentice Hall, Inc., 1969.

Lai, H.M. "A Historical Survey of Organizations of the Left Among the Chinese in America." *Bulletin of Concerned Asian Scholars,* Fall 1972.

Lai, H.M. and Philip Choy. *A History of the Chinese in California*. San Francisco: Lawton and Kennedy, 1969.

_____. *Outlines: History of the Chinese in America*. San Francisco: Chinese American Studies Group, 1971.

Lan, Dean. "The Chinatown Sweatshops: Oppression and an Alternative." *Amerasia Journal,* November 1971.

Lee, Rose Hum. *The Chinese in the United States of America*. Hong Kong: Hong Kong University Press, 1960.

Lichauco, Alejandro. "The Lichauco Papers: Imperialism in the Philippines." *Monthly Review,* July-August 1973.

Light, Ivan. *Ethnic Enterprise in America*. Berkeley: University of California Press, 1972.

Loewen, James W. *The Mississippi Chinese*. Cambridge: Harvard University Press, 1971.

Lyman, Stanford. *The Asians in the West*. Reno: Western Studies Center, University of Nevada, 1970.

———. *Chinese Americans.* New York: Random House, 1974.

Maykovich, Minako. *Japanese American Identity Dilemma.* Japan: Waseda University Press, 1972.

McGovney, Dudley. "The Anti-Japanese Land Laws of California and Ten Other States." *California Law Review,* Vol. 35, No. 7 (1947).

Melendy, M. Brett. "Filipinos in the U.S." *Pacific Historical Review,* November 1974.

Miller, Stuart. *The Unwelcome Immigrant—The American Image of the Chinese, 1785-1882.* Berkeley: University of California Press, 1969.

Murphy, Betty. *Chinese-Americans: Schools and Community Problems.* Chicago: Integrated Education Associates, 1972.

Nee, Victor and Brett DeBary Nee. *Longtime Californ': A Documentary Study of an American Chinatown.* New York: Pantheon, 1973.

Owens, Norman G. *Compadre Colonialism: Studies on the Philippines Under American Rule.* Center for South and Southeast Asian Studies, Ann Arbor: University of Michigan, 1971.

Pearlstone, Norman. "The 'Quiet Minority'—Tokyo-U.S. Differences Stir Fear and Militancy in Japanese Americans." *Wall Street Journal,* August 8, 1972.

Peterson, William. *Japanese Americans.* New York: Random House, 1971.

Saxton, Alexander. *The Indispensable Enemy—Labor and the Anti-Chinese Movement in California.* Berkeley: University of California Press, 1971.

Sue, Stanley and Harry Kitano. "Asian Americans: A Success Story?" *Journal of Social Issues,* Vol. 29, No. 2 (1973).

ten Broek, Jacobus. *Prejudice, War and the Constitution.* Berkeley: University of California Press, 1970.

Thomas, Dorothy and Richard Nishimoto. *The Spoilage: Japanese Evacuation and Resettlement During WW II.* Berkeley: University of California Press, 1946.

Tong, Ben. "The Ghetto of the Mind: Notes on the Historical Psychology of Chinese America." *Amerasia Journal,* November 1971.

Vicente, Domingo. "The Philippines and Martial Law." *Bridge: The Asian-American Magazine,* April 1974.

Wei Min She Labor Committee. *Chinese Working People in America.* San Francisco: United Front Press, 1974.

Wu, C.T., ed. *"Chink!"* New York: Meridian Books, 1972.

Yu, Connie. "The Chinese in American Courts." *Bulletin of Concerned Asian Scholars,* Fall, 1972.

CHICANO

BIBLIOGRAPHY

Acuña, Rodolfo. *Occupied America: The Chicano's Struggle Toward Liberation.* New York: Harper & Row, 1972.

Castañeda, Carlos E. *The Mexican Side of the Texan Revolution.* Dallas: P.L. Turner Co., 1928.

Castillo, P. and A. Camarillo, eds. *Furia y Muerte: Los Banditos Chicanos* (English Text). Los Angeles: Aztlan Publications (University of California, Chicano Studies Center), 1973.

Day, Mark. *Forty Acres: Cesar Chavez and the Farm Workers.* New York: Praeger, 1971.

Emmerich, Andre. *Art Before Columbus.* New York: Simon and Schuster, 1963.

450 Years of Chicano History in Pictures. Albuquerque, New Mexico: Chicano Communications Center, 1976.

Galarza, Ernesto. *Merchants of Labor—The Mexican Bracero Story.* Santa Barbara, CA: McNally & Loftin, 1964.

Grant, Ulysses S. *Personal Memoirs.* New York: Webster, 1886.

Grebler, Leo, Joan W. Moore and Ralph Guzman. *The Mexican-American People, The Nation's Second Largest Minority.* New York: The Free Press (Macmillan Co.), 1970.

Herrera, Rafael Trujillo. *Olvidate De El Alamo.* Mexico, D.F.: La Prensa, 1965.

Landon, Joan and Henry Anderson. *So Shall Ye Reap: The Story of Cesar Chavez and the Farm Workers' Movement.* New York: Crowell, 1971.

Lopéz y Rivas, Gilberto. *The Chicanos.* New York: Monthly Review Press, 1974.

Lord, Walter. "Myths and Realities of the Alamo." *The American West.* Vol. 5, No. 3 (May 1968).

Martinez, Elizabeth and Enriqueta Vasquez. *Viva La Raza!* New York: Doubleday, 1974.

McWilliams, Carey. *Factories in the Field.* Boston, Little, Brown & Co., 1939.

————. *North From Mexico: The Spanish-Speaking People of the United States.* New York: Greenwood Press, 1968.

Meier, Matt S. and Feliciano Lopez. *The Chicanos.* New York: Hill and Wang, 1972.

Morin, Paul. *Among the Valiant.* Alhambra, CA: Borden Publishing Company, 1966.

Price, Glen. *Origins of the War with Mexico.* Austin: University of Texas, 1967.

Rendon, Armando. *Chicano Manifesto.* New York: Macmillan, 1971.

Ruiz, Ramon, ed. *The Mexican War: Was It Manifest Destiny?* New York: Holt, Rinehart and Winston, 1963.

Samora, Julian. *La Raza—Forgotten Americans.* Notre Dame, IN: University of Notre Dame Press, 1966.

Scott, Winfield. *Memoirs.* New York: Sheldon, 1864.

Swadesh, Frances. *Los Primeros Pobladores.* Notre Dame, IN: University of Notre Dame Press, 1974.

Valdez, Luis and Stan Steiner, eds. *Aztlan.* New York: Knopf, 1972.

Valliant, George C. *Aztecs of Mexico.* Baltimore: Penguin Books, 1944.

Weinberg, Alfred Katz. *Manifest Destiny: A Study in Nationalist Expansion.* Baltimore: Johns Hopkins Press, 1935.

Wolf, Eric. *Sons of the Shaking Earth.* Chicago: University of Chicago Press, 1959.

BIBLIOGRAPHY

NATIVE AMERICAN

Akwesasne Notes. Mohawk Nation, Rooseveltown, NY 13683.

Aptheker, Herbert. *The American Revolution 1763-1783.* New York: International Publishers Co., Inc., 1967.

Brown, Dee. *Bury My Heart at Wounded Knee.* New York: Bantam Books, 1972.

Cahn, Edgar S. *Our Brother's Keeper: The Indian in White America.* New York: New Community Press, 1969.

"Coast Dig Focuses on Man's Move to the New World." *New York Times,* August 6, 1976, p. 33.

Cohen, Felix. *Handbook of Federal Indian Law.* U.S. Dept. of Interior, Washington, D.C.: Government Printing Office, 1941-1942.

Collier, John. *Indians of the Americas.* New York: W.W. Norton and Co., 1947.

Cook, Sherburne F. and Woodrow Borah. *Essays in Population History: Mexico and the Caribbean.* Berkeley: University of California Press, 1972.

Council on Interracial Books for Children. *Chronicles of American Indian Protest.* New York: Fawcett, 1971.

Deloria, Vine, Jr. *Behind the Trail of Broken Treaties.* New York: Dell, 1974.

_____. *Custer Died for Your Sins.* New York: The Macmillan Co., Collier-Macmillan, 1969.

_____. *God Is Red.* New York: Grosset and Dunlap, 1973.

_____. *Of Utmost Good Faith.* San Francisco: Straight Arrow Books, 1971.

Dobyns, Henry F. "Estimating Aboriginal American Population: An Appraisal of Techniques with a New Hemispheric Estimate." *Current Anthropology,* VII, 1966.

Fact Sheets on Institutional Racism. New York: Foundation for Change, 1975.

Forbes, Jack D. *The Indian in America's Past.* Englewood Cliffs, NJ: Prentice-Hall, 1964.

Jacobs, Paul and Saul Landau. *To Serve the Devil, Vol. I: Natives and Slaves.* New York: Vintage Books, 1971.

Jacobs, Wilbur R. "The Tip of an Iceberg: Pre-Columbian Indian Demography and Some Implications for Revisionism." *William and Mary Quarterly,* January 1974.

Josephy, Alvin. *The Patriot Chiefs.* New York: Viking Press, 1961.

Kappler, Charles. *Indian Affairs, Laws and Treaties* (5 Vols.). Washington, D.C.: Government Printing Office, 1904-1941.

Katz, William. *The Black West.* New York: Doubleday, 1971.

Kickingbird, Kirke and Karen Duchereau. *100 Million Acres.* New York: Macmillan, 1973.

LaFarge, Oliver. *A Pictorial History of the American Indian.* New York: Crown, 1956.

Levine, Stuart and Nan O. Lurie (eds.). *The American Indian Today.* Baltimore: Penguin Books, 1972.

McNickle, D'Arcy. *They Came Here First: The Epic of the American Indian.* Philadelphia: Lippincott, 1949.

Talbot, Steve. "The Revolution and the American Indian Frontier." *WASSAJA: A National Newspaper of Indian America.* San Francisco: The American Indian Historical Society, August 1976.

Tebbel, John and Keith Jennison. *The American Indian Wars.* New York: Harper and Row, 1960.

U.S. Senate. *Indian Education: A National Tragedy—A National Challenge.* Washington, D.C.: Government Printing Office (91-501), 1969.

Vogel, Virgil. *This Country Was Ours.* New York: Harper and Row, 1974.

Washburn, Wilcomb E. *Red Man's Land, White Man's Law.* New York: Charles Scribner's Sons, 1971.

WASSAJA: A National Newspaper of Indian America. San Francisco: The American Indian Historical Society.

White Roots of Peace. *The Great Law of Peace of the People of the Longhouse.* Mohawk Nation, Rooseveltown, NY 13683: Akwesasne Notes, 1970.

Witt, Shirley Hill and Stan Steiner. *The Way.* New York: Vintage Books, 1972.

Wrone, D.R. and R.S. Nelson. *Who's the Savage? A Documentary History of the Mistreatment of the Native North Americans.* New York: Fawcett, 1973.

Young, Mary Elizabeth. *Redskins, Ruffled Shirts and Rednecks.* Norman: University of Oklahoma Press, 1961.

PUERTO RICAN

BIBLIOGRAPHY

Alvarez, José Hernandez. *Return Migration to Puerto Rico.* Berkeley: Institute of International Studies, Univ. of California, 1967.

Brameld, Theodore. *The Remaking of a Culture: Life and Education in Puerto Rico.* New York: Harper, 1959.

Bulletin of Interracial Books for Children. Council on Interracial Books for Children. 1841 Broadway, N.Y., N.Y. 10023.

Centro De Estudios Puertorriqueños. *Taller De Cultura: Conferencia de Historiografia: Abril, 1974.* New York: City University of New York, 1976.

————. *Taller De Migracion: Conferencia de Historiografia: Abril, 1974.* New York: City University of New York, 1975.

de Negrón, Aida Montilla. *Americanization in Puerto Rico and the Public School System 1900-1930.* Rio Piedras, Puerto Rico: Editorial Edil, 1970.

Diaz Soler, Luis M. *Historia de la Esclavitud Negra en Puerto Rico.* Rio Piedras: University of Puerto Rico, 1965.

Illinois State Advisory Committee of the U.S. Civil Rights Commission. *Bilingual/Bicultural Education: A Privilege or a Right?* May, 1974.

Jacobs, Paul, Saul Landau and Eve Pell. *To Serve The Devil: Vol. II: Colonials and Sojourners.* New York: Vintage Books, 1971.

King, Lourdes Miranda, "Puertorriqueñas in the United States," in *Civil Rights Digest,* Spring, 1974, pp. 20-27.

Lewis, Gordon K. *Puerto Rico: Freedom and Power in the Caribbean.* New York: Monthly Review Press, 1963.

López, Adalberto and James Petras. *Puerto Rico and Puerto Ricans: Studies in History and Society.* Cambridge: Schenkman Publishing Company, 1974.

Maldonado-Denis, Manuel. *Puerto Rico: A Socio-Historic Interpretation.* New York: Vintage Books, 1972.

Pantoja, Antonia, Barbara Blourock and James Bowman, eds. *Badges and Indices of Slavery: Cultural Pluralism Redefined.* Lincoln, Nebraska: University of Nebraska, 1975.

Presser, Harriet. *Sterilization and Fertility Decline in Puerto Rico.* Berkeley: University of California, 1969. Doctoral Dissertation.

Puerto Rican Independence Party & Socialist Party of Puerto Rico. *Memorandum Supporting the Petition of the Puerto Rico Independence Party & the Puerto Rico Socialist Party in Relation to the Colonial Case of Puerto Rico.* August, 1972.

Puerto Rico Libre! Committee for Puerto Rico Decolonization. Box 1240, Peter Stuyvesant Station, N.Y., N.Y. 10009.

"Puerto Rico Seeks Way Out As Economic Woes Mount," *New York Times,* October 15, 1975, pp. 1 & 86.

Rubenstein, Annette T., ed. *Schools Against Children: The Case for Community Control.* New York: Monthly Review Press, 1970.

Silén, Juan Angel. *We, The Puerto Rican People: A Story of Oppression and Resistance.* New York: Monthly Review Press, 1971.

"Sterilization Abuse of Women: The Facts," in *Health/PAC Bulletin,* No. 62, January/February 1975. Health PAC, 17 Murray St., N.Y., N.Y.

U.S. Civil Rights Commission. *A Better Chance To Learn: Bilingual-Bicultural Education.* Clearinghouse Publication No. 51, May, 1975.

————. *Puerto Ricans in the Continental U.S.: An Uncertain Future,* 1976.

We would like to recommend an excellent book for students:
Williams, Byron. *Puerto Rico: Commonwealth, State, or Nation,* Parents' Magazine Press, 1972.

WOMEN

BIBLIOGRAPHY

Carroll, Berenice. *Liberating Women's History*. Urbana: University of Illinois, 1976.

Chafe, William. *The American Woman: Her Changing Social, Economic and Political Roles, 1920-1970*. New York: Oxford University Press, 1972.

Davis, Angela. "Reflections on the Black Woman's Role in the Community of Slaves." *Black Scholar*, December 1971.

DePauw, Linda Grant. *Founding Mothers: Women in the Revolutionary Era*. Boston: Houghton Mifflin, 1975.

Fact Sheets on Institutional Sexism. New York: Foundation for Change, 1976.

Flexner, Eleanor. *Century of Struggle*. New York: Atheneum, 1973.

Gornick, Vivian and Barbara Moran. *Women in Sexist Society*. New York: Basic Books, 1971.

Josephson, Hannah. *The Golden Thread: New England Mill Girls and Magnates*. New York: Russell, 1949.

Kraditor, Aileen S. *Up From the Pedestal*. New York: Quadrangle, 1969.

Lerner, Gerda. *Black Women in White America: A Documentary History*. New York: Vintage, 1973.

———. *The Woman in American History*. Reading, MA: Addison Wesley, 1971.

Merriam, Eve. *Growing Up Female in America: Ten Lives*. New York: Dell, 1971.

O'Neill, William. *Everyone Was Brave*. New York: Quadrangle, 1969.

Ryan, Mary P. *Womanhood in America: From Colonial Times to the Present*. New York: Franklin Watts, 1975.

Sanger, Margaret. *Margaret Sanger: An Autobiography*. New York: W.W. Norton & Co., 1938.

Scott, Anne Firor. *The Southern Lady: From Pedestal to Politics, 1830-1930*. Chicago: University of Chicago Press, 1970.

———. *Women in American Life*. Boston: Houghton Mifflin, 1970.

Smuts, Robert. *Women and Work in America*. New York: Schocken, 1971.

Sochen, June. *Herstory: A Woman's View of American History*. New York: Alfred Publishing Co., 1974.

Spruill, Julia Cherry. *Women's Life and Work in the Southern Colonies*. Chapel Hill: University of North Carolina Press, 1938.

Terrell, John Upton and Donna M. Terrell. *Indian Women of the Western Morning*. New York: Dial, 1974.

U.S. Commission on Civil Rights. "Sexism and Racism: Feminist Perspectives." *Civil Rights Digest*. Spring 1974.

Williams, Selma R. *Demeter's Daughters: The Women Who Founded America*. New York: Atheneum, 1976.

Witt, Shirley Hill. *The Tuscaroras*. New York: Crowell-Collier, 1972.

In addition to the materials listed above, we would like to recommend:

Women in U.S. History: An Annotated Bibliography, The Common Woman Collective, 5 Upland Rd., Cambridge, MA. 1976

The Bibliography of the History of Women, Gerda Lerner. Bronxville, NY: Sarah Lawrence College, 1975.

Women & Work in U.S. History: An Annotated Bibliography, Business and Professional Women's Foundation, Wash. DC: 1976.

Two issues of *Black Scholar* have appeared on the subject of Black women: December 1971 and March 1975.